NEW YORK UNIVERSITY STUDIES IN
FRENCH CULTURE AND CIVILIZATION

General Editors: Tom Bishop and Nicholas Wahl

Also by Erika Ostrovsky

Céline and His Vision
Voyeur Voyant: Portrait of Louis-Ferdinand Céline
Eye of Dawn: The Rise and Fall of Mata Hari

Under the Sign of Ambiguity: Saint-John Perse/ Alexis Leger

Erika Ostrovsky

NEW YORK UNIVERSITY PRESS
WASHINGTON SQUARE, NEW YORK
1985

Library of Congress Cataloging in Publication Data

Ostrovsky, Erika.
Under the sign of ambiguity.

Bibliography: p.
Includes index.
1. Perse, Saint-John, 1887–1975. 2. Poets.
French—20th century—Biography. 3. Diplomats—
France—Biography. I. Title.
PQ2623.E386Z79 1985 848′.91209 [B] 85-8946
ISBN 0-8147-6163-1 (alk. paper)

Clothbound editions of New York University Press books are Smyth-
sewn and printed on permanent and acid-free paper.

Pour toi

CONTENTS

ILLUSTRATIONS

PROLOGUE

THE COMPLEX IMAGE

O Poète, ô bilingue, entre toutes choses bisaiguës . . . homme parlant dans l'équivoque!
—*Saint-John Perse*[1]

J'ai toujours pratiqué . . . le dédoublement de personnalité.
—*Alexis Leger*[2]

In this dual pronouncement of duality, Saint-John Perse/Alexis Leger offers us the key to his life. From birth to death, ambiguity, complexity, and paradox were the marks of his destiny. Yet, by an ironic twist of fate, which often plagues great men, his admirers have imposed a static, unilateral image upon him. He is today preserved as in a reliquary, poised on a pedestal, contemplated in awed silence or discussed in hushed tones, examined with the latest instruments (but always with the forgone conclusion of eminence), fêted in officialdom and academe. His signature deemed an emblem, his handwriting calligraphy, his sayings scripture, he is in danger of lying forever in state, encased in a great gilded sarcophagus.

Plants wither when too much watered. A human life may be diminished by excessive reverence. Turned into a grandiose statue without a flaw in its superb outlines, an impurity of color, a chisel mark, or an unexpected shadow, he has been fixed in a sublime pose fit for a shrine or a mausoleum. And praises sung by a chorus of voices with hardly one discordant note, a hint of laughter or irreverence, shroud his own words with a chant that endlessly echoes solemn hymns of adoration.[3]

An outrage, perhaps. An injustice, surely, to thus condemn to monumental fixity a man who prized nothing so much as movement and life's vibrant diversity, to embalm one who celebrated change and mortality, to make a monolith of him who never ceased to love multiplicity.

Fortunately, there is a way to reverse this fate—though at the price of some risk. One must dare to hew the statue asunder; lift off the golden funeral mask; speak in a new voice; reveal flaws, scars, shadows. Only thus can the living image of this man emerge once more in all its vigor and complexity. Paradox, once liberated, will bring him back to life. Dissonance, irreverence, laughter will resurrect him—not in his deified state, to be sure, but as a vital human force that will not cease to exist and to change.

There lurks, however, as in the treatment of any great life, the perennial danger of new statues, the glorious frozen pose, the return to fixity. It can be skirted only by constant flexibility, by allowing that which disconcerts, shocks, or contradicts to enter. One must juggle a myriad of pieces preserved in all their disparity so that the puzzle that constitutes this destiny may come into being.

To begin, let us return to the statement: "J'ai toujours pratiqué . . . le dédoublement de personnalité." It provides the first clue—a clue that, under threat of rigidity, may have to be discarded somewhere along the way but that for the moment serves to open the game. It obviously suggests consideration of a double image, a split identity or personality (without the implications of pathology), two names—patronym and pseudonym, Alexis Leger/Saint-John Perse—a simple dichotomy. Instantly, however, the initial pieces of the puzzle take on a disconcerting shape, do not fall into the usual place, defy obvious rules. For, in this instance, the pair of patronym and pseudonym does not form a stable construct (as is generally the case) but undergoes a series of changes, moves, evolves, is subject to jugglery.

A first paradox involves the patronym. Traditionally a fixed entity, it provides a solid base for identification and is indeed linked to a sense of identity. Not so in the case of—one is almost instantly at a loss of how to refer to him—the poet-diplomat. Born Marie-René Alexis Saint-Leger, he becomes Alexis St.-Leger, Alexis Leger, or simply Leger. (Love of pun would incite one to suggest a gradual *allégement*, or lightening, of the patronym.) One finds, however, no predictable progression in these changes of the family name but rather an alternating use of the longer or shorter version, sometimes in letters addressed to the selfsame correspondent within a short span of time.[4] And, if one is tempted to associate the name Alexis Leger with entry into diplomatic service, one must abandon this notion, for the varying patronyms occur throughout life in an undulating pattern that is impossible to pin down.

The complex play of names, however, has just begun. Besides the various patronyms, pseudonyms come into view. These, as well, are multiple and subject to change. They evolve from Saintleger Leger to St.-J. Perse to Saint-John Perse, and even the last and best known of the pseudonyms is once jokingly qualified by its bearer as "S.-J. P. (le vrai)."[5] Their progression, moreover, does not follow a straight line: at times they alternate; at other times they exist side by side,[6] and, in at least one case, the poet (indulging in vagary or mystification) claims to have used his second pseudonym when, in fact, we know he signed his work with the third.[7]

Pseudonyms, in and of themselves, are of course a fascinating problem. With their power to name or rename, hide, and reveal; with their esthetic and psychological value, their origins and uses, their links with the work of art, they have tantalized critics and continue to do so. Several have turned their attention to Saint-John Perse but none so successfully as Jean-Pierre Richard who, in a recent study,[8] has pointed to the paradox implicit in the most famous of his pseudonyms, linked the poet's names and titles, and explored the evolution from the Saintleger Leger of *Eloges* to the Saint-John Perse of *Anabase,* avoiding the traps of reverence and credulity in which some other critics have been caught.

Conjectures in this realm are tempting, and one tends to construct one's own hypotheses. Thus, while not agreeing with one critic that the choice of the quasi-Anglo-Saxon "John" was determined by a desire to facilitate publication during eventual exile in the United States,[9] one might suggest that "Saint-John," returned to its French form, i.e., "Saint-Jean," evokes "la Saint-Jean" or Midsummer Night, the time of the summer solstice and sacrificial rites—important elements in the thematics of Saint-John Perse's poetry.[10] Or one could affirm that an important clue is found in the latter's comment on the name of a fellow poet: "Fargue! . . . L'éclair du nom,"[11] especially if one notes that the complete name of this poet—Léon-Paul Fargue—has the same rhythmic and tonal distribution as Saint-John Perse and that "l'éclair" is one of they key images of the latter's imagination.

Perhaps the most interesting leads, though, are the poet's own statements concerning his choice of pseudonyms. Typically alternating between the lofty and the facetious, they both help and hinder our efforts at elucidation. Thus, refuting attempts to link his assumed name to an interest in the country (Persia) or the Latin poet (Aulus Persius Flaccus), he ascribes its origin to simple coincidence, not to affinities, reminiscences, or references, and insists that:

échappant à tout lieu rationnel, il fut librement accueilli tel qu'il s'imposait mystérieusement à l'esprit du poète, pour des raisons inconnues de lui-même, comme dans la vieille onomastique: avec ses longues et ses brèves, ses syllabes fortes ou muettes, ses consonnes dures ou sifflantes, conformément aux lois secrètes de toute création poétique.[12]

Such linking of the pen name to a poetic construct and attributing its genesis to mysterious forces contrasts sharply with another, lusory pronouncement: "J'ai songé d'abord au pseudonyme 'Archibald Perse' pour pouvoir mieux me renier."[13] Here playfulness is coupled with, or masks, serious considerations—the ability to repudiate one part of the self or split one's image.

A third statement, metaphoric in nature, speaks equally of the pleasures of secrecy, the lure of anonymity: "Etre [en littérature] comme ces navires qui offrent seulement leur poupe à la curiosité des passants: un nom, un port d'attache, c'est là tout leur état civil. Le reste est aventure et n'appartient qu'à eux."[14]

It seems quite evident that pseudonyms are fair game both for this poet and his critics.

If one returns now to the already complex play of patronyms and pseudonyms, one finds that there is another—most curious—piece in the mosaic of names. It is located somewhere between the two, yet is neither one nor the other, falling, as it does, into a special category. Its origin dates from the years that Alexis Leger spent in the Orient as a diplomat and is the transposition of his name into Chinese; Lei Hi-gnai ("La Foudre sous la neige").[15] This transposed name evidently had a more than passing appeal for Saint-John Perse—perhaps because of its poetic quality, its incongruity, the estrangement it provides, its link with thunder and lightning—for, among the rare possessions that accompanied him during his entire nomadic life was a stele with the Chinese calligram of this name,[16] a calligram that also adorned one of the flags he flew over his last abode.[17]

Finally, though, the most striking instance of such play between patronyms and pseudonyms occurs when the poet (apparently not content with a dichotomy of images, explanations, and languages) juggles four different names—in referring to himself—on a single page.[18]

What a long way we have already come from the monolithic statue bearing only a single inscription. Yet, we have but touched upon the simplest part of the puzzle. We must go on to other pieces if we are to further construct its outlines.

Among the basic marks of identity, usually just as unequivocal and easily identified as the name, is a person's birthplace. In the present case, however, fact and legend, nature and artifice, the singular and the multiple coincide—as if in defiance of the rules that apply to such a definitive location. Factual accounts state simply that Saint-John Perse "was born on an islet off the coast of Pointe-à-Pitre, Guadeloupe."[19] He himself enumerates half a dozen variants: "L'Ile des Feuilles," "L'Ilet-à-Feuilles," "Saint-Leger-les-Feuilles," "Ile Feuilles," "Ilet Petreluzzi," "Les Iles des Vents."[20] As if variety did not suffice, he adds a mythical aura to his birthplace by stating that no land, but the Atlantic, spawned his race and that its watery expanse (an open space rather than a closed site) was the most suitable element to engender "l'homme incirconscrit."[21]

Yet, even this homeland of ebb and flow, this shifting, unstable abode would not be permanent. It would give way to other, farther shores—France, the Orient, the Americas—and a largely aquatic circumnavigation of the globe lasting a lifetime. (What is more, a legendary dimension—already established in the quasi-miraculous sea-birth—is added to these voyages by curious parallels with the mythological hero journey where the crossing of various thresholds occurs at critical points along life's way and is accompanied by symbolic death and rebirth: the initial transition took place at puberty; the second, at the age of thirty; the third, and most dramatic, in the thirty-third year; the final one at the time of the climacteric[22]—and all were accompanied by exile and metamorphosis.) Nor would the undulating pattern of these voyages, akin to the flux and reflux of the sea, disappear even in old age, for during the final years of his life the poet-diplomat resided alternately in France and the United States, his sojourn in each continent coinciding with the two halves of the year. Thus, lack of fixity was maintained to the very last, and paradox continued to reign.

The multiple facets of the name, the impossibility of attributing a single port of call to this man, have contributed adventure to our game. We must nevertheless consider still other means of identification if we are to play within the rules.

A third mark of identity is generally a person's handwriting.

As unique as the name, as recognizable as a geographic site, as characteristic as a fingerprint, an expression of personality, it tends to remain virtually unchanged during a lifetime. No so, however, in this case. We are once again confronted with a curious and unusual phenomenon. In the year 1911 the young poet, who had developed a distinctive handwriting, felt compelled to alter it drastically. The reasons given for this metamorphosis are, typically, multiple and contradictory: The best known is linked to his publication of *Eloges*—reputedly, the manuscript written in a "disconcerting" hand, barely legible but unusually beautiful, resulted in various printer's errors in the published version; whereupon the poet, concerned with clarity and legibility, imposed upon himself the arduous task of "reeducating" his handwriting.[23] The lesser known, equally important reasons are found in more obscure utterances, such as a letter of the period where the young poet admits: "Je m'entraîne en ce moment, à changer mon écriture, afin qu'il n'y ait absolument rien de moi qui puisse, même au premier abord, me faire croire singulier."[24] The extraordinary decision to develop a pseudoscript is, then, also motivated by a desire to mask his true nature by means of different writing (paralleling the assumption of a pseudonym). The new writing creates a public image—opposed to the secret, personal one—and formal script resembling calligraphy,[25] even more outstanding in its beauty than the former writing and thus, paradoxically, more likely to be considered "singular." It might also be compared with a poetization of the everyday and, therefore, a fitting instrument for writing by a poet. Oddly enough, though, this pseudoscript would not be limited to literary use. It also appeared in letters of an official nature (then always handwritten in France) and even in personal notes to friends. In addition, as proof that the public and private selves remained in constant dual motion, one finds (in unpublished correspondence)[26] first drafts of letters written in a script entirely—almost startlingly—different from the final version. Thus, official and private handwriting, script and pseudoscript are juggled in such complex fashion that it would be difficult to say which best mirrors the man. And graphologists would be at a loss which to analyze.

As if such riddles were not enough, we find ourselves confronted by several lives, one of which often hides or repudiates the other. The most obvious and best known of these dual existences is, of course, that of the diplomat and the poet. Distinguishing himself from numerous other French writers who had such double careers (Paul Claudel, Jean Giraudoux, André Malraux), however, Alexis Leger/Saint-John Perse felt it necessary to cover his poetic tracks, deny his creativity, forbid publication of his work in France during his diplomatic career, even attempt to destroy the poet within ("étrangler en moi le seul être qui me soit au fond vraiment naturel").[27] Fortunately for poetry, this execution by garroting did not take place. And exile, combined with the cessation of diplomatic functions, allowed the poet to gain the upper hand. Then, in turn, the diplomat was repudiated by Saint-John Perse, and any reference to him was prohibited in studies of his poetry.

Moreover, all biographical accounts of either the poet or the diplomat were either discouraged or disparaged by him,[28] as if an embargo had been declared on any discussion of this double life. And yet, in a very odd move—not dissimilar to the reshaping of his handwriting—it was Saint-John Perse himself who composed his "biography" for the Pléiade edition of his complete works in 1972.[29] In a sense an official or public biography, as close to calligraphy as the transformed script, it is completed by extensive notes and a voluminous correspondence, the latter (some believe) edited, censored, or otherwise arranged to produce a certain image. Rather than calling this artifice, inauthenticity, or hypocrisy, it seems far more pertinent to speak of jugglery, of splitting identity into a number of facets—a penchant not unknown to us by now.

To further complicate matters, the multiple lives of this man are also replete with masks and a variety of guises. Masks are

perhaps most interesting in this instance, for they provide secrecy, create distance, preclude a static self in that they can be
changed with ease, insure fluidity and metamorphosis. But they
are also the hallmark of the actor, the hierophant, the shaman—
indeed, of all the roles known to the poet, this poet. (The persona of the poet as actor, hierophant, and shaman, in the work of
Saint-John Perse, has been skillfully treated by such critics as
Henriette Levillain[30] and Marie-Laure Ryan.[31] Little attention,
however, has been paid to this phenomenon as it occurs in the
life of Alexis Leger, although it is capital to the formation and
development of his multiple identities.) The most interesting
examples are of Leger in the guise—or disguise—of a "magneti-
seur," a kind of sorcerer with strange powers over animals,[32] or
achieving such closeness that they both virtually become one
being, exchange identities, reverse roles, and undergo totemic
identification.[33] The latter is particularly arresting, since simul-
taneous existence, the assumption of animal guises, and totemic
practices are all part of the shaman's vocation. Moreover, he
traditionally engages in extraordinary travel (astral voyages and
journeys into the underworld)—a factor that may not be unre-
lated to Leger's enigmatic expedition into Outer Mongolia, "aux
frontières même de l'esprit,"[34] beyond the limits of the human
world, nor to his bringing back two ritual objects from this voyage: a horse's skull and a "pierre de foudre de chaman."[35]

Compared with such extrahuman exploits, the life of the diplomat, with its masks worn for political expediency, may seem
mundane indeed. Yet, it also takes one to great heights, thrives
on personal magnetism, creates an aura of secrecy, is an "art
d'absence,"[36] casts one in a variety of disguises. In the case of
Alexis Leger/Saint-John Perse, all this is intensified by the fact
that the masks of the diplomat hide the poet's features. The two
faces of Janus seem simple indeed when compared with such
complex maneuvers as these. Even during exile, when the diplomat no longer conceals the poet (but the opposite then is true),
one notes a continuing predilection for the dual image and,
stranger still, the divided mask. This tendency appears to be all-

pervasive; it applies to major as well as to minor matters. Thus, it occurs in the famous definition of the Poet in Saint-John Perse's *Vents:* "O Poète, ô bilingue, entre toutes chose bisaiguës! . . . homme parlant dans l'équivoque!"[37] as well as in a detail concerning a pet animal: "Grattez, je vous prie, l'échine de . . . ma petite amie la chatte bimasquée à face de Picasso."[38] The first pronouncement in its loftiness and the second in its whimsy speak of a similar penchant.

Old age itself does not diminish this tendency, for the roles played by the septuagenarian are as varied as those of the young man. Among the most unusual is that of bridegroom—in a first marriage at the age of almost seventy-one—who called his wife by two different names (Dorothy or Diane), depending on which continent they lived.[39] But perhaps the most amusing role (yet treated with utter seriousness by reverent visitors) is that of ship's captain—played on shore. It entailed the raising of various flags, including one with the initial *P* (for Perse?), named "blue Peter" in nautical jargon, that signals to the pilot a ship "en partance" (i.e., ready to cast off).[40] Thus, at the brink of the last voyage, the final parting, the poet still juggled names, masks, roles, and identities with as much zest and humor as he did in his youth—and, one imagines, he would condone our also doing so.

Paradox flourishes not only because of the plurality of masks, roles, and images created by their owner; it also arises from the impressions made upon others and the resulting diversity in how the same man is seen. This is especially so if the perceptions are those of astute observers—as one can assume writers to be. Should one decide to complete the puzzle by putting side by side some of the most striking statements made by the latter, the resulting image is disconcerting, extraordinarily varied, often totally contradictory.

Let us, then, consider a few of the most succinct and interesting of the pieces:

"Il y a dans Leger je ne sais quoi   "Un type très bien."
de princier qui m'intimide."   Louis Aragon[42]
            André Gide[41]

"The aristocrat of our age."
W. H. Auden[43]

"Il se plaît . . . dans la compagnie des gens les plus simples."
Katherine Chapin[44]

"Une volonté si cruelle."
Alain Fournier[45]

"Ce qui me frappe chez lui, c'est sa présence tranquille."
Pierre Emmanuel[46]

"Supreme pantheist . . ."
Kathleen Raine[47]

"Dieu est un mot que Saint-John Perse évite, dirai-je religieusement?"
Paul Claudel[49]

"Nous aimons les mêmes dieux."
Michel de Ghelderode[48]

"Regard de papillon des îles, arrêté dans l'étonnement."
Anna de Noailles[50]

"Homme de l'antiquité, de l'antiquité héroïque, et de l'antiquité finissante."
E. M. Cioran[51]

"Ulysse moderne."
Romeo Lucchese[52]

"Il y a dans sa démarche quelque chose du marin."
Pierre Guerre[53]

"Cher impossible ami."
Colette[54]

"Admirable mais obscur."
Marcel Proust[55]

Such polarity of views would probably have neither surprised nor displeased Saint-John Perse. On the contrary, it coincides with the persona of the Poet (as we have already seen) and is most fully developed in two striking portraits of fellow poets that he himself created. These concern figures diametrically opposed in a number of ways (the age in which they wrote, their poetic vision and style, even the degree of their renown): Léon-Paul Fargue and Dante Alighieri. And yet, Perse singled out traits in both that are peculiarly similar, so much so that they seem almost mirror images of each other and—one might venture the guess—reflections of Perse the poet, himself. A back-and-forth movement between these two portraits results in the clearest picture, as well as providing some revealing glimpses of their creator's silhouette.

The description of Fargue focuses on the following characteristics:

[Il] sait d'instinct . . . qu'une fatalité heureuse régit l'équation poétique entre l'abstrait et le concret, entre l'imaginaire et le réel, comme entre l'esprit et la lettre, et qu'à solliciter seulement l'un des deux termes du rapport, le poète brûlant l'une ou l'autre de ses ailes, s'exposerait mortellement.[56]

The portrait of Dante climaxes in the following definition:

[Poète], homme d'absence et de présence, homme de refus et d'affluence. . . . Homme de pleine vocation . . . rebelle né . . . le Téméraire, et Taciturne . . . le Transgresseur. . . . Sous le signe des Gémeaux, pour son double destin d'homme de songe et d'action, homme d'amour et de violence, homme d'enfer et de ciel, naquit, un jour de Mai, Dante degli Alighieri, homme de poésie.[57]

It is more than evident that, in the eyes of Saint-John Perse, the Poet is a living paradox and that his power resides precisely in this play of opposites. While both portraits emphasize traits of this nature, that of Dante mirrors Perse so closely that one is tempted to see it as an instance of oblique self-portrayal: so many details coincide (particular juxtaposed characteristics, titles, even the sign of the zodiac—Gemini)[58] that the two poets appear as twins in more than one sense of the word.

Going beyond such unusual confluence, however, is the suggestion (which we must heed) that it is the oblique look that is most revealing, and is frequently the best way of obtaining meaningful insights. From this we might conclude that the real key to the life of Saint-John Perse/Alexis Leger can be found only by means that allow antitheses and unexpected pairings to come into view, while never losing sight of fluidity and movement.

One realizes, at this point, that the game must change. The original notion of the puzzle, while valid for an initial glance at this personality, can no longer apply. For puzzles are limited both by their two-dimensional quality and by their fixity (once the pieces are in place).

How, then, are we to obtain greater depth of field, a truer image, additional dimension? We need an instrument by which the elements at play are kept in motion, assume importance by their relative place, create shifting patterns, can produce figures of infinite variety. It seems evident that the puzzle must now give way to something resembling a kaleidoscope, for by virtue of its particular qualities we can gain a better view, perceive configurations hidden before, and see everything in a new perspective.

Let us look through its lens, then, at what was formerly a monolithic statue, fixed in a static pose, obscured by veils of idolatry. Now broken into a myriad of fragments, its components full of intricacy and far more richly colored than originally surmised, moving in ever changing patterns before our eyes, it is transformed and brought to life. Defying the repose of funeral masks, it disturbs—by a play of mirrors—the motionless sanctity of the reliquary.

Let us also listen to diverse new voices, speaking in discordant tones that admit laughter, irreverence, and sacrilege to drown out the tedious chant of praise. For they render, by their variance, the only fitting homage to this man, whose very essence is ambiguity.

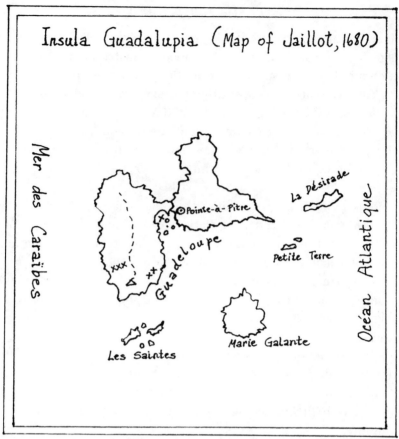

Insula Guadalupia (Map of Jaillot, 1680)

Mer des Caraïbes

Océan Atlantique

Pointe-à-Pitre

Guadeloupe

La Désirade

Petite Terre

Marie Galante

Les Saintes

X   Ilet de Saint-Leger-les-Feuilles
XX   "Le Bois Debout"
XXX "La Joséphine"
△   "La Soufrière"

Map of Guadeloupe, indicating the location of the birthplace of Alexis Saint-Leger Leger (Ilet de Saint-Leger-les-Feuilles) and various sites of his childhood (Le Bois Debout at Capesterre; La Joséphine near Matouba, the volcano La Soufrière, etc.)

CHAPTER 1

SON OF THE ATLANTIC
(1887–1899)

O fable généreuse, ô table d'abondance!
—*Pour fêter une enfance* (*OC*, p. 28)

Some might say it resembled a birth at sea.[1] Saint-Leger-les-Feuilles, where the child was born on the last day of May 1887, was so small that one was never out of the sea's reach. The odor of brine permeated the rocky terrain and tall groves of trees that distinguished the islet from the flat coral reefs of the environs;[2] the sound of the surf resounded as far as the great house without windowpanes[3] opening onto the water to catch every breeze in the hot and humid season, penetrating even into the remote bedchamber where the young mother lay in labor. So strong was the impact of the sea that her very body surely mimed its rhythms—the ebb and flow, the crest and trough of waves, the breakers' thrust—and the child seemed like some creature of the deep about to surface.

Perhaps, during the long hours of travail, a wind had risen from the Atlantic and fanned her face, as if a reminder that her forebears had settled the "Isles des Vents"[4] or a prophecy that she would bear a son—for the men of the islands called themselves "Hommes d'Atlantique"[5] as though the ocean were their birthplace. She may have mused on all this, and on the birth sign of the child, foretelling a life divided, an innate dichotomy.

Or, as labor progressed in a movement as inexorable as the tides, she may have imagined the vast expanse of the deep that the women of her family considered "terre sainte"[6]—both cradle and burial place, site of fortune and tragedy, passage and passing, immense as death, and birth. And, though in childbed, a deathbed scene might have flashed across her memory: the aged ancestress who, as she lay dying, called for the shutters of the great bay window facing the Atlantic to be thrown wide, to give her last blessing to the ocean that reigned over the fate of all her kin.[7]

The child about to be born was of that lineage. Surely, it would bear the imprint of the sea. And seamarks guide the unfolding of its destiny.

The infant's first voyage appeared to substantiate this prophecy. For it was a sea crossing: the son of Amédée Saint-Leger Leger and his wife Françoise-Renée (née Dormoy) was taken by ship, when he was only a few weeks old, from the islet owned by his father's family to Pointe-à-Pitre where his birth would be officially registered.[8]

His journey thus took place close to the summer solstice when the sun seems to stand permanently at the zenith. The procession would have set out from the great house at the highest point of the island, in the late afternoon when the air was cooler, and wound its way down to the wharf—the mother holding the infant; the father following close behind, with the three sisters of the boy; a group of servants, varying in color from yellow to bronze to deepest black,[9] bringing up the rear.

Although the vessel lay perfectly still in the calm waters, the young mother surely advanced with caution across the gangplank and glanced somewhat anxiously at the sea, the sky, the intense light (as if expecting adverse effects from the elements for her child) and, as the ship made ready to cast off from shore, crossed herself piously.

As soon as the prow headed toward the open sea, the wind freshened. An odor of salt filled the air. Soon the outlines of the island blurred, and the servants on the shore were only a brilliant patch of color against the foliage. Then all traces of land disappeared, and one saw nothing but the sapphire expanse of sea. The child, asleep before, seemed to stir as soon as they were afloat. His eyes opened and looked, unblinking, into the light, as if he not only tolerated the sun but was drawn to it. And he appeared to breathe in the salt air with relish. Alert when he should have been drowsy, exhilarated when others would have shown discomfort, his behavior would certainly have been deemed unusual. Very likely the father announced that his son would become a great seafarer; surely the mother shuddered at this augury and gazed with open hostility at the deep.[10]

As always, a number of seabirds followed the vessel's wake. Outlined against the sun, they cut a bright pattern across the sky, dipping and swerving in search of invisible prey. Quite probably, their presence also affected the child and caused him to follow their course with his eyes, untiring in his intense perusal of their flight.

Only when they approached port would he again doze off. But he seemed to sleep more soundly than before, as if sun, sea, and salt air had soothed him; and waves rocked him more gently than any cradle.

It has been said that no voyager could enter the port of Pointe-à-Pitre without being struck by its splendor. For it was a visual feast of which one never tired, a triumphant mingling of colors: green foliage, golden sunlight, a sea of pure silver; and the city itself, which lay like a gem on the shore, ringed by a circle of lush vegetation.[11]

The prow of the ship headed toward this dazzling scene. It wound its way among sailboats, great ocean liners, and the figures of "Ti-canotiers"[12] (young boys who dived for coins with the litheness of marine creatures); then crossed the newly constructed boat basin, of which all Pointe-à-Pitre was justifiably proud.[13] At the landing place there was the usual group of native washerwomen who made their way toward ships at anchor, descended like a flock of brightly colored birds and asked for soiled clothes in tones so musical that they belied the women's arduous trade.[14] One also saw less merry women, in somber attire, staggering beneath sacks of coal that they carried out of the holds of merchant vessels.[15] Still others, balancing baskets, trays, or jars on their heads, who appeared to dance as they walked, were the granddaughters of recently freed slaves[16] who moved as majestically as if their ancestors had always strolled in palace gardens.

Carriages awaited voyagers at the wharf to transport them into the heart of the city. The usual route was through the Place de la Victoire with its newly constructed theater[17] and the church with its Greek peristyle where most important religious ceremonies took place. It then entered the streets of the city. There, wealthy mansions stood side by side with modest abodes (for Pointe-à-Pitre made no distinction between aristocratic and lower-class districts, as did other commercial cities in this part of the globe).[18] All, whether poor or luxurious, had shops on the ground floor and living quarters above; and all sported balconies.

Toward sunset the city became crowded with carriages drawn by magnificent horses. Evenings would be calm, for here as everywhere in the Antilles there was little nightlife except for the riotous period of the Carnaval.[19] But now, activity was at its height, especially in the marketplace.

The Place du Marché was filled with crowds of numerous races and nationalities (Africans, Indians, Chinese, Europeans), there to buy, sell, barter, argue, or simply enjoy the spectacle.[20] Natives from the country offered the colorful produce of the tropical soil. Fishmongers sold the incredibly varied species of the local waters. Sailors from ships all over the world bid for provisions in French, English, Spanish, and many other tongues.[21] Besides the people of the marketplace, there were also the street vendors. Mostly women, they balanced trays on their heads and wore the long robes of the region, gathered up to give free movement to the legs and adorned with gay jewelry. More than their colorful garb, however, it was their cries that intrigued the visitor: the seller of herbs hawked products with strange, delightful names ("Balai doux," "Bois d'homme," "Bonnet carré")[22] and promised cures for all imaginable ailments; the pottery vendor

Open-air market in Pointe-à-Pitre, virtually unchanged today from its appearance in the nineteenth century. (Photo by Judy Gurevitch. Courtesy French West Indies Tourist Bureau).

swore to take her life if her wares were not appreciated; the pastry cook's chant matched the sweets she sold.[23]

The carriage transporting the Saint-Leger family across the town must thus have wound its way among this throng from all corners of the earth, proceeded in the midst of calls, peals of laughter, the sounds of the "bamboula,"[24] the songs that sprang up spontaneously on every occasion, the whispering noise of many bare feet; surrounded by odors of sugar and garlic (typical of Creole cuisine) and the heady scent of tropical flowers.

The teeming life of Pointe-à-Pitre surely assailed all their senses (accustomed to the serene pleasures of their private isle). It probably affected even the newborn child, for he could not help but hear the babble of varied tongues, the lilting chant of Creole, the beat of drums, the vendors' calls, and somehow already shared the life of the simple people of the streets.

The gathering, on the day of his baptism, would assemble a

quite different crowd. For this occasion, all the notables of the city would surely be present: the jurists who were his father's colleagues, dignitaries come to honor the old and distinguished family, fellow plantation owners from the islands—representatives of the class of the masters, the rulers of the Isles of the Winds.

The church would be filled with tropical flowers. The stained-glass windows, illuminated by the brilliant sun of the tropics, would shine with jewel-like splendor. Numerous paintings (especially the copy of a work from the Louvre that Napoleon III had donated) formed a backdrop in which the privileged class of the city took great pride.

Those come together here, however, reveled also in the pride of their heritage. For both sides of the child's family laid claim to an ancient and noble lineage, and centuries of prominent rule in the Antilles. The father's forebears went back to a branch of the Castellane of Castille, to barons of Provence, bishops and cardinals of Savoie, members of Parliament and counselors to the king, Hungarian counts, aristocrats established in the Antilles since the seventeenth century.[25] The mother's ancestors were no less illustrious, for her family tree went back to d'Ormois le Bourguinon, included a hero in naval battles against the British (shipwrecked off the coast of Africa, first prisoner, then chieftain of one of the tribes), owners of great fleets of ships, and aristocratic planters settled on the isles since the eighteenth century.[26]

Gathered around the altar for the christening would be the most recent representatives of both great families: the infant's parental grandparents—Alexis Saint-Leger Leger (whose name the child would bear) and his wife Augusta (the former Mlle de Caille whom the poet Lamartine had admired in her youth)[27]— as well as his maternal grandfather, Paul Dormoy.[28] Flanking the parents of the newborn and his three sisters, Eliane, Paule, and Marguerite, they surely viewed the infant with much satisfaction, for he was the first male child born to the couple and would carry on the family name.

All crossed themselves piously, but the mother did so with special fervor[29] when the priest, after uttering the ritual formula of baptism, ended by pronouncing the child's full name: "Marie-René Alexis Saint-Leger Leger."[30]

Once the ceremony had ended, the gathered dignitaries, landowners, and planters of wealth and renown filed out of the church, proudly exhibiting the youngest member of their great clan.

Alexis Saint-Leger had now officially entered the world.

A life of less official but far greater splendor would await the child in the years that followed.

Eden (on the sea) might have resembled the realms of his childhood days. On the Ile des Feuilles, to which he soon returned, and the great plantations of his family (La Josephine and Le Bois Debout),[31] the dawn of creation seemed to coincide with the start of his young life. Everything had an auroral freshness in this landscape where blues and greens predominated. Fecund valleys, swift rivers and waterfalls alternated with primeval forests and mighty mountain chains.[32] As far as the eye could see there were vast expanses of sea and sky. In this world seemingly without end, all was "si calme et pur, si tiède . . . si continuel aussi"[33] that space and time seemed to stretch to infinity or had not yet come into existence.

Life must have been fuller each day. As the various senses awakened, the child encompassed new riches and pleasures unknown. The eye encountered flora of infinite variety: royal palms, giant rubber trees, blossoming coffee plants, "flamboyants," "balisiers," "frangipaniers," "sabliers," acacia and vanilla trees, riotous cactus blooms, and giant lianas.[34] The ear became attuned to birdcalls of every tropical variety, the many sounds of the sea, the changing voices of the wind (from the gentle "alizé" to the wild typhoon that made everyone flee to the "cases à vents" of the plantation).[35] Taste brought a whole other array of discoveries: spices, salt, hearts of palms, the rose-apple sweet-

Typical nineteenth-century plantation house in Guadeloupe showing windows without panes open to catch every passing breeze. (Photo courtesy French West Indies Tourist Bureau).

ness of his nurse's mouth,[36] the savor of "lambis" and other "fruit of the sea." Touch revealed the smoothness of women's arms, rough coral, and slimy seaweed, of the soft mouths of horses and the hard carapace of an insect in his small palm. Odors marked the passage of the day: morning coffee, the smell of sweat in the sun, the pungent sea scent of women's loins, the perfume of L'Herbe-à-Madame-Lalie that surrounded his mother at evening time.[37]

The doors of his body brought ever new adventures as they opened to the plenitude of his life. And he, himself, seemed king of all this universe.

As the only son of the master, surrounded by nursemaids, doting servants, as well as a retinue of native children, his every wish was surely anticipated and instantly fulfilled,[38] as though it emanated from divinity. It would have been natural for him to have basked in the glory of being, to all appearances, the center of creation. But young Alexis—or "Allan," as his mother liked to call him[39]—appears not to have followed this path.

A restless child, impatient of too much tender solicitude or restraints imposed by excessive care, it seems that he preferred to go off alone, to wander and explore, turning his sharp gaze at the sun; the mysterious volcano, La Soufrière, veiled in vapor until a cloud suddenly crowned it with gold,[40] the giant Matouba waterfall with a rainbow across its cascades;[41] the movement of sea creatures; the shapes of seedpods and the structure of stones; a fruit tree devoured by crabs;[42] fish more splendid than the peacocks of Solomon or ocelots fed by Montezuma on human flesh;[43] the strange animals his family had imported from Guyana to enhance their island.[44]

He spent long hours in the company of animals. They fascinated him and seemed, in turn, mesmerized by the boy. A horse, his large dog, even a lizard in the sun came under his spell. The servants muttered about witchcraft. The adults in the family called it "magnétisme animal" (a term used by the local doctor who had first spotted the boy's aptitude).[45] To Alexis, it was probably simply communication without need for words between kindred creatures. But he also knew it as a form of solitude, setting him apart from others of his species.[46]

Yet, solitude seemed to be an imperative need. He roamed for days, accompanied only by his dog, in the remotest parts of the island. Or he rode alone across the beaches that stretched for miles without a human trace. So great was his desire for space, the vast openness of nature, the freedom of the air, for everything that defied enclosures and limits that he was soon nicknamed "Ban-moin-lè" (the Creole equivalent for "Donnez-moi l'air, l'espace") by an old black stable hand.[47]

But it was also the unleashing of forces (his own or those of nature) that moved him. He even relished cataclysms[48]: the mighty winds that decapitated the "palmistes" and lashed the waves into white fury; storms that lifted ships out of the deep and tossed them, toylike, unto the land; the threatening rumble of the volcano that had already, several times, devastated the is-land;[49] earthquakes that could engulf whole villages and reveal the earth's firey core. All these manifestations of nature's power seemed to him part of the enormous vitality pervading every-thing, and to be reflected in the strength of his young body.

The sense of his own invulnerability was so great that, when illness one day struck him down,[50] he probably reacted with the same sort of anger and surprise as he would have if a robber had suddenly stolen a treasure he owned. The attack of typhoid that wracked him with fever, leaving him weak and defenseless, must have terrified the boy. His parents, who remembered the dread epidemics that had ravaged the island (such as the wave of chol-era in 1866 that claimed 12,000 victims),[51] anxiously watched the family doctor as he examined the patient. As soon as the wind changed, though, and blew in from the Atlantic, his fever dropped dramatically. The sea had done its work. The boy's strength returned, and he heard the doctor joyously exclaim: "Celui-là, s'il lui arrive jamais quelque chose, qu'on le porte à la mer, et il se relèvera aussitôt sur la tête!"[52]

Thus the first seven years of Alexis's life passed. The eighth marked the end of those days out of time when everything had seemed infinite and inviolate. But it was also the beginning of a new mastery: on his birthday that year he received three gifts that gave him power over sea, earth, and sky, in the form of his own boat, horse, and telescope.[53]

Now the sea was not only a force that vanquished illness and restored vigor but an infatuation to which he could give full reign. Tutored early in life to its ways, he now determined to achieve superior mastery. He often set out alone. Sometimes his voyages seemed to take him to a domain that lay beyond the profane. Far out at sea when the waves' clamor alternated with a great silence, his heart pounded with a strange joy. He felt that he had crossed into an awesome realm and inhabited "la gorge d'un dieu!"[54]

Now also, having long admired his mother galloping on Tzigane, her splendid mare,[55] he had a horse of his own. He delighted in the way they appeared to form a single being as they moved, and spent a long time contemplating the beauty of its face, the moon-shaped imprints his knees made on its coat, the head lifted as if to strange gods[56] that turned it into a creature of bronze, mysterious and awe-inspiring.

The telescope gave rise to other explorations. The whole sky was now revealed in its vast, unexpected complexity. New constellations, clusters of stars, the intricate design of the moon became visible. He marveled at the magnitude of the unknown.

Having so many added riches might have made him conclude that each day could only bring forth further abundance and joy.

But death entered his life that year. It claimed his younger sister, whom he probably considered part of a world where everything thrived as easily as tropical vegetation. Yet she had withered and died. And while, given his age, it must have been impossible to imagine that the word "death" described a permanent state, and besides, she had been placed in a coffin of fragrant wood[57]—not unlike a small boat for a journey from which she would shortly return—it was his mother's grief that taught him anguish.

Sadness now shrouded the house. The women were in deep mourning, their eyes constantly reddened by silent tears. One heard only the murmur of prayers, hardly ever the familiar laughter in the sun that had echoed all throughout his childhood days.

When his mother and sisters left for France in the summer and he remained, as was customary, on the island, a great weight seemed to lift, and relief brightened the hours. He turned once more to the activities he had known before the crevice, made by death, had opened. But he had become more pensive and thought of those who had died while he was still too young to understand[58] or gazed with concern at his grandmother's wrinkled hands. And, while in the past, a bloated dead cat in the water or a live dog on a hook as bait for sharks[59] had primarily aroused his curiosity, he now saw the destruction of life quite differently.

It was at this time that a Hindu servant, whose beauty had already struck him when he was a young child, began to observe the boy closely. In the evenings, in her soft, melodious voice, she told him the stories of her gods. Often, she spoke of Shiva, the great creator and destroyer, Lord of the Three Faces, who had created the world by dancing and, with the lightning that issued from his third eye, destroyed it. She also spoke of the endless cycle of birth, death, and rebirth that governed everything in the universe. The boy listened, spellbound, to her tales. There was a profound harmony there, a movement so vast that it encompassed all space and time.

Now that his family was absent and they were alone, the woman began to double her interest in the boy. Her attentiveness was certainly reciprocated, for he surely appreciated the languid grace of her copper-colored body, her magnificent dark eyes, the swaying motion of her hips as she walked; and he probably daydreamed for hours over her mysterious presence, imagining her the priestess of a secret cult into which he desired to be initiated.

One night this dream was realized. It seemed that, as he lay on his bed in the state between sleeping and waking, he saw her float into the room, magnificently dressed and with a small bowl in her hands. In silence and with solemnity she proceeded to paint the palms of his hands and the soles of his feet with ochre.[60] When he was thus anointed, she beckoned him to follow her out of the house. Like shadows, they made their way through the silent plantation. Even his dog did not stir as they passed. Near the edge of the woods they came to a small structure he had often passed in his wanderings without ever venturing inside.

Now a door slowly opened. An old Indian led them without a word into the sanctuary. In the middle stood an elaborate altar, surrounded by idols in the form of tall pillarlike stones that the

Hindu temple at Changy (not far from Capesterre and the Saint-Leger Leger family's plantation of Le Bois Debout) still in use today. (Photo by the author).

woman, in a whisper, referred to as "lingams." Worshipers anointed these with butter and honey, touching them reverently in passing. There were also statues of voluptuously shaped women twined about male figures like vines; others were seated in hieratic poses, their exposed genitals outlined in carmine, which the faithful touched with expressions of awe as they entered the shrine. His guide, in a low voice, referred to them as "yonis." Then she spoke of the sacred union of Shiva and Shakti, symbolized by the male and female emblems in the temple, celebrating the creative energy of the universe through the act from which all life originates.[61] Her radiant smile, as she spoke, seemed to illuminate the entire shrine.

Alexis felt as though the sacred energy suffused his own body as he stood among the worshipers. He found himself chanting in honor of Shiva, who sat enthroned on the central altar in a state of divine afflatus that, from chaos, had made the universe arise.[62]

In the morning it must all have seemed like a mirage. Fragments of his dream—or memory—returned confusedly: the third eye of Shiva; Deva, the great goddess in her various incarnations, both smiling and terrible; sexual union as a form of worship.[63] But it felt as if it were a figment of his imagination, an erotic fantasy, except for the ochre that still clung to his palms and to the soles of his feet. Then, too, there was the secret smile of a conspirator that the beautiful Hindu gave him as soon as they were out of the others' sight.

Church services seemed dull and insipid in comparison to the clandestine ceremony. He guarded the night of Shiva as one would a contraband treasure. And he never forgot the rites of his pagan initiation.[64]

Soon, however, he was initiated into less exotic rites. His education that, until then, had been in the hands of private tutors (an old naval officer to teach him some mathematics and physics; a priest to supervise his readings of the classics; Father Duss who encouraged his love of botany)[65] would now be formally pursued at the lycée of Pointe-à-Pitre. He encountered the rigors of the classroom, contrasting with the idyllic ways of his early schooling.

He surely regretted the latter, so different from the dry disciplines to which he was now subjected. In the close rooms, among walls of books in dusty libraries, his body must have ached for movement. Yet his mind became trained by the exercise of the intellect. He succeeded admirably in the feats prescribed. But, though he excelled in all his studies, only one subject interested him passionately: natural history.

As soon as classes were dismissed, he hastened into the streets of the city; most of all, toward the wharf to which he was always drawn. There, mountains of sugar flowed onto the dock; men staggered under the weight of red-and-purple carcasses of animals; gleaming bodies of an endless variety of fish tumbled from

The bustling harbor of Pointe-à-Pitre as it appears today, still an important port-of-call (Photo courtesy French West Indies Tourist Bureau).

nets into carts. He saw mules and cattle swim from barges to shore and rise from the water, magnificent as statues. He watched prophets and sorcerers and heard a black witch doctor chant.[66] But his heart leaped when, past the throng of people, he suddenly caught sight once more of the sea—unplowed and uninhabited—whose clamor drowned out the fishmongers' cries.[67]

He began to spend most of his free time in the port. The variety of ships there was fascinating: whalers from America, ocean liners from Europe, freighters from all corners of the globe. But it was not only the vessels, their form and rigging, the beauty and efficiency of their lines, their names and ports of call, that intrigued him, but also the sailors and ship's captains that held him spellbound. Their faces had the look of conquerors; their wind-swept, sun-etched features distinguished them from the dwellers on land; their walk mimed the rhythm of the waves; even their voices had a different ring (more distant and mysterious, as though wrapped in fog or tinged with the roar of storms). He never tired of watching their gestures, as they tied intricate knots, secured a rope, folded a sail, or touched the instruments of navigation. Whenever he could, he engaged them in conversation.

Alexis found that these encounters fired his imagination. He started to jot down his impressions, in his desire to capture this world. Then he found that he could give them life by images, rhythms, the sorcery of language. At first, he kept these writings to himself because he had an intense sense of privacy and was reticent to share anything so personal—and probably also because he knew, intuitively, that he was only groping his way in a new domain and that these gropings must be protected as a premature child would be.

Some of his schoolfellows, however, curious about the small notebook he carried with him at all times, managed to discover his nascent talent. They urged him to participate in the small magazine published at the lycée. He hesitated at first but finally agreed to write a chronicle entitled "Mouvement du Port,"[68] mostly because it gave him the opportunity to interview the captains of the great ships anchored in port but certainly also because words (with their mysterious allure) had begun to cast a spell over him, far greater than any he had known. And created a new world.

1897

It seemed as if the end of the world had come. The earth was torn open. Huge chasms opened under one's feet. The whole island trembled. The sea rose in gigantic waves that blocked out the sky.

An earthquake shook Guadeloupe. It was not for the first time in the century. The Isles des Vents had been devastated before: Martinique in 1839; Guadeloupe in 1843 (almost wiping out Pointe-à-Pitre).[69]

Alexis had probably heard the old people speak of these catastrophes but treated them almost as legends. He could not have imagined the sight that lay before him now. True, he loved the cataclysms of nature, the wild unleashing of the elements. And the observer in him made him watch, with fascination, walls fall in slow motion, objects appear at weird angles defying gravity, and listen to the ominous rumble of the earth's entrails, to ships' sirens wailing like terrified animals. But when it was all over (in an endless moment that lasted less than two minutes in chronological time), he stood before a Dantesque spectacle.

Bodies looking like flayed animals were carried through the flames. Cadavers were piled up in heaps in the marketplace. Others, thrust into tin boxes, were borne along the main thoroughfare that now resembled a river of greenish water, for the sea had risen and entered the city. In the main square, where most of the dead lay, he saw the tall, dark figure of a man, aloof as a prophet, ready to sound a conch—as if doomsday had come. The sky, by its menacing colors, announced another quake for that night.[70]

What remained most vivid was the look of horror on a woman's face as she carried a child, resembling a disjointed doll, through a sheet of fire.

Horror, mingled with dismay, reigned also in Alexis's family. A great deal of their property had been devastated; financial ruin had come to several members of the clan. There was constant talk of disaster, for grave economic crises were anticipated. The end of an epoch seemed in view. Family councils occupied much of the time in the months that followed. Surely, the children sensed that momentous decisions were in the air; the weight of foreboding was such that they hardly dared to venture out to visit their favorite haunts. The island suddenly seemed to be a precarious shoal that might disappear at any moment. A lush paradise before, it now threatened one with extinction or with expulsion by violence. Trees, sea, sky could all prove treacherous; even familiar animals seemed to assume a threatening guise. The adults provided no solace, for they spoke in low tones and were extremely preoccupied. There was much discussion behind closed doors, mostly among the men of the family. They emerged, after such meetings, with somber faces and clothes reeking of cigar smoke.

One day Alexis's father called together the members of his immediate family to announce that they must seek another domicile and way of life. In order to prepare for this great change, he would shortly journey to France where he hoped to explore new possibilities and, he added, better schooling for his son. He concluded with some optimistic comments on the place from which his ancestors had come to the islands long ago. But, to Alexis, it must have seemed as if another earthquake had shaken his world and that the deep roots he had in this soil were being torn up as violently as those of trees that succumb in cataclysms.

The months that passed during his father's absence were surely full of anxiety. It seemed that the family lived in a state of suspended animation: no longer part of their native land, which had betrayed them; not yet oriented toward a new existence, which somehow had the feel of exile. They sometimes spoke in forced, cheerful tones of the possibilities of the future; at other times they gazed with melancholy at the island they might soon have to leave forever.

It was the decision of departure that prevailed. When Alexis's father finally returned from Europe, he announced that Saint-Leger-les-Feuilles would be sold. A buyer, named Petreluzzi, had already expressed interest in the property. The boy was speechless when the announcement was made. No words could express the loss he felt.[71] There was only a great emptiness, as though everything had given way.

The other members of the family certainly also reacted with dismay at the dramatic exodus. Although nowhere an angel with a fiery sword was visible, there was the distinct feeling of being exiled and, after centuries of being lords of this corner of creation, chased from what had once been a fair replica of Eden.

1899

It was the time of leave-taking. The island sold, the great house emptied of its furnishings, the library carefully crated and awaiting departure, the children's old toys distributed among the servants, the past seemed abandoned—or liquidated. In some ways, this caused the boy some sense of exhilaration, a giddy sensation of embarking on unbeaten trails or uncharted paths.

Only when it came to leave his horse must the break have manifested itself in all its raw pain. As, for the last time, he stroked the beloved face and the animal turned its knowing eyes upon him, he turned suddenly and almost ran from the stall. He refused to look back once as he took the downward path that led to the place of embarkation.

The boat going to Pointe-à-Pitre, where a transatlantic liner waited, took the same course as on Alexis's very first journey. Now—twelve years later—he could not help but respond to sun, wind, seabirds, and ocean as intensely as he had during infancy.

As the last traces of Saint-Leger-les-Feuilles disappeared on the horizon and the prow of the ship headed toward the Atlantic he would soon cross, he probably already found himself wondering whether, for the loss of his childhood paradise, he would gain worlds unknown.

CHAPTER 2

CRUSOE IN FRANCE
(1899–1907)

D'un exil lumineux . . . comment garder les voies . . . ?
—*Images a Crusoé* (*OC*, p. 20)

The sound of the siren was stronger than organ tones. It rent the air, made the tall ship tremble, drowned out all lesser sounds. Like the cry of a vast sea creature, full of anguish and triumph, it enveloped the boy who stood on the deck of the great transatlantic liner. Slowly, with infinite majesty, its giant prow swung around. Minute tugs pushed their noses against its sides, nudging and guiding it like so many sheepdogs herding a mammoth strayed from the herd. At the edge of the harbor they were left behind, and the ship, free of all restraints, moved into its true element—the open sea.

Pointe-à-Pitre was soon no more than a shining dot on the seacoast, the island of Guadeloupe an ever thinner line on the horizon—until they vanished entirely and there was nothing but the endless expanse of water. When the sun set, a great stillness hung over sea and sky. Alexis stood for a long time at the ship's rail watching the silvery wake—the only remaining trace indicating the direction of his homeland. Even that was quickly lost as the vessel veered around. There was nothing to orient one now. The stars had not yet risen by which one could determine one's course. The hour was uncertain. It was that strange time of the day, called *entre chien et loup*, when the light had begun to fail and the heavens appeared endless and lonely, an unfathomable hollow space.

A sense of longing had come over him. For past or future? He did not know. He only felt that, Januslike, he faced in two directions at once. His mind moved backward, to the Isles des Vents, and forward, toward an unknown that lay beyond an infinite series of waves. The ship's progress, on the other hand, seemed resolute, inexorable as fate in motion, carrying him along in its headlong flight. When the first constellations appeared in the sky, he saw that they were headed due East, in diametric opposition to the land of his birth. Now childhood had truly come to an end. It must be forsaken—or interred in the memory.

He tore himself from his musings and entered the ship's brightly lit public rooms where the passengers had assembled on this, the first night of their journey. A babble of voices engulfed him, issuing from the Spanish and French admirals who had left Cuba and Martinique,[1] as well as from various other colonialists abandoning the islands. The talk centered on natural disasters and financial ruin, on the recent war that had put an end to Spanish sovereignty in Cuba—a situation lamented by the old French families from Guadeloupe and Martinique who were related to those of Spanish origin.[2] There was also much conjecture about life on the European continent, for to the majority of the expatriated it was a foreign land despite their ancestral links with that soil. One sensed a mixture of hope and melancholy in all those gathered here. They seemed to hover between two lives, two worlds.

Alexis slept fitfully that night, turning in his berth (from east to west and back again). He dreamed alternately of his native isle and the shores of Europe he had never seen. Palm trees and sugarcane mingled with fir and oak described in botany books, the brilliant hues of the tropics with a gray imaginary landscape. Eventually, however, his youth and the rocking motion of the ship won out, and he sank into a deep sleep before the sun rose.

In the morning all his agitation had vanished. A fresh salt breeze blew in through the porthole, and the roar of the waves and the calls of seabirds delighted his ear. He dressed and climbed swiftly to the top deck where he surveyed the ever new marvel of the deep. As he stood there, he felt the wind and sun sweep his former doubts and misgivings away. The unknown had become adventure, the future a challenge to be met with joy. The sea had once again cured him. The anguish of the night was gone. He felt himself surge forward, as full of power as the vessel itself. He eagerly anticipated each lap of the journey to the point where the sad faces of the passengers he saw irked him and he felt a twinge of ferocity in their presence. A wild laugh seized him each time the spray flew in his face or a wave rose to particularly great heights. Irritated by the supine figures in deck chairs (for whom the sea spelled sickness) and by the greenish faces in the dining room, Alexis began to seek out the members of the crew and spent most of his time in their company. He preferred their rough oaths to the polite but lugubrious conversation of the passengers in the stuffy salons where morose phrases mingled with stale cigar smoke. The men of the sea had other tales to tell. Their dealings were with far greater powers than rival nations; their battles were waged with the elements; the only badges of their victories were to be found in the deep lines of their faces and in the calm gaze reminiscent of seabirds.

They, in turn, enjoyed the rapt attention of the boy, his insatiable curiosity, his delight in new experiences, such as the day when, during their Atlantic crossing, Alexis (forever on deck) encountered what was, for him, an entirely unknown element. As they passed the Azores, which lay on their course, he saw a strange new sight. On the top of one of the mountain ranges, a soft sheet of white was spread, shimmering and pure, resembling nothing he had ever seen before. He turned toward one of the seamen, a query on his face. "Snow,"[3] the man said with a smile, noting the amazement of the boy who stood mesmerized at the ship's rail.

The voyage continued for many more days. Fog alternated more frequently now with fine weather, overcast skies with starry nights. The ocean, ever changing, shifted its colors with each hour, its surface in accordance with the winds and tides. One could not conceive of ever tiring of its infinite variety. And yet, it was changeless also. It was forever different and the same, the sum of all possible contradictions.

Alexis had grown so enamored of life on board ship that he could hardly imagine a landbound existence again. He seriously considered remaining with the crew (as many a boy his age had done) and making his life at sea. It certainly seemed more tempting than being a *lycéen* in some landlocked French town. Just as he had acquired the rolling gait of a sailor and successfully imitated the raucous tones of the salts he frequented, the first traces of the European shore appeared on the horizon. The captain announced that they would touch land at Santander[4] and then proceed along the coastline until they sighted the great lighthouse of Cordouan.[5]

With some emotion, the passengers gathered on deck to greet the initial signs of the Continent. For some it was a new experience and, as the landmass loomed larger, their excitement increased. They strained forward, craned their necks, even jostled each other in an effort to catch a glimpse of European soil. Alexis was more interested in the vegetation and the rock formations. Having never seen the flora of these regions—the pine, cypress, olive, and plane trees—except in the pages of his botany books, he trained his binoculars on the shore and peered with great intensity at forests and cliffs as they drew nearer.

The agitation of the landing, the transport of trunks and crates, the cries of infants, and the shouts of longshoremen were of no import to him. He had eyes only for the strange new landscape. It was gray and wrapped in mist, stones outlined against a lead-colored sea from which a chill wind blew; the houses appeared forbidding, with their shining, cold windowpanes and gardens shut in by high walls—small and mean in comparison with the rambling luxuriousness of the plantations he had known.

When he heard the voices that rose from the wharfs, he was struck by their strangeness also. They had a sound quite different from the lilting Creole chants of Pointe-à-Pitre he associated with seaports. These accents were far more clipped and harsh, as if to echo the landscape. Only now and then the melodious tones of one of his compatriots brought a note of warmth to the chorus of cold voices—and a disdainful smile from the French of the Continent. Alexis began to wonder how his own speech would be received and felt a mixture of reticence and defiance as he considered his status that of a stranger in this land.

As he walked down the gangplank and, for the first time, set foot on French soil, he was not certain whether he was fated to play the role of explorer or exile.

Pau, 1899–1905

Fortunately, Pau was a cosmopolitan city. During the "season" especially, it seemed a world of legend filled with glamorous exiles: Russian émigrés mingled with Latin expatriates; Austrian music lovers rubbed elbows with German philosophers; British eccentrics encountered African explorers; colonialists from all parts of the globe brought the flavor of far-off lands to the scene; moreover, the great sportsmen of many nations gathered here, especially champion riders wishing to compete in the most arduous race in all of France.[6]

The Saint-Leger family soon settled into this new life, and a fine house (at 37, rue de Bordeaux)[7] finding much stimulation in the international society. The children began the European education their father had sought for them: Alexis entered the lycée of Pau but continued to live at home; his sisters became boarders at the convent of the Ursulines.[8] As the belongings of the household began to arrive, their dwelling gradually acquired the look and feel of a home once more. Objects and furnishings they had long loved surrounded them again—with one notable exception—Alexis's father's library, which had met with a most strange fate.

The day of the books' arrival, long awaited and joyously anticipated, had finally come. The workmen unloaded the numerous crates and piled them up in the courtyard of the house. Then a bizarre thing happened (which Alexis would remember all his life). The tin-lined cases containing the precious cargo began to emit an odd and horrid odor, almost as though they harbored corpses, not books. So great was the stench that no one dared to venture what the contents would reveal. Alarmed by this turn of events, M. Saint-Leger Leger called in the local police. They gathered around the crates looking suspiciously on as the men broke the lids open, ready to spring into action if some dread secret came to light. When planks and covers were finally removed, a compact black mass appeared (obviously in an advanced state of putrefaction). No one could have guessed what the original contents of the crates had been. The only indication was a single sheet of paper, miraculously preserved in the midst of this sickening pulp—the title page of the original Poulet-Malassis edition of Charles Baudelaire's *Les Fleurs du mal!*

Strange flowers of evil had indeed sprouted in this sunken library. After long inquiries, it was revealed that nine of the cases of books had fallen into the sea while being loaded on board at Pointe-à-Pitre; the insurance company, with an exaggerated faith in its packing expertise, had shipped them in their sodden state across the Atlantic without suspecting their contents' fate.

What struck Alexis most in all this was his father's mute grief as he surveyed the ruins of his library, the books he loved turned into a repugnant, rotting mess. The boy's gorge rose at the sight. He suddenly felt a violent revulsion for all books, as though they were, by nature, destined for stagnation and decay. It was an aversion so powerful that it would last for the rest of his days.[9]

Yet, in the years that followed, his life was lived among books, and turned out to be highly rewarding in many respects. He completed his two *baccalauréats* with distinction, excelled in Latin and Greek, and received the Grand Prix de Rhétorique, the highest honor the lycée bestowed; he also brilliantly passed his examination in philosophy in Bordeaux where he was questioned by Professor Drouin, the brother-in-law of André Gide.[10]

Despite such successes, books would surely have become prison walls for young Alexis had there not been other worlds to

explore. If winters had to be spent in scholarly pursuits, summers restored the equilibrium between the life of the mind and
that of the body. As soon as classes were over, he left the confines
of libraries and cities for the countryside, fled from dusty rooms
and dark corridors into the wild, sunlit landscape of the Basque
region and the adjoining northern reaches of Spain. The Pyrenees especially, attracted him, for he had a passion for mountaineering. He found the exhilaration of the ascent, the solitary
splendor of the summit where one's only encounters were with
eagles, hawks, or other birds of prey, as intoxicating as the head-
iest wines.

During one of these expeditions, he encountered a fellow trav-
eler who would become his first real "compagnon" (as he liked
to call those with whom he had deep affinities). The meeting
took place far from all other humans, in the remote grottoes
of Bétharam[11] where their love of natural science and mountain
climbing had brought both of them. This place and these predilections formed the first link. In talking, they soon discovered
others: both had ancestors in Guadeloupe;[12] they shared an intense interest in botany; they both wrote poetry. It seemed almost instantly that such affinities could lead to friendship. Yet,
the differences between them were as striking as the similarities:
Francis Jammes, who was born in 1868, was more than twice
Alexis Leger's age; he was already a well-established poet who
had published several volumes of verse which Mallarmé and
Gide admired[13] by the time the two men met in 1903, while
Alexis (although he had been writing poetry since the age of
ten)[14] was totally unknown and certainly unpublished; Jammes
was a fervent Catholic whose main concern in writing was a
return to God and nature, while Leger had quite different notions concerning religion and poetry.

It was probably fortunate for their friendship that Jammes's
early verse (which Leger first encountered) was marked by a
kind of pagan sensuality[15] that corresponded quite well to the
latter's own penchants and preoccupations. The young man also
responded to his older friend's simple, direct, and unassuming

manner of celebrating his region and his people or, as he termed it, Jammes's "élocution au sol, à hauteur de vaches, les faces terreuses, les oiseaux de passage."[16] And he was impressed by the latter's independence, his freedom from current literary trends, his "penchant naturel à vouloir retrouver . . . sa contrée et sa race par-dessus toutes convenances des lettres du jour"[17]— in other words, to live outside the narrow circle of the young French literati. Most of all, however, Leger admired the spontaneity of creation in Jammes, who seemed to him one of that rare species, "un poète pur."[18]

The two men began to spend much time together and to frequent each other's families. At Orthez, where Jammes lived, Alexis found a warm welcome in this household that maintained its Creole heritage. His own ancestry endeared him to them. They found him refined, discreet, and charming with his lilting speech and ways of the islands. When Jammes gave his young friend a gift of one of his volumes of poetry (which the latter would preserve in his personal library during his entire lifetime), he inscribed it with words that expressed all these feelings: "A mon ami, Alexis Leger, qui a le coeur délicat de Créole."[19]

As their friendship developed, they shared excursions into the countryside enhanced by their common love of botany. They also exchanged ideas on poetry. In the latter domain, it must have been more difficult to arrive at a meeting ground than in the choice of specimens for herborization. For Jammes insisted that poetry was exclusively the result of inspiration, not to be tampered with once put on paper. Leger, in the process of writing his first major poem, "Images à Crusoé,"[20] wrestled with his difficult subject of exile and memory, subjected his inspiration to rigorous poetic discipline, saw poetry as the fruit of long labor and extensive revision. And, while the former spoke easily of his work, as a farmer might of his sowing, the latter was secretive about his writing, played down his involvement with creation, treated it almost as something he gave in to despite himself.[21]

There is some doubt that Jammes realized that a great poet was maturing before his eyes. But his principal merit was to encourage a youthful talent (which would far outstrip his own). And, probably most important of all, he was instrumental in arranging a meeting that brought together Alexis Leger and Paul Claudel.

Orthez, 1905

It all happened quite naturally. Claudel was visiting Jammes at his home. He had recently returned from the Far East where his diplomatic functions had taken him. Those years had been a time of great crisis, both in religious and in secular terms. For the profoundly Catholic Claudel (who had undergone such a dramatic conversion in 1886)[22] had experienced a passionate, illicit love that had shaken him to the depths of his being. Vanquished, transmuted into poetry, it had become the major triumph of this period in his life and given impetus to the works he had brought back from China, considered among his most remarkable creations: *Cinq grandes odes*[23] and *Partage de midi*.[24]

Jammes hastened to present Leger to Claudel. On the surface, the two men seemed hardly suited for empathy: Claudel was thirty-seven (the same age as Jammes),[25] a mature writer, and a scholar with extensive culture and knowledge—an expert translator of Aeschylus, a perceptive interpreter of the Far East, an adept of Christian philosophy, Virgil, Dante, Shakespeare, and the Spanish authors of the Golden Age. Leger, a youth of less than half Claudel's age, had just written "Images à Crusoé," his first major poem, and begun to delve into literature and philosophy. The distance between them seemed enormous. Moreover, to be presented by Claudel, at their initial meeting, with a copy of "Les Muses"[26] (the first of the *Cinq grandes odes* and probably the most magnificent) must have overwhelmed the youthful Leger.

As must the man himself. Claudel, at this point in time, was a massive force of almost unbearable power. One astute observer (Gide) described him thus: "He looks like a sledge-hammer. . . . He gives the impression of a solidified cyclone. . . . He has the most gripping voice I have ever heard. . . . He talks endlessly; someone else's thought does not stop him for an instant; even a cannon cannot divert him."[27] Leger, on the other hand, was then "un jeune homme . . . silencieux, refusant un sourire . . . d'un mutisme presque insolent . . . [il a] un petit air transcendant et sûr de lui . . . [et] une voix douce, solennelle et qui tombe sur la fin des mots."[28]

One can only conjecture about the impact of such diametrically opposed characters—the vociferous, dominating Claudel and the laconic, aloof young Leger—the sledgehammer meeting a polite wall; the cyclone raging against the soft, solemn tones; the torrent of words confronted by insolent muteness.

Yet, these were surface manifestations. Beneath the obvious differences, they shared many experiences and convictions of a deeper variety. (Perhaps they sensed this, and knew of the underlying awareness that could make a meeting possible—an awareness outweighing disparity of age, personality, and outlook.) Both men had broken early ties, and both had a fierce sense of independence and shunned literary trends of the day. They shared a rapport with earthly things and the concrete; a keen appreciation of the life of the senses; the experience of suffering and triumph over suffering; and, perhaps most of all, the knowledge of the power of laughter as liberation, pure joy, creation, even a manifestation of the sacred.[29]

Indeed, their most recent poems, despite the evident contrasts, had a fundamental parallelism of motifs that could provide the reasons, even the necessity, for their encounter. For, if "Images à Crusoé" is essentially the outcry of a very young man in exile, and "Les Muses" the cry of a mature poet wrought from crisis, both nevertheless reveal a preoccupation with severance, the power of memory, and the genesis of poetic creation—expressed in ways that, surprisingly, suggest a natural meeting of sensibilities.

One of Claudel's preoccupations, however, almost destroyed the possibility for further encounters. It was his religious faith— verging on fanaticism—and the compulsion he had for convert-

ing those whom he met to Catholicism. He had recently succeeded with Jammes and now turned his attention to Leger. Was
it because he detected an opening in some of the lines of "Images
à Crusoé" (taking the voice of Crusoé for that of the author of the
poem) where Leger had written: ". . . D'un exil lumineux . . .
comment garder les voies, ô mon Seigneur! que vous m'aviez
livrées?"[30] Or was it because he attributed the same pious penchant to the young man as he had seen in the women of the
latter's family? Probably it was simply because he himself felt the
need to fish for souls.

   The conversion attempt took place on a hot summer afternoon. The day was oppressive, the air stifling, as before a storm.
Claudel invited Leger to accompany him to one of the rooms of
Jammes's house that was located high up, under the eaves. From
there, one could survey the whole countryside—God's earth—as
well as the sky. He began, in his powerful voice, to pour out
Cartesian logic followed by Thomist demonstration, attacking his
companion. The younger man listened politely, if somewhat distantly, to the older, who "had a striking way of first masticating
his phrases and then spitting them out with a sort of exasperated
authority."[31] Claudel's invectives grew progressively more violent. Suddenly, the summer storm broke. Flashes of lightning
were followed by claps of thunder; the treetops swayed in the
high winds; the windowpanes trembled; the roof shook over
their heads. Claudel raised his voice even more, competing with
the storm, feeling perhaps that this cataclysm of nature was a
sign of divine intervention in order to underscore his sermon.
He noticed that the youth intently watched the heavens—and
probably concluded that these upward glances were proof of the
triumph of his argument. In actuality, however, Leger was absorbed in the grandiose visual spectacle (the changing colors in
the sky, the movement of the trees, the designs the lightning
made) and was far more impressed by the unleashing of nature's
forces than by the theological argument. Lightning and thunder
had, since the start of his life, been far more persuasive "de la
puissance du dieu caché au coeur des choses que l'argument de

Saint-Anselme." "Le feu divin," he would say, recalling the incident, "m'apparaissait déjà dans l'immédiat du monde. Je n'avais besoin d'aucun intercesseur." And, he would add with a smile: "Je n'ai jamais pu me sentir tout à fait chrétien: comme les vrais enfants des îles . . . *je suis sauvé de naissance.*"[32]

At the moment, however, the young man did not smile. Some even report that he left the house weeping.[33] Claudel, at any rate, did not intercede for or save Leger, and the conversion attempt left a painful rift in their relations. Yet, the impression made by Claudel was a lasting one. Eventually, the two men would form a friendship that endured a lifetime. Now, though, the chasm between these two powerful and unyielding natures was deep.

Shortly after the stormy afternoon, Leger sent Claudel a letter that expressed the distance between them in poignant terms:

Je suis seul, sans que je le veuille. . . . Que vouloir de vous?—Je ne sais pas. Je crois que je resterai seul. . . . Si je songe à vous, c'est un peu avec une aigre détresse . . . vous êtes pour moi . . . celui qui a "fini," celui qui est "sorti," qui est "arrivé," tandis que moi je commence. Et je serai sans doute seul jusqu'au terme. Vous êtes de ceux qui ont disparu pour moi derrière le Lac de Soufre de vos Livres Saints. . . . Rappelez-vous votre jeunesse et vous retrouverez ce deuil que laissent ceux qui nous précèdent.[34]

February 1907

Far greater mourning struck Alexis shortly after, as suddenly as winter lightning. "J'ai trop aimé mon père pour n'avoir pas souvent imaginé sa mort,"[35] he said, but the imagined suddenly became a reality. For long hours the son sat at the father's side in the somber sickroom, watching the drawn face grow wan and distant, hearing the breath come more and more laboriously from the gaping mouth. All the while, he heard the steady drone of women's voices in other rooms, praying for him to live—as he lay dying. "Nous nous sommes aimés, je crois, jusqu'à en souffrir,"[36] he would one day say. Now, the love and suffering were inextricably bound. As he stood beside the still figure that seemed about to enter an unattainable dimension, he fully knew the essential loneliness of all beings. True, they had always been "seuls, l'un près de l'autre,"[37] separated by the manly reserve their stations required. But now each was utterly and irremediably alone—the one to die, the other to live.

From the day of his father's death, Alexis's life changed entirely. The ritual of his passing was a rite of passage. Youth had truly come to an end.

Gone were the childish dreams he had harbored (such as being a gaucho in Chile),[38] gone the relatively carefree moments of army life[39] when he toyed with Oriental "nihilism" and the study of the violin,[40] gone the gay student days in Bordeaux (where he lived in the "quartier de pauvres grues, de cartomanciennes et d'étudiants malsains,"[41] plunged into Roman law, philosophy, and science), gone the summers of mountaineering and geological exploration (when meeting a rare bird[42] or near death by drowning while crossing a lonely lake[43] were the most memorable events of the season).

Now he must take his father's place. He had to become the head of a household of women paralyzed by grief and helpless in face of the world's harsh demands. Heavy material worries compounded the torment of suffering.

All his youthful energy, his well-trained body—that "bonne machine"[44]—seemed insufficient to rouse the women from their despair and apathy. Month after month, they wept silently. Sorrow enveloped the house as in a vast shroud. And Alexis remained alone (as he had with his dying father), struggling to act, not founder into grief-stricken passivity, to assume the grave responsibility of his family's future.

At times, he almost despaired of his ability to infuse them with his strength. "Je ne puis rien," he wrote, "pour quatre coeurs de femmes, que me tenir là, près d'elles, dans notre amour. On ne fortifie personne; on ne se fait que dur, et on souffre de blesser."[45] (It seemed that his efforts to rouse them with his vitality had either failed or been misinterpreted as hardness.)

Perhaps he had also shown impatience with their form of piousness (which, to him, might have been tantamount to passivity or concern with the prosaic), for he went on to say: "Les femmes aussi sont trop peu 'capables' de leur religion. . . . Elles prient, je sais, et elles demandent 'des choses'. . . . Pendant que j'assistai seul mon père mourant, dans les chambres on priait qu'il vive; maintenant l'on priera que je réussisse dans telle entreprise, dans une combinaison d'argent, à un examen peut-être!"[46] He himself saw these matters in quite another light: "Si j'étais exactement religieux, la religion ne serait pas pour moi le moyen de réalisations terrestres, mais . . . aspiration à l'absolu."[47]

The disparities between Alexis and his family were numerous. Perhaps the greatest, though, concerned their manner of mourning. The women were weakened by their grief, inert, incapable of feeling any other emotion. While he, although experiencing pain as deep as theirs, found that it fostered growth, increased strength and capability: "Porter le deuil de quelque chose ou de quelqu'un. . . . Grandir et s'émouvoir! (Deuil = capacité.)"[48] It also did not exclude feeling its polar opposite—joy: "J'ai appris qu'on peut souffrir sans s'attrister . . . —bien plus, la joie!"[49] Moreover, all this seemed to him in the natural order of things. Did not day coexist with night, laughter with weeping, birth with death in the same way that, in the great round of existence, cyclical movement established a fundamental and necessary balance between destruction and creation?

Thus, when winter had once more given way to spring, even though the shadow of death still hung over the house, he exclaimed: "Mais la lumière devient belle!"[50] (As he would, during another period of mourning, the following year, write: "Comme la lumière est belle . . . et comme elle aide, et comme elle est 'solide'!")[51] In the same way as light balanced darkness, or both coexisted side by side, he insisted on a complex (and delicate) equilibrium between suffering and joy.[52] This need for parity could take the form of hatred for sadness (or for the basic self-indulgence that sadness might imply) and result in some of the fiercest pronouncements to be heard in his later poetry,[53] which probably had their roots in the realizations made at this crucial time.

At this point also he began to understand that the capacity to feel grief without sadness had been among the things that Claudel had tried to convey to him during their conversations shortly before the death of his father. Perhaps it had taken this tragic experience for him to grasp their full meaning. "Vous m'avez dit l'essentiel," he wrote to Claudel at the end of the year of mourning, "et c'est maintenant seulement que je sais vous remercier."[54] Perhaps also, now, "cette force, sur la vie, qui se passe même de compréhension,"[55] of which Claudel had then spoken, was beginning to win out. The life force, however, for Alexis, was not the sole property of a particular divinity but the vital energy that infused all creation.

Nor had this force ever been absent. It had already manifested itself earlier—though perhaps not as clearly, nor thus verbalized. For, in an intuitive move, at the height of mourning (in the summer of 1907), Alexis had taken the women of his family to the Pyrenees. He had done so in the hope that the change of surroundings would bring them new vigor and interest in life. But he must also have known, in some instinctive way, that the enduring power of nature, the sense of its presence in these high places, was essential to his own survival—in the same way as was the process of creation.

Thus, in the valley of Ossau, among the timeless mountains, in a realm of pure light, he began to write. There, the first of the luminous poems of *Eloges* began to take form. In their unconditional celebration of life, the shadows of death receded. Pain was balanced by brilliant visions. "Et l'ombre et la lumière alors étaient plus près d'être une même chose."[56] At this time when mourning had closed "toute époque de fête, de complaisance et d'images,"[57] Alexis wrote "Pour fêter une enfance."[58] The feasts of childhood, stored in his memory, arose with new splendor. And, crossing into adulthood, he cast a backward glance toward those days of long ago[59] when everything was new and grave and noble, when the entire world was matter for praise and could be summed up in the ecstatic exclamation: "O j'ai lieu de louer! O fable généreuse, ô table d'abondance!"[60]

Through poetry, the poet's death work proceeded. Slowly, as they emerged, the poems affirmed—and resurrected—the past, the endless childhood days, the time of legendary splendor. Moving against the flow of time, retracing its course upstream toward the place of origin, by anamnesis and reiteration, renewal was achieved. The curative powers of such a journey (known to healers and shamans everywhere) must have been intuited by the artist Alexis had become.

As the circle of the year turned, creation triumphed. It was manifest in the budding of the trees, the bursting of eggs, even in the stones that seemed to expand in the sun. In poetry, it expressed itself in lyricism that, for Alexis, was essentially a "mode de joie envers soi."[61] It was in this mode that he now wrote, fashioning "éloges" (instead of elegies) and odes—filled with and to—joy. Just as death was slowly being inscribed in the vast cycle of existence, so his dead father (preserved in and by memory) could once again arise, transformed, at the core of that early paradise that his loss had resuscitated.

Eloges—the very title of the group of poems (whose beginnings date from that summer)—expresses this acquiescence and this victory. And the word itself—of which Alexis would say, "il est si beau que je n'en voudrais jamais d'autre, si je publiais un volume—ni plusieurs"[62]—contains the root and essence of his entire poetic creation: praise wrought from pain, joy from grief, and celebration from the unending round of destruction and creation in the universe.

CHAPTER 3

CROSSROADS
(1908–1916)

Homme . . . le plus secret dans ses dessins; dur à soi-même,
et se taisant, et ne concluant pas de paix avec soi-même,
mais pressant, errant . . .

—Amitié du Prince (OC, p. 67)

1908–1911

In his early twenties, life to Alexis seemed both a wide-open field and a series of hurdles—something resembling a steeple-chase where even the most intrepid rider would at times have stumbled or been at a loss at how to leap. Often, when a path seemed to lead straight to the finish line or an advantage urged him to press on, an obstacle loomed up, a rut appeared in the terrain. Passes were blocked; handicaps arose in unforeseen places; the course pursued depended not on the excitement of the race but on the necessity for caution as to its outcome.

True, he was at the height of his powers. In the prime of youth, fit for the most rigorous tests, able to strain his body to the limit,[1] he was ready to forge ahead, to attain nearly any goal. Yet, though he sought challenge and did not shrink from arduous tasks, the demands upon him sometimes outstripped even such capacities. Strength and inventiveness did not appear to suffice. For he was constantly solicited by fragility and ineptitude. And this was in the form of women he loved—his mother and sisters—who looked at him as their only source of solace, of salvation even, unable to fend for themselves at all. They continued to sit in darkened rooms, hardly spoke or touched their food, gazed at him in mute appeal each time he returned to the house from the sunlit world outside, as if whatever little life remained hinged solely on his presence.

Especially painful was the sight of his mother: "Une mère qui n'a guère plus de vingt ans que moi et que je vois insupportablement vieillir,"[2] struck down by mourning twice in the space of one year,[3] whose only occupation was to grieve. While he himself suffered without outward signs, a double loss equally great,[4] they gave themselves up to sorrow in such an exhaustive way that he often found their ways hard to tolerate. He tried to console them (when no consolation seemed possible) and undertook, at the same time, to insure their livelihood. He had to learn to manage funds, budget their meager income, juggle investments,[5] fight lawsuits with debtors,[6] scheme almost constantly how to thrash out financial problems.

Alexis considered various projects to solve their situation, deprived himself of even the slightest luxuries, allowed himself not the least indulgence. Secretly, however, he once again harbored dreams of departure. He remembered his old plan to become a rancher in South America—abandoned when his father had insisted that he finish his studies[7] (but preserved in the poetic persona that appeared in "Ecrit sur la porte," a work written during that period).[8] He also thought of various other distant shores, warmer climes, wild pagan existence,[9] grandiose quests. Most of all, he craved a life far from France, whose climate, in more ways than one, did not suit him well: "Je creverai d'ennui dans ce pays: d'ennui, de froid, et d'impersonnalité."[10] But any cry of leave-taking had to be stifled. Not a sign of this yearning for action, for space, must appear on his face. The women needed, even demanded his presence. Emotional outweighed financial support in the scale of priorities.

A road had to be chosen. "Il me faudra bientôt précipiter, de quelque façon, l'engagement de ma vie d'homme,"[11] he wrote to a friend. He must throw himself into an arena where he would not necessarily have chosen to battle otherwise. Departure to far-off lands was impossible. Writing was out of the question as a means of assuring his family's livelihood; even the mention of such an activity must be suppressed[12] (it could only continue in secret, underground). The consensus of opinion was that, as the head of the household, he should follow his father's footsteps (or step into his shoes, in more ways than one) and embark on a career in the law. Since he could finish his legal studies by returning to the Université de Bordeaux, he would also remain within easy reach of his relatives.

Hardly a panacea, leaving Pau was at least a form of liberation. On the day of departure, he felt as if he had stepped out of a dim enclosure into a pristine, diurnal world. Even academe seemed exhilarating when compared with somber family councils and the mournful silence of his house. It would be a relief to occupy his mind with matters other than budgets, accounts, and legal suits.

He launched into his studies with great energy and almost instantly found a way of avoiding confinement to the field of law by expanding into political science and sociology, ethnology and anthropology.[13] Even his former violent dislike of philosophy[14] began to lessen. He started to explore Nietzsche, Spinoza, and Hegel (when all the rage, at the time, was Bergson).[15] Nietzsche especially intrigued him. There was much in the former's work that coincided with his own current thoughts and discoveries: "Joyful knowledge"; superiority based on the capacity to endure suffering and rise above it by creative effort; cyclical patterns of existence. His only criticism of Nietzsche was "de ne pas aller lui-même assez loin dans Nietzsche," not pursuing contradiction to its utmost limits. He regretted that "ce Grand Maître Inquisiteur n'a pas su mener plus loin l'inquisition de ses inconséquences: jusqu'à ce point final d'explosion et de fulguration,"[16] and wished that Nietzsche had taken "ce dernier saut, sans perte de sandales, dans le cratère de l'absurde."[17] Nevertheless, he was greatly attracted to this powerful "compagnon,"[18] whose vitality combated quietus and sloth. Alexis found him admirable— not as a philosopher in the narrow sense of the word, and certainly not as a poet[19]—but as an "inquiétant lyrique"[20] and as the creator of heroes and supermen (not unlike the central figure of the Prince in a poem he was currently writing).[21]

It was not only in pursuits of the mind, though, that Alexis sought "compagnonnage" or a community of interest. As always, these were only one side of his life and needed to be balanced by explorations of an opposite kind. Now a new passion had taken hold of him: aviation. It combined a number of his penchants— his enduring fascination with birds, the love of air and space, his predilection for risk, the exciting conquest of a new element. He began to follow the accounts of the Wright brothers and their extraordinary exploits, which filled the newspapers at this time. Often, when poring over his books in dusty libraries, he thought how gladly he would have traded academe for such high adventure, and success in bar examinations for transatlantic defiance of gravity. He had to content himself, however, with a single visit (on ground) to Wilbur Wright, at the latter's solitary encampment in the flatlands of Pont-Long.[22]

Other flights were nevertheless at his disposal: the realms of the imagination were, fortunately, not subject to the laws that governed bodily levitation. Moreover, they could be pursued while pretending to be involved in prescribed occupations. He turned to poets and poetry, probing ever more deeply the domains they explored, the elements with which they wrestled. Pindar, Claudel, Fargue, Rimbaud, Laforgue became his companions in this venture.

Pindar—whose work had already interested him as a *lycéen*— now became for him "une puissante aide à vivre."[23] He translated his *Pythic Odes* as a personal exercise, a study of meter and word structure, for he considered Pindar's "la plus forte métrique de l'Antiquité."[24] Not that he did not have some reservations: while he admired the ancient poet's harmonious moderation and his continent style, he was bored by his thematics. Alexis had come to prefer "une conception plus moderne du grand lyrisme individuel, à base de jubilation, d'exultation, et d'ivresse";[25] and it seemed to him that Pindar's was an "ivresse à froid . . . imposant la retenue du souffle"[26] and, in the final analysis, merely an "ivresse des nombres, et leur sagesse pure—rien d'autre."[27]

The "conception plus moderne du grand lyrisme individuel" he sought was certainly better expressed by Claudel—and Fargue.[28] True, Claudel still evoked ambivalent feelings (probably because his hellfire sermon continued to rankle, to the point where Alexis exclaimed: "Claudel m'annonce la naissance d'un fils. Quelle proie pour cet homme!").[29] But his poetry was cause for admiration. Alexis could not help but recognize his greatness and bow before the "immobile éclat . . . le poids . . . la sublime extrémité" of Claudel's latest creations.[30] He also had to admit that it was a source of some pride to him when "cet homme" spoke with praise of his first poems—although he would probably have resented Gide's saying that these were "violemment influencés" by Claudel.[31] If influence there had been, he might more easily have conceded it in another realm: the interest that Claudel undoubtedly awakened by his references to Rimbaud. For the former constantly made such remarks as: "I am always moved when Rimbaud's name is mentioned—I've lived with him so long and feel myself bound to him by the most secret of fibers";[32] or "he is the man to whom I owe everything."[33] Claudel even indicated that it seemed to him that Rimbaud was a part of himself.[34]

But Alexis formulated his own reasons—less self-centered and more precise than Claudel's—for feeling affinity with Rimbaud. Although they were in some ways diametrically opposed (as in their fundamentally divergent vision of childhood),[35] he recognized their mutual penchant for powerful dualism, admirably demonstrated, he felt, in those "impérieuses *Illuminations* de Rimbaud, où le style très cursif et toujours décisif . . . tient sans faille ni trêve une fulguration durable, libérant d'un seul jet une même substance, intellectuelle et spirituelle, entre deux pôles réversibles—aérien et terrestre."[36] But he also singled out other traits that fascinated him: "Rimbaud . . . est précisément le plus amusical, sinon antimusical de nos vrais poètes";[37] "Il y a dans la divine maîgreur de sa langue cursive, tout le sens insonore et fulgurant de l'abstrait."[38] Alexis would even, as he himself became more deeply involved with Rimbaud's poetry, criticize the utterances of Claudel and give his own definition of what he considered central in the former's work: "Claudel n'a pas su parler assez pauvrement de Rimbaud pour le grandir absolument. . . . Le vrai Rimbaud: toute cette 'fièvre d'intelligence' . . . cette hâte . . . cette maîgreur et cette hâte . . . ce poète de l'ellipse et du bond."[39] By thus underlining the qualities he valued in Rimbaud, the young poet revealed the traits that he himself would, or had already begun to, cultivate in his own creations.

There were other important penchants, however, that Alexis shared with a poet less known than Rimbaud and quite different from him in most respects. At first glance incongruous in this group of giants, the Pierrot of nineteenth-century verse, wry, whimsical, full of incongruities—Laforgue—appeared to Alexis "admirable, incomparable."[40] This was perhaps because Laforgue was a master of laughter, transmuted suffering into a clown's capers, masked sensitivity by irony, excelled at incongruity and paradox. But it was most likely, as is shown in a remark to a friend, for stylistic reasons: "[Leger] admire ce que la langue de Rimbaud a de dépouillé et même de cursif. Pour la même raison il admire beaucoup Laforgue."[41]

Evidently, the exploration of other poets' work clarified many of Alexis's own ideas on poetry at this time. But, as vital as this was to his development, it could not suffice. He had to undertake his own struggle with creation. The poems of "Eloges" were behind him now. His homage to childhood had been paid. New realms were opening. His work must change.

The poetry that began to emerge now was inspired by other moods, revealed quite different preoccupations. Transposing thoughts and feelings of his current life, it produced utterances far less idyllic than before (although the note of celebration, the sense of nobility, the forceful imagery remained). Its very titles were proof of the direction his imagination was now taking: "Récitation à la gloire d'une Reine," "Amitié du Prince," "Histoire du Régent," collected under the heading of *La Gloire des Rois*.[42] More than any of the others, it was the first two of these poems— when seen as a diptych—that best disclosed the predominant imaginings of this time in his life.

The first, "Récitation à la Gloire d'une Reine," which Alexis (obviously somewhat worried about his choice of subject, especially as it might strike Claudel)[43] claimed to be "surtout un effort musical, un travail de la matière verbale, considérée comme sonore,"[44] revealed concerns of a quite different nature (which might indeed have disconcerted Claudel by their sexual explicitness). Here, woman appeared as an object of violent physical desire. At the same time, she seemed a hieratic figure of enormous proportions resembling the fertility goddesses of the most ancient kind: voluminous and gravid as the Venus of Willendorf (yet, paradoxically, sterile), the Queen of this poem was a paradigm of various telluric divinities, if not the Terra Mater herself whose earth-body is a holy altar of sacrifice.[45] Her epithets—"Tiède," "un-peu-Humide," "Douce"[46]—suggested, in no uncertain terms, that she was the embodiment of sexuality, indeed of the female sexual organ (reminiscent of the sacred yoni of Hindu doctrine).[47] Awesome and munificent, desirable and terrifying, maternal and virginal, this pagan goddess was—as a number of her avatars—surrounded by a group of youths (sons), aspiring to be her consorts, whose chants expressed the intense yearning underlying this poem, essentially a recitatif in honor of the Queen of Desire.

(In the domain of desire, only conjecture is possible concerning the activities of Alexis Leger—always extremely discreet, if not secretive about his involvements with women—during these years when the sexual drive is at its most intense. Was it turned toward those *filles de joie* (knowing how to earn their title by rendering physical encounters joyous) in the student quarter of "pauvres grues"[48] where he had first lived in Bordeaux? Had he joined a band of those "healthy" young males he had met who knew how to "limiter les femmes à leur vagin"?[49] Most likely, desire did not find its object in literary women, for his disdain for this breed was passionate: "Je n'aime pas l'encre femelle, ah! fichtre non!" he wrote, "[elles] se nourissent de fleurs de papier, de morceaux de tapisserie comme les chèvres des rues . . . il ne semble pas que le goût féminin s'affranchisse jamais de la boîte à mouchoirs ou du papier à lettres."[50] Evidently, his tastes led him to more robust and earthy encounters. As startling as the contradictions between the young man's direct view of women and the transposed, poetic image at first appear, they are quite natural in view of his already complex personality, and their very paradox seems proof of their verisimilitude.)

The second poem, "Amitié du Prince"—especially when coupled with the first—offered further insights into the world of the youthful poet's imagination and his major preoccupations. It centered on the figure of the Prince (also referred to as "the King"—and thus the consort or equal of "the Queen" of the first poem), depicted as an ideal leader of men. His portrait emphasized traits diametrically opposed to (or complementing) those of the female figure in "Récitation à la gloire d'une Reine": physically, as well as morally, he was defined by "maîgreur" (akin to the "divine maîgreur" that Alexis had seen in Rimbaud),[51] acuity, life on a knife edge or "au tranchant de l'esprit"; his epithets— "Très-Maîgre," "Subtil," "Guérisseur," "Enchanteur," "Dissident," "Prince taciturne,"[52] "Honneur du sage sans honneur"[53]— further defined the persona of this male counterpart of the female divinity in the earlier poem. But his predominant characteristics also seemed to reveal an ideal to which—one suspects— the young poet aspired. In this respect, the vision of the Prince was also an instance of self-portraiture. Certainly, Alexis, at this time, was (every bit as much as the figure he had created) "[l]'homme le plus secret dans ses desseins, dur à soi-même, et se taisant, et ne concluant pas de paix avec lui-même."[54]

The tendency toward secrecy, harshness, silence, and lack of inner peace came to a critical pass in the year 1909. It was a time of grave self-doubt for Alexis, the refutation of past work, the rejection of former certainties. In other words, it was an existential crisis that he (in true French fashion) referred to as "une crise philosophique."[55] His latest poems seemed worthless to him. They were jettisoned as soon as they were put on paper. Among them there was probably one inspired by a painting by Gauguin[56] that had haunted him for a long time, completed just as he had decided "une deuxième fois au renoncement littéraire complet."[57] He might have destroyed all his early work, even "Images à Crusoé," if it had not already been in the process of publication.[58] Only the urgings of his friends to salvage at least some of his poems prevented him from demolishing everything, so great was his disaffection for writing at this time. He felt an "insurmontable et physiologique dégoût de toute oeuvre"[59] and an even greater distaste for being published, which, according to him, was "to be stinking [sic]"[60]—something akin to the rotting books in his father's sunken library. "L'art a une tête d'Ubu,"[61] he cried out, for it seemed to him as grotesque as Jarry's epitome of all man's vices. It could only be summed up in the equation "Art = onanisme"[62] (the complete opposite of an equally terse formula, "Deuil = capacité," which he had devised during another period of crisis). It seemed to him definitely linked to disgust, putrefaction, impotence, decrepitude. It was a symptom to be feared as intensely as any other sign of decline, "comme la menace d'un dentier."[63]

(And yet, in a typically paradoxical move, he permitted some of his early poems to be published at this time, perhaps because, despite his railings, he could not totally deny his own past. Perhaps it was because he heeded the voices of his friends[64] who pleaded with him not to let his present doubts and misgivings wipe out everything he had created.)

Aside from this bout with disgust and futility, the "crise philosophique" had other outcomes. It led him back to philosophy—quite fittingly. He turned once more to Spinoza (who had already interested him in the past)[65] and found in his "Traité théologico-politique"[66] ideas that mirrored his own concerns: an "extraordinaire jouissance 'etymologique' . . . un sublime Mot-à-Mot";[67] a "prodigieux marchandage juif défendant pied à pied

le divin contre l'humain (si ce n'est pas déjà tout l'humain contre
le divin) . . . Abraham rusant avec son Dieu, le pressant âpre-
ment." "Je ne vois pas page plus extraordinaire dans toute l'histoire humaine," he exclaimed, "plus humblement hautaine ou
plus sublimement basse!"[68] voicing once more his own predilections for paradox that he saw mirrored in Spinoza's treatise.

Even more than philosophy, however, it was music that—at
this critical moment—sustained him. During the months when
he had to return to the silent house where the women of his
family still observed an interminable period of mourning, he felt
an intense need to pierce the stillness with Gregorian chants,
the preludes and fugues of Bach,[69] and most especially, the music of d'Indy. His admiration for the latter grew each day,
"jusqu'à l'étonnement, de ne pouvoir 'épuiser' un tel art—iné-
puisable en effet dans ce qu'il a de peu fortuit."[70] He eagerly
followed d'Indy's experiments at the schola cantorum[71] and often
wished that he could resume his old plan for studying the violin.
It was not that he was particularly gifted as a musician himself,[72]
but because he would have wanted to be actively involved in an
art form whose most prodigious strength came from its being
"irréductible et inasservissable"[73]—qualities he treasured in all
aspects of life. When he compared music with the art of writing,
it seemed to him far superior. Yet he would admit of no fusion (or
confusion) between the two: the "musical," he felt, must be distinguished from the "verbal" method, and poetry must never
move outside its own laws. Such fusion which "était bonne pour
une génération à demi musicienne, a trop souvent avachi notre
langue dans le goût de l'à-peu-près,"[74] he would insist, thus also
clarifying his earlier (rather enigmatic) remark that Rimbaud was
"précisément le plus amusical, sinon antimusical de nos vrais
poètes."[75]

The year was not only a time of crisis, however. It also brought
Alexis, aside from a deepening of insights and a clarification of
convictions—which sometimes resulted in a parting of ways with
old friends, such as Jammes[76]—the birth of new friendships. As
if severance were balanced by fresh bonds, and solitary struggles

by "compagnonnage" (the highest form of encounter—being a link that does not bind but fecundates by cross-fertilization—a privileged form of reciprocity that he would prize all throughout life).

The first of these encounters involved Jacques Rivière, whom he had met in 1906[77] but did not truly establish contact with until this time. Rivière, only a year older than Leger, was already an accomplished essayist and critic with wide interests and discriminating tastes, capable of pitiless self-scrutiny and great individuality. Moreover, he had a complex, contradictory personality that resisted facile analysis.[78] In other words, he was a fitting counterpart for Leger. The latter saw in him a being of "parfaite noblesse . . . parfaite vigilance . . . [et] une incapacité de s'user aux contacts de la vie"; he liked his "enthousiasmes, ses naïvetés, ses actes de foi . . . et cette perpetuelle maïeutique de la transfiguration . . . autant de garanties d'une force personnelle," as well as "sa grande réserve, son honnêteté et ses scrupules . . . sa force secrète, comme son art même, comme son cœur."[79] It was obvious that the two men were meant for true companionship.

They could exchange views on literature, share their interest in music, speak of the problems of creation.[80] Rivière, associated with *La Nouvelle Revue Française* by this time, could hear Leger's invectives against publication[81] and yet encourage him not to abandon poetry. The latter could also fantasize to the former (a gifted critic and perhaps the model for such fantasy) about the ideal critic, and define him thus:

Le critique auquel je songe . . . assume de restituer, de recréer . . . "trouvant" à son tour comme le poète trouve . . . relié à l'inconscient et au mystère, "voyant" enfin. . . . C'est ainsi, par l'usage du rapport et par un jeu d'analogies, que la critique peut accomplir un acte propre, cesser d'être un parasitisme pour devenir un compagnonnage; une "anabase" si vous voulez, ou retour à la Mer, à la commune Mer d'où l'oeuvre fut tirée (dans sa définitive, et peut-être cruelle, singularité).[82]

(This definition, striking in its originality and in the insights it offers into the use of the important term "anabase"—long before it became the title *Anabase,* one of Perse's most famous poems[83]—describes the perfect companion whom Alexis needed, and found, in this year of crisis.)

Rivière would continue to accompany the young poet in his first ventures into the literary world. After becoming secretary of *La Nouvelle Revue Française* in 1911,[84] he was instrumental in the publication of *Eloges* in this review (then under the aegis of Gide). And while Gide's relationship with Leger was problematic at the start (for reasons that shall shortly be elucidated), Rivière remained the trusted companion and confidant with whom Leger could share joys, rages, and outrages.

1911–1914

The greatest outrage occurred at the moment when *Eloges* was published: in January 1911, the young poet had sent the hand-written manuscript of his work to Gide.[85] In April, after acceptance of the poems for publication, he wrote to the latter: "[les] poèmes que je vous avais addressés en janvier: je vous supplie qu'il n'en soit rien fait sans que je reçoive des épreuves."[86] When these arrived, he realized that a poem, "Cohorte," which he had sent to Rivière and allowed him to show to Gide (for his personal perusal and *not* for publication)[87] had nevertheless been included. Leger wrote to Gide, urgently demanding that the poem be immediately withdrawn and hinting that if this were done he would "invent" a way to show his gratitude.[88] When Gide complied, the young poet indeed invented an inimitable gift (the first of such gifts which would include one made to Valéry—fitting his "cristallisations"[89]—in the form of a crystal skull seen in the British Museum,[90] and another to Claudel, in the form of a stark rocky island, and of silence[91]): the photograph of a row of palm trees,[92] accompanied by the following text:

Je vous donne cet arbre, le neuvième en partant de la gauche, et qui est une des choses les plus incomplètement belles, je veux dire les plus belles, qui se puissent fonder. C'est l'un des miens qui l'a planté . . . dans une petite île qui n'a qu'un nom local. Je "le" connais. Ces arbres sont de race pure—tourmentée par le voisinage de la mer—la grande espèce *Oreadoxa*. Je vous donne cet arbre, je veux dire: je lui ferai donner votre nom sans plus d'explications. . . . Et votre nom connaîtra la joie, quelque part, de ne signifier rien.[93]

(This was a most revealing gift, revealing of the giver, for it showed so many things he himself held dear: trees, his native isle, a pure race arising from contiguity with the sea, the joy of a name signifying nothing.)

Gide was apparently so taken with this present, and especially with the words of the young poet, that he preserved it for almost four decades and published it in a homage to Saint-John Perse in 1950.[94] Unfortunately, he also treasured and kept the manuscript of "Eloges" that Leger had sent him, for, as he said, "ces pages de Saint-Leger me parurent, indépendamment de leur apport et déjà par elles-mêmes, si belles que je ne pus consentir à m'en séparer."[95] He thus decided to send, not the original, but a copy to the printer. The secretary charged with this task made many errors in the process of transcription. To Gide's horror (and even more so, that of the author), "d'effroyables 'coquilles' dés-honoraient le texte d'*Eloges* tel qu'il parut d'abord dans la N.R.F."[96] Upon seeing the June 1, 1911, issue of the review, Saint-Leger (or Saintleger Leger, as he had signed his work) was consumed with rage. The very next day, he wrote to Rivière:

Tout détaché que je me croyais, lorsque j'ai eu jeté les yeux sur cette première page de fou que l'on donnait là sous mon nom, j'ai eu envie de crier comme un enfant. Non, je n'oublierai jamais le tour que l'on m'a joué, à cette revue de cuistres . . . Ces extravagances et détraque-ments qu'il me faut endosser à la N.R.F., ah! voilà bien qui me dégoûte encore plus de publier.[97]

Two weeks later he had mastered his fury. But, as for the guilty handwriting (which had been the cause of all this dreadful iniq-uity), he decided on a chastisement characteristic of his unusual personality: he would subject it to harsh discipline and force it to undergo a complete reeducation "aussi pénible que cela lui parût."[98] He practiced for hours, for days. The new writing was slow in undergoing the desired transformation. He tried differ-ent angles, reshaped the letters, judged its legibility with a schoolmaster's severity, an inquisitor's zeal until he finally arrived at a new form—still beautiful but obviously the result of rigorous training.[99]

Gide, in the meanwhile, had also pondered over ways to repair the damage and make amends. The only way, it seemed to him, to rectify publication of a disfigured text was to immediately reprint *Eloges* correctly and distribute copies to the subscribers of La *Nouvelle Revue Française*[100]—and also (to, perhaps, even further assuage his guilt) propose publication of the work in book form by the Editions N.R.F. (Gallimard).

Leger, justifiably suspicious now, before entrusting Gide with such a task, asked Rivière to send him a photograph of the man in order to study his face[101] (evidently confident in his judgments of physiognomies). When he had subjected the photograph to thorough examination, he arrived at the conclusion that Gide was "inguérissablement sérieux" and that there was "derrière cette forme assidue de visage . . . plus d'attentif appel au mensonge, plus de tentatives et de ruses, de sollicitations enfin, qu'on n'en prêta jamais a l'impatient Ulysse"; he saw a man with "un goût de séduire," full of instability, "insatisfaction et . . . irréductible solitude . . . énorme 'bon sens' . . . obstination . . . tristesse"; and he concluded that someone "de cette espèce se grise de l'amitié plus qu'il ne s'attache à un ami."[102] Decidedly, this was not a portrait that would inspire great confidence. Yet, in a typically paradoxical move, he decided to allow Gide to go ahead with the publication of the first volume of his poems.

He had, however, some hesitations about the name he wanted to use. A pseudonym seemed wisest, for a number of reasons, although Claudel, whose advice he had sought, counseled him to use his own name.[103] "Saint-Leger Leger" was hardly disguised by "Saintleger Leger" with which he had signed the poems that had appeared in *La Nouvelle Revue Francaise*. There must be other ways to insure at least partial anonymity. He remembered having seen Claudel use an interesting maneuver and requested, similarly, of Gide to print only the title of the work on the outer cover of the book, thus leaving it "libre du nom de l'auteur" (which would only appear on the flyleaf inside). "Ne croyez pas à la manie," he wrote to Gide, "il me paraît seulement que des poèmes devraient toujours garder quelque chose de leur affleurement initial dans l'anonymat"[104] (thus already voicing a lifelong predilection, expressed in the use of various pseudonyms, and disproving the notion that his nom de plume arose from the exigencies of his diplomatic career).

While the appearance of *Eloges,* in book form, was a major event in itself, it also brought the young poet another friendship—although quite different from that with Rivière, but equally fecund—that of Valery Larbaud. The two men met in April of that year. Each retained quite different details of their initial encounter: Leger remembered their meal in a deserted hotel dining room where they had been the only guests, and were observed, it seemed, by a "poupée fétiche vêtue de laines rouges sur un petit meuble droit, et qui était fixement derrière nous."[105] Larbaud recalled that they had spent three hours together and that Leger was "d'abord assez froid et ne fai[sai]t pas de gestes . . . [comme] un de ces jeunes Anglais de grande famille"; that he spoke "de la France comme d'un pays détestable où il souffre"; that when he pronounced the name of Paris, one seemed to see "un immense tas d'ordures sous un brouillard éternel"; that he seemed to have a "grande sagesse . . . la courtoisie d'un monarque de cinquante ans et la modestie d'un vieux mondain rassasié par la gloire." Larbaud also noted that the young poet refused to talk about art, judging that life alone had any importance and that "l'art n'étant qu'ellipse et l'ellipse tendant au silence—mieux vaut ne rien écrire, et simplement goûter la vie. Pour lui, publier des vers dans une revue, c'est 'jouer du piano sur le pont d'un paquebot'."[106] (This, nevertheless, was exactly what Larbaud hoped to convince Leger to do— not to play piano on the deck of an ocean liner, but its parallel— publish more of his poems.)

Evidently, Leger's originality had intrigued Larbaud, who was himself a highly creative and original being: extensively traveled, a polyglot, quite a good poet also. Larbaud had recently published a collection of verse indebted to Whitman and the French Symbolists (*Poèmes par un riche amateur*) as well as having written an unusual sort of biography ("Journal de A. O. Barnabooth," in progress at this time); he was also an excellent translator and—perhaps most important for his rapport with Saintleger Leger at this time—a uniquely self-effacing man of letters who took as much pleasure in the literary reputation of others as in his own writing career.

It was probably the last of these qualities that caused him to take up the work of the young poet shortly after they met and to write the first important critical article on him. It appeared in *La Phalange* on December 20, 1911,[107] following close upon the publication of *Eloges* by the N.R.F. From the outset, Larbaud evoked Homer, Virgil, the best of Whitman and Hugo, for comparison with the work of Saintleger Leger. He then proceeded to analyze the qualities that made for its excellence: the aliveness, the plenitude, the rhythms based on respiration (drawing parallels with Homeric and Pindaric verse), the permanence of the language, the vital quality of each word, the power, the total lack of preciosity, the exactness of image, the singular maturity of this lyricism that, nevertheless, kept the sense of childhood intact. The article concluded by invoking Heredia and Malherbe.[108]

Leger considered it too full of praise. At least he wrote to Rivière in this vein, adding that Larbaud's evaluation of his work had already evoked "des sottises qui m'affectent plus . . . que n'ont pu faire toutes les lettres élogieuses de Claudel." And, he added: "Il n'est possible à personne de penser autant de mal que moi de mes poèmes, mais je voudrais être seul à le penser."[109] Evidently, both publication and criticism had resulted in the kind of exposure (it mattered little whether good or bad) from which his proud and reserved nature shrank. In the same letter to Rivière he resolved to undertake nothing more in France than the preparation of a career "qui m'aidera un jour à m'en aller."[110]

The career that he had begun to think of in this respect was one in the diplomatic service. It seemed to combine the training he had with the possibility of travel he desired. He had written to Claudel, asking him for advice in this matter, since the latter had successfully managed to combine the career of a diplomat with the life of a poet. In the letter, he mentioned the various options offered him thus far and his reaction to them: a magistrate's position in the colonies (which did not appeal to him at all); life as a settler in Chile, Borneo, or Australia (impossible for him because of family responsibilities). He wondered what Claudel thought his chances were of preparing for the examinations that decided entry into the Ministry of Foreign Affairs, on his own in Pau, despite the fact he had lost his father, lacked any fortune, and was a stranger in France.[111]

Claudel was somewhat cautious in his response (perhaps remembering the young man's reactions at their initial meeting and feeling some disapproval of the subject matter of some of his poems). Instead of answering directly, he informed himself—via Jammes—about Leger's character, his family, his financial situation. Only then did he concede that his plan seemed possible, "mais à condition d'avoir du caractère."[112]

Strength of character was certainly not what the young man lacked. Before making his final decision to plunge into the arduous task of preparing for the examination, however, Alexis decided to go on an exploratory trip to Paris—despite his disparaging view of that city—to reconnoiter the fields of finance, politics, law, and diplomacy. He visited friends of his father there, heads of banks and various overseas enterprises, apparently not yet decided which road to choose.

It was the diplomat Philippe Berthelot who, essentially, convinced him to pursue a career in the Ministry of Foreign Affairs. Their meeting seemed fated to produce an almost immediate sense of affinity, for no two men could have been better suited for "compagnonnage." Berthelot was a powerful and complex personality—a man of dream and action, sensitivity and enormous willpower. The son of a famous scientist (Marcelin Berthelot), he himself possessed truly encyclopedic knowledge as well as a mind that was constantly in search of new ideas. Not content with having degrees in philosophy and law, he was also a poet and an admirer of poets (Heredia, Ménard; Claudel whom he had met in China). A man characterized by great courage, he welcomed challenges and habitually took risks. While he often appeared insolent, he was actually deeply respectful of the liberty and wishes of those he cared for; aristocratic by nature, he had a natural gift for communication with simple people (laborers, peasants, coolies). He seemed impenetrable to many, distant, reserved, discreet, a master of silence, surrounded all his life by a zone of solitude, for he protected himself by irony against familiarity or vulgarity. Not a believer and with no use for established religion, he believed in perpetual flux and becoming, an endless chain of being. Besides these qualities, he was also a tireless walker and a fine swimmer. A lover of animals and, most of all, of women—who, in turn, found him extremely attractive—he could have recounted many adventures and conquests in the latter domain, but he was as discreet in this respect as in his political life. "Anonymity was his signature," it was said of him. He would even refuse to write his memoirs.[113]

The parallels between the two men were so unusual that Berthelot, as well as Leger, must have been struck by their kinship of spirit. (And if the former was not an actual model for the latter, it is certain that he profoundly influenced the paths that Leger would choose to follow.)[114]

They very likely then spoke of the advantages that a career in the Ministry of Foreign Affairs offered, the travel to distant places, and Berthelot's mission to the Orient. His year-long stay in China must have especially intrigued Leger. Berthelot had visited the interior of the country, closely observed the life of the people, and traveled all the way to the edge of Tibet; he had also formed a friendship with Claudel (then consul at Fou-Tcheon), sharing his literary tastes, but differing radically in his opinions when it came to religion. And, very likely, the younger man listened to his elder with rapt attention, imagining himself already in similar exploits. His old dreams must have come crowding back, and a diplomatic career seemed the perfect way to realize his secret desire to "s'en aller."[115] He resolved, then and there, to choose this road and to do everything in his power to attain his goal.

It meant a great deal of concentrated study. He found a way, however, of making his work less abstract and more interesting by taking several "study" trips outside France to balance book learning. The first of these took him to Spain, the second to England. During the former, he dutifully studied the country's industrial and mining development, irrigation, and port organization, as well as the evolution of social issues (aided by his knowledge of Spanish, which he spoke fluently ever since childhood). But he also indulged in a private quest—the search for an unpublished partita of Monteverdi and a rare text of Philo the Jew.[116] During the latter, although he spent some time studying the great industries, mining centers, and the organization of labor unions, he became far more involved in the literary scene. He visited Joseph Conrad in Kent and found that they had many profound affinities; he also met William H. Hudson and Arthur Symons, the critic, there. Other friendships included those of G. K. Chesterton, Hilaire Belloc, Arnold Bennett, and William Butler Yeats.[117]

His most interesting sojourn was in London, which was, before World War I, "une étonnante chronique humaine en même temps qu'un splendide emporium. . . . La grande ville impériale demeurait bien le vrai carrefour, et comme le lieu géométrique, où se tenir entre deux courses, attentif et lucide, à la croisée des pistes de ce monde."[118] Somewhere at this crossroads, this geometrical locus, the intersection of the paths of the world, where he halted as between two races, lucid and attentive, both laughter and a mythical encounter awaited young Leger.

The first involved a most curious place: "Un 'John Donne Club' franco-britannique . . . fondé en pleine Angleterre post-victorienne, par une Californienne pétrarquisante, à la gloire d'un élisabéthain!"[119] It amused Leger no end to be nominated as the youngest member of this club (presided over by Agnes Tobin), whose other French adherent was Gide, by Larbaud.[120]

"It is really too funny! So let's go!" (sic)[121] he exclaimed. And go he did, for laughter determined many of his choices—in situations, people, and literature. (This is probably why he was so delighted with Edward Lear, the author of the *Book of Nonsense Songs and Stories*, whose poem, "The Jumblies," Conrad had recited to him, affirming with utter seriousness that he found more of the spirit of great adventure there than in the best sea sagas, such as Herman Melville's.[122] Leger himself loved citing the work and communicated his enthusiasm to Gide concerning the poet: "Si je pouvais me permettre jamais de citer mon plaisir ou mon goût, je ne recommanderais qu' [Edward] Lear, seul poète d'une race qui me semble la race même poétique"[123]—high praise indeed for one as selective as he, and quite revealing in terms of the important links he saw between poetry and laughter.)

The second experience was of a quite different nature. It involved another "poète d'une race qui . . . semble la race même poétique," Rabindranath Tagore. Leger met Tagore during this same stay in London and was deeply affected by "ce grand vieillard pèlerin, d'un charme délicat et d'une distinction très sûre."[124] Tagore, "le Sage de Santiniketan,"[125] spoke to the young poet and his friends "en musicien autant qu'en philosophe, avec cette douceur étrange, dans le regard, des âmes très altières." He seemed to them to stand "à la croisée des routes de deux mondes, et de deux âges . . . un peu comme une figuration mythique . . . il fut . . . l'image même du Poète antique, sous la double couronne de l'Aède et du Sage."[126] To Leger, he must have appeared an incarnation of all that he had (since childhood) absorbed of the spirit of India, its myths, its great concepts of human and cosmic scope.

Though their meeting was brief, the exchange was timeless. In a few short hours, in a peaceful house in South Kensington, the two men—knowing no difference of age, East or West, renown or acclaim—achieved a lasting encounter. Afterward, the younger of the two pored for a long time over the other's work, the *Gitanjali*. It appeared to him an "'offrande lyrique' . . . toute fraîcheur et toute essence, comme prise au feuillage même d'un grand arbre d'Asie."[127] He decided, then and there, that this offering must be brought across the sea, to France.

Gide seemed to Leger the best suited for carrying out this task. He would be able not only to translate Tagore but also to introduce his work in those circles that could best receive his gift—admittedly an elite. He saw the possibility of an association between writers, not unlike that which had linked Baudelaire and Poe or Nerval and Goethe[128] and wrote to Gide about the project, including a copy of the *Gitanjali*. Gide, although warned away by Claudel who said, "I am very suspicious of your Rabindranath Tagore! What I have read of his seemed to me rather nauseating, and I so despise that sort of Asiatic!"[129] fortunately did not heed these words of disparagement. He read, greatly admired the work of Tagore, and accepted with joy to undertake its translation.

Thus, the *Gitanjali*—thanks to Leger—was published by the N.R.F. in 1914, with this dedication by Gide to the former, acknowledging his indebtedness: "Il est bien naturel que j'inscrive ici votre nom, cher ami. Grâce à vous, je fus peut-être le premier en France à connaître Rabindranath Tagore, alors que bien peu de lettrés le connaissaient encore en Angleterre."[130] Leger had indeed recognized the genius of Tagore before he was known in either country, and a year before the former was awarded the Nobel Prize for literature (in 1913). Interestingly enough, he had wanted to share his discovery with France—the country of which he had spoken so harshly on numerous occasions.

Back in France, he continued to meet poets and further showed the broad range of appreciation he was capable of in this realm. For the next friendship he formed was with Paul Valéry, who had an entirely different view of literature than he. Valéry's rationalist orientation, his Cartesian strain, involvement with the Self, disembodiment, the single note, monologue, were in diametric opposition to Leger's emphasis on the irrational, involvement with the Cosmos, embodiment, polyphony, and dialogue.[131] Yet, the two men felt a bond of sympathy, perhaps because this was a period of silent reflection for Valéry, of abstention from poetry for a whole decade—a position that Leger surely respected and would one day share. Valéry's great poem, *La Jeune Parque* (which was to be his farewell to poetry but became a return instead), was already germinating in his mind. It is not unlikely that the fecund soil created by this encounter with a kindred spirit was instrumental in its fruition.

During the years that followed, Leger had many other preoccupations aside from poets and poetry. He lived in Paris now—where his mother and sisters had also taken up residence—and was absorbed by his studies, hoping that he would pass the highly competitive examinations that determined entry into the Ministry of Foreign Affairs. Time was drawing short, for there was an age limit (which he was fast approaching) beyond which it became impossible to begin such a career. He traveled again to England, and also to Germany, in order to research port installations, as a part of his preparation. But, although he was interested in such problems, part of him inevitably drew him again to poets.

Thus, he managed to visit Claudel who was then consul in Frankfurt. The two men met in Hamburg in 1913, and while they studied this great port together, Leger made Claudel a gift of a rare edition of Pindar,[132] and their most meaningful conversation took a much more poetic than industrial turn; it occurred as they were returning on foot, through a tunnel beneath the Elbe. A strange impulse caused both of them to stop at the same moment, and talk.[133] Leger spoke of the sea, from which he had come and upon which he would reembark once again. Suddenly Claudel, as if speaking to himself pronounced, "ce mot de grand terrien: 'La mer . . . la mer, c'est la vie future.'"[134] And perhaps Leger (repeating what he had written to Rivière) spoke of that "anabase" that he had defined as "un retour à la Mer, la commune Mer d'où l'oeuvre fut tirée"[135] or reiterated once more what he had already confided to Claudel, sometime earlier: "J'aimerais qu'il me fût donné un jour de mener une 'oeuvre' comme une *Anabase* sous la conduite de ses chefs. (Et ce mot même me semble si beau que j'aimerais bien rencontrer l'oeuvre qui pût assumer un tel titre. Il me hante.)"[136]

But even more haunting was another experience—also linked to the river Elbe—which Leger would remember (and recount) almost half a century later, on the other side of the world. It happened one night after he had dined at the home of the German poet Richard Dehmel (to whom Leger had been introduced by Claudel). The night was dark, damp, and cold. He had decided to walk to the port to see some of the great old schooners anchored there. Leaving the hospitable warmth of his friend's home, he wandered through the badly lit, snowy streets in search of the port. Advancing almost with desperation, groping his way like a blind man, slipping and overturning vague objects in the mist, he sensed nevertheless that the sea could not be far.

Suddenly, in the silence broken only by the sound of a foghorn, he heard distant music—broad, solemn, slow. Someone was playing a harmonium. An invisible artist was performing a piece by Handel that, in this solitude, took on a hallucinatory splendor. He tried to locate the site of the music. It was not easy. Finally, the feeble light of a lantern helped him to orient himself. A man—at first only a vague shadow—played the instrument on the deck of a ship with lowered masts, some distance away. At the risk of falling into the water, Leger arrived on deck by crossing a frail gangplank. He advanced a few steps and greeted the musician. The latter did not stop playing, as if his visitor did not exist. A lantern, hung by a rope, lit up his graying beard. He was shrouded in a dark seaman's cape; his eyes were hidden by the visor of his cap.

When the piece was over, the man closed the cover of the harmonium. Leger drew closer. The old mariner showed no surprise at his presence. Without being questioned, he explained, speaking in the rough local accent: "—L'enfant. . . . C'était pour l'aider à mourir." And he showed his visitor a meager heap of blankets and old rags next to the instrument. He brought the lantern closer. Leger lifted one corner of the blanket. There lay "un pauvre petit singe, un spectre de petit singe, au poil grisâtre, la bouche entrouverte [qui] nous regardait, avec la fixité des yeux de mort."[137]

He would never forget the incident.

1914–1916

The year 1914 was one of personal triumph and world disaster. Alexis Leger—shortly before the outbreak of World War I—succeeded in passing his examinations and entered diplomatic service. His elation knew almost no bounds. He wrote:

J'ai maîtrisé ce que j'entendais maîtriser de ma vie. Je n'aurai pas été dupe de mes songes ni du regard d'autrui. Je suis très simplement heureux d'avoir trouvé en moi assez de haine et de dégoût pour l'habituelle lâcheté et l'écoeurante suffisance des hommes d'imagination, qui gardent envers leur vie des façons, des espoirs de mendiants. Peut-être vaut-il mieux encore prendre et mener sa vie comme une femme que de la suivre comme une fille. . . . *So, glad I won that!*[138]

The Quai d'Orsay, where he would soon make his entry, must have seemed to Leger like a battlefield to a victorious general; or a sanctuary whose portals opened to an initiate. He had mastered the obstacles that guarded the access to this hermetically sealed place, this "house without windows," this sacred ark, this Sanhedrin of which most spoke only on bended knees.[139] Even a good imitation of a dragon would probably not have been able to turn him from his path.

Something like it awaited him when these doors actually opened: he saw a gallery of strange creatures, seemingly forgotten there since the days of Louis Philippe.[140] The first figure he encountered was Monsieur le Grand Hallebardier, chief of the bailiffs, whose entire uniform seemed covered with shining braid and was decorated with over a dozen medals of the mightiest nations on earth, replete with sword and halbert. There were many others with official functions, pointed out to him, who had odd, amusing titles and specialties: Monsieur le Conseiller Ecclésiastique, Monsieur le Géographe-Adjoint,

Monsieur l'Archiviste-Paléographe, Monsieur le Calligraphe Officiel. Last, but most important of all, there was Monsieur le Directeur du Protocole (who supervised the various dramas of etiquette).[141]

Leger would certainly have outraged the latter if he had deigned to notice the young man, for he almost instantly disregarded official protocol by not furnishing the Quai d'Orsay's training commission with any personal references or letters of introduction, as was traditional.[142] While this intrigued some, others who had long been established there resented the freedom that the newcomer already showed. The reactions Leger evoked were, from the outset, far from lukewarm. To some—the most nonconformist, or the most generous—he seemed "un être apart . . . [une] comète! . . . au firmament de l'esprit," having appeared "dans le ciel diplomatique comme un astre de la constellation nouvelle, un signe du temps."[143] Others, such as his colleague, Paul Morand, who had entered the Ministry of Foreign Affairs at the same time as Leger,[144] were fascinated by "ce précoce Créole" who seemed "déjà un esprit complètement formé" and spoke of Gide and Claudel as his equals, as well as by "sa pudeur, les longues perspectives de son esprit, sa pensée élevée et tendue, son imagination joyeuse et sa sagesse de vieillard, son désintéressement, sa vie secrète, ses appartements sans meubles, avec des malles, son enfance nomade."[145] It was quite evident that here was a man of quite unusual gifts and traits of character.

His beginnings in the diplomatic service were certainly not concomitant with his noticeably superior qualities. The first position he occupied was a relatively modest one—in the Press Service. Rather quickly, however, it was noticed that he seemed to transform everything he touched to a higher plane. Especially when he spoke, he appeared to outdistance all those around him, dwarfing them with his stature. "Il suffisait à Leger," one observer noted, "de faire entendre sa basse chantante, d'introduire dans un dialogue, devenu soudain monologue, quelques-unes des paroles coulées dont il sait le charme, d'appuyer sur son interlocuteur un regard de perroquet . . . pour donner entrée à un personnage d'une envergure telle que ses collègues devenaient ce qu'ils sont, de simples apparences de l'annuaire."[146] Obviously, such overshadowing could not help but irritate his less brilliant colleagues at the Quai d'Orsay—as did the interest that Berthelot and Claudel showed in this novice.

It must have been a relief to many when, shortly after his entry into the Ministry of Foreign Affairs, Leger was sent out of Paris, to Bordeaux, with the cabinet of his minister (Delcassé).[147] It was a move, however, that was not determined by petty jealousies or sabotage of a minor nature but by far greater struggles and conflict on a much more grandiose scale: World War I had broken out. France faced one of its bitterest battles. The war would decimate its youth, ravage its countryside, and create an upheaval of the nation's entire societal structure. The "guns of August" had begun to sound.[148] France seemed already entirely changed.

As for Leger, finding himself once more in Bordeaux, the city where he had spent his student days, was in many ways a personal triumph. To return to the site of so many of his former struggles and doubts—now that he was victorious—must have given him a sense of elation; elation hardly mitigated by the danger France was facing. For it seems unlikely that he considered this country sufficiently a homeland to feel great allegiance to it as a nation and to take extreme sides in this war. His view of world events was a far broader one, and he was certainly not swayed in his objective appraisal of events, as were many of his colleagues who were motivated by zealous patriotism. Besides, work in the Press Service exposed him constantly to the opinions and interpretations of journalists from other nations, giving him varied insights into, and perceptions of, everything that took place in this conflict.

The time in Bordeaux passed rapidly. It was enlivened by a visit from Claudel—repatriated, because of the war, from Germany—who shared his most recent work, "Le Pain dur" (still in manuscript form), with his young friend.[149] Some months later,

Leger was brought back to Paris with the cabinet of his minister.

He was now assigned to work at the Maison de Presse, where he read and analyzed the articles of foreign correspondents from around the world, selecting those which would be of interest to his superiors.[150] Assignments such as these most probably reactivated his old longings for far-off places. As the reports came in from every part of the globe, his wanderlust—dormant awhile but never stilled—undoubtedly awakened. He found it difficult, quite likely, to be confined to Paris.

Life in the French capital (at least for members of certain circles) was quite enjoyable and seemed hardly affected by the war[151]: dinners and spectacles proceeded as though there were no rationing—or death either. The Ritz and Chez Larue were crowded with high society, diplomats, aristocrats, and artists of renown. Those who dined and rubbed elbows there were named Proust, Giraudoux, Cocteau, Bergson, Gide, Morand, Claudel, Jammes, Diaghilev, Bakst, Stravinsky, Berthelot, Anna de Noailles, Nathalie Barney, Mata Hari, Misia Sert, Colette . . . and Leger.[152] Women of beauty and renown enlivened these evenings, and the handsome young diplomat's Creole charms were not lost on many of them. He—with all his reserve—was not indifferent to their allure. True, he might have been irritated by gossip that centered around his conquests, as when Misia proclaimed: "Je crois que Leger m'aimait. Hélène Berthelot me l'assure. Il m'embrassait les bras, et, la veille d'un voyage en Espagne, n'a pas voulu partir," sitting in her room at the Meurice, "très 1895, très Renoir, avec un vaste corsage, des mèches, les cheveux en casque et se curant les dents avec des ciseaux";[153] or when Cocteau claimed that Misia had plans for "la petite Mimi Godebska," such as marrying the latter to Leger.[154] And, while he certainly enjoyed this social whirl, the varied encounters with such colorful characters—and his success with women—he had quite other plans in mind. The lure of distant places had not lessened because of excellent dinners, great spectacles, fascinating conversations, or female allure. He had not forgotten that the main attraction of diplomatic service had been—and still was—that it allowed one "de s'en aller." The mundane existence that, on the surface, he led so well, could not for long content his nomadic spirit, nor his innate yearning for solitude.

It was thus with great excitement that he learned that he had been selected for a mission to China, in the fall of 1916. He was to be sent to Peking, where he would assist the local chargé d'affaires to settle the current crisis in Franco-Chinese relations (over the French concession of T'ien-Tsin).[155] All the tales he had heard about the Orient, from Claudel and Berthelot, came rushing back to him. He could hardly contain the flights of his imagination. Paris paled in the shadow of the Orient. He already saw himself in a series of adventures on the other side of the globe.

True, the mission to Peking was only temporary. But he had heard Berthelot predict that his stay would last a long time. "Leger a voulu partir pour la Chine," he said, "eh bien, il y restera dix ans!"[156] (He could not know that Berthelot would be only half right, but the prophecy was one that augured well for his desires.) Inwardly, the call "s'en aller! s'en aller!" echoed all throughout his remaining days in Paris and gave an aura of leave-taking to everything in his life. His most secret wish, so long denied, was being realized.

At the Quai (as it was familiarly called), being sent to the Orient was no small matter. As in everything, strict hierarchies existed: a system of zones determined the importance of the place to which a diplomat traveled. An expert in these matters explained the complex and solemn rules that prevailed: "Le globe terrestre est divisé en 4 zones, dont le périmètre varie par rapport à Paris et où le Quai d'Orsay est considéré comme le point zéro . . . la troisième zone est Pékin et Tokyo. . . . Plus on s'éloigne, plus le traîtement est élevé."[157] Thus, even being named third secretary [158] in the third zone (as was Leger's case) was great cause for celebration.

This celebration took the form of a farewell dinner, given at Chez Larue. The list of guests was quite impressive: officers of various sorts, at least one princess, the wife of the Italian commercial attaché (probably because she wrote verses), and a number of Leger's colleagues in the diplomatic service. He, of course, was the star of the evening and enlivened the dinner by his gifts as a storyteller and by his humor. One of the guests noted some of the highlights of the memorable evening in his *Journal:*

Leger n'apprendra pas le Chinois, nous dit-il. "La vie est trop courte, laissez-moi être dupe de mes travaux et de mes plaisirs." Puis il nous enchante, ou plutôt nous incante, en évoquant son enfance antillaise, l'éruption du mont Pélé. Il parle de la Martinique, de Saint-Leger-les-Feuilles, de l'îlot au nord de Pointe-à-Pitre où il naquit. Il parle aussi du rhum, de la forme et du gréement des yachts, de la supériorité de la goélette, des fourmis du Gabon, de Claudel, . . . raconte des histoires de corsaires, de crabes "creux et gris." . . . Une immense envie de voyage prend tous les convives.[159]

The guests' yearning for travel, awakened by the enchantment of the stories told by this master of tales, was surely exceeded only by the longing of the teller himself. For this was the moment he had fervently awaited: a farewell to the past, to France, to the continent where he had long lived as a stranger. Leave-taking. The start of a new life. Terra incognita. Risk. Adventure. Space. Solitude. China.

Truly, he felt that he now stood at the crossroads of the world.

CHAPTER 4

THUNDER BENEATH THE SNOW
(1916–1921)

Nous n'habiterons pas toujours ces terres jaunes, notre délice.
—*Anabase* (*OC*, p. 105)

Peking, Winter, 1916–1917

It seemed like the "capitale astronomique du monde, hors du lieu, hors du temps, et frappé d'absolu."[1] He had reached the city around the time of the winter solstice, when the sun is at its nadir and the earth seems about to disappear into the primordial Void. Never had he known such cold[2] nor such perfect dryness; neither had he ever encountered light so pure, skies so clear, a land so ancient. Everything had an air of strangeness, of irreality. It was as though one walked on another planet.

"La 'Ville Tartare,'" totally alien still, appeared as a place of "abstraction—camp de pierre pour les dernières manoeuvres de l'esprit et dernier 'lieu géométrique' de ce monde."[3] (How different it was from that other "lieu géométrique"[4]—London—where he seemed to have been in another life.) He wandered alone through the labyrinth of streets and saw only a kingdom of shades where everything dissolved into nullity: "Des couples qui ne s'étreignent pas, des aventuriers qui ne s'aventurent pas . . . on ne fait rien . . . ne réalise rien."[5] He himself seemed to evolve in nothingness, detached from the globe, floating in end-

less space. An immeasurable distance separated him from everything in his past life. His former love for space (seemingly
innate, so early had it declared itself)[6] now appeared to him
unfathomable. For all around him there was "l'espace, tant d'espace qui se fait épaisseur et durée" that it occurred to him that
"peut-être la notion d'espace se confond-elle un jour avec celle
d'insularité, où, pour un Antillais né, s'abîme toute solitude."[7]

He had already felt this abyss of loneliness during the long,
long journey more than halfway across the world. He had then
thought that it was perhaps the crossing of so many seas or the
succession of numberless ports of call—Djibouti, Colombo, Singapore, Saigon, Haiphong, Hong Kong—or the ancient ship,
filled with "sa faune légendaire de vieux routiers d'Extrême-
Orient"[8] who seemed to live on another planet. Perhaps it was
the numerous detours they took that wiped out all sense of direction, or the change of time as they crossed various meridians.
Everything added to the feeling of the unknown, the alien. Even
he himself was becoming a stranger who felt that he journied
"chaque jour, avec un peu plus d'un autre homme en [lui]-
même, et ce sentiment, chaque jour accrû, de la relativité des
choses de ce monde."[9]

Solitude had struck him, with sudden force, during a brief halt
at the Suez Canal. There, the final link with the past had broken
and detached itself from his being. As he and the last of his kin
sat, for a whole night, facing the narrow sea strait, speaking
words of parting, he saw the Canal as the "suture dernière . . .
entre deux mondes, entre deux âges, entre deux tournants de
[s]on destin."[10] The timeless, nocturnal scene marked the point
of no return, the great divide. It seemed as awesome as that
moment in Claudel's *Partage de midi* when the passage from
world to otherworld was consummated.[11] As he gave his last
recommendations to his relative for his family's care, he felt as if
he were making a testament. When the ship's siren sounded and
he stepped across the gangplank, he knew that he had irrevoca-
bly chosen the path of the "voyageur et de l'absent" and that,
from that day on on, he would inhabit "ce côté du monde où l'on
se tait, où il me semble qu'on n'ait droit que de se taire."[12]

In China silence, absence, and solitude seemed indeed to reign. It was the immensity of the country, its agelessness, its strangeness—but also the absolute transparency of the air—that made everything appear unreal and spectral to the newcomer. Perhaps it was also that the land, "à première vue, n'est que poussière, terre usuagée, terre arasée, de temps immémorial . . . (Moi qui ait toujours rêvé d'écrire un livre sur la poussière, je suis ici servi!)"[13] Most voyagers would feel total alienation in the midst of this phantom scenery, which appeared even more incorporeal because of the blinding light.

Yet this voyager was also strangely drawn to this landscape. Dust had long haunted his dreams. The soil was volatile, subject to instant transformation when a wind rose ("le 'vent jaune,' mon délice").[14] It became an entirely new "element"[15] then (loess, which had fascinated him ever since the days of his first geology books). Besides, he relished the extreme contrasts that existed in this land; between the disembodied, lunar aspect of the scenery and the totally corporeal, earthy beings it produced.

At first, he saw them only as vast frescoes of humanity. Viewed from a distance, the creatures swarmed and made indistinct sounds. What came to mind was Claudel's harsh description: "cette Chine à l'état de friture perpétuelle: grouillante, désordonnée, anarchique . . . avec sa saleté épique, ses mendiants, ses lépreux, toutes ses tripes à l'air."[16] But, as he drew nearer, he saw their vivacious, talkative nature, their sense of adventure, their gaiety, and he remembered that "la grande leçon . . . l'humour vint à Claudel de la Chine."[17] Moreover, their level of activity seemed prodigious—there was movement everywhere. They seemed so singularly vital that he exclaimed: "C'est la vie même, courant en bottes de feutre, parmi tant de cendre accumulée!"[18]

What made this people even more fascinating to Leger was that it was in the process of mutation, of metamorphosis. One could watch "l'histoire à vif et convulsive d'un très grand peuple usé par sa trop longue soumission, et maintenant lancé en pleine transformation."[19] Upheaval constantly threatened, and certainly intrigued his penchant for cataclysm. And, once he knew them better, the Chinese revealed other traits that coincided admirably with his own: for them, contradiction seemed second nature; they had an inborn taste for inconsistency and for the absurd. "Why not?" appeared to be always the last word in a discussion among this nation of "possibilistes." Yet, at the same time, these born rationalists were open to "toute incidence du subconscient, qui fait d'[eux] les premiers praticiens d'une sorte de surrationalisme."[20] (Thus, he found in them many of the qualities he had regretted seeing incompletely developed in Nietzsche, some time ago).[21]

Obviously, then, there was much to see and learn on this side of the globe. He remembered, with gratitude, the parting words of Berthelot: "Il n'y a pas de formation professionelle, ni humaine, complète sans un séjour en Extrême-Orient."[22] And began to frequent the Chinese—more than was usual, or well thought of (especially by officials with old prejudices and adages who preferred to live among themselves in the enclosure of the Diplomatic Quarter). In the evenings, whenever he could escape from the social events that his profession called for, he started to play chess with native politicians and to spend his time in their company. He found them joyous and devoid of haughtiness; they taught him more about China than the members of the legations and, besides, they never bored him. On the contrary, they intrigued him with their logic, so different from that of Occidentals, and revealed to him "quelque chose de ce vieux fonds humain, si variable toujours."[23]

The oldtime French diplomats, on the other hand, irritated him by their stultification, their smug lethargy. He criticized them severely when he wrote to Berthelot:

C'est à hauteur d'horizon qu'il faut tenir le regard . . . bien au-dessus la vision de ce Corps diplomatique de Pékin . . . qui s'est forgé dans les limites du Quartier diplomatique, un mode de vie . . . comme en cocon, qui peut être assez piquant pour le snobisme de ses résidents, mais qui demeure totalement étranger à la Chine. D'où l'isolement, l'inattention et la paresse d'esprit des plus vieux Chefs de mission . . . tournés comme ils sont, en dilettantes, vers une Chine antique dont les assises leur semblent immuables.[24]

Yet, despite such negative appraisal of their life-style and attitude, he was forced to move in this diplomatic world each day—
and in the evenings as well. Endless social obligations were part
of his job: formal dress dinners (even in subzero weather) must
be attended in evening attire; all openings of festivities demanded his presence. He even had to make his living quarters
with his superiors.[25]

The only relief from this mundane life came at dawn. Then, he
escaped on his horse to the outskirts of the city and rode full
speed in the open spaces. He scanned the horizon for further
vistas in the semidesert at the northeast of Peking, which, during free weekends, he hoped to explore; and he turned to the
uninhabited for contrast from the "civilized," to solitude for re-
freshment from the overly gregarious, and to animals for deliverance from what passed for the human. It was in the last of the
three domains, however, that he found the deepest meaning.

For he now owned an extraordinary horse—with whom he
would achieve an extraordinary form of "compagnonnage." At
first, he had bought him simply as a mount—but perhaps also as
a challenge, for no one could approach the animal, neither the
stable boys nor the acupuncturist-veterinarian. He was certainly
unprepossessing in looks and could not have captured the attention of Leger (who was used to magnificient steeds) by his appearance: homely and small, massively built with a barrel chest,
thick neck, and short, stubby legs, his head hung low, and he
had a heavy, undistinguished face. When running, Leger noted
laughingly, he had "la silhouette d'un gros rat sur roulettes."[26]
But he had also seen the horse's eyes, "admirables yeux de co-
libri ou de caniche, vraiment les plus attendrissants qui
soient."[27] He began to observe the "monster" (as he had been
dubbed by his would-be trainers) more closely than before. The
character of the animal revealed itself to him when he saw, one
day, "la douceur amusée avec laquelle il acceptait les pires inso-
lences d'un très petit enfant chinois se glissant sous son ven-
tre."[28] From that time on he knew that an entente with humans
was possible.

Slowly, the friendship between the Mongolian horse and the man from the Atlantic began to grow. They seemed, after a while, to sense each other's every mood. There was no need for commands, for outward gestures even. One look from the man and the animal responded with perfect understanding. It was moving to see how trusting he had become. "Il vient maintenant à moi," Leger wrote, "avec ses yeux d'enfant, insoucieux de sa laideur et de son manque de manières. Il entre jusque dans ma maison, glissant sur le carrelage du hall, où je dois seulement lui masquer une glace qui le terrifie."[29]

Alexis named his horse Allan—"ce nom," he wrote to his mother, "que j'ai porté pour vous dans mon enfance."[30] The closeness between them became so great that it seemed, sometimes, as if they not only shared a name but were of one body. "Mon cheval," he said, "me semble parfois faire tellement corps avec moi, que c'est moi, l'homme, qui me sens devenir cheval, et lui, cheval, qui me tient pour son totem."[31] Everything about Mongolian horses now fascinated him. He researched their ancestry and discovered that they were of the pure Kirghiz race and descended from the fabled horse of Central Asia, "dit 'cheval de Prjevalsky,' l'ancêtre de tous les chevaux" (an animal that fascinated him and that he dreamed of encountering, somewhere in the desert, during that expedition into Mongolia and Turkestan that had haunted him ever since his arrival in the Orient.)[32]

For the moment, however, it was Allan himself who fascinated him sufficiently. He had begun to notice that the horse intuited his wishes and feelings in an almost uncanny way: sometimes they both stopped suddenly, in some deserted spot on the vast Chinese plain, and, as if moved by secret vibrations, both turned instinctively toward what the man's compass showed to be the direction of the sea.[33] It was as though the animal, though never having been near the shore, sensed the human's love and nostalgia for that element. At other times, the horse seemed to look expectantly for some intelligible words from the man, as though he could speak the language of animals. But his gaze also appeared to be that of a creature mesmerized. He seemed to be responding to a form of "magnetism" that this human being possessed.

Leger had found that numerous animals, including the wild horses brought fresh from the depths of Mongolia, fell under the spell of his gaze before he had ever touched them. It did not exactly surprise him, for this "gift" had been his ever since childhood (and had even been confirmed by a scientist friend of the family).[34] And, while it amazed those who saw it in action—saw that, without words, by a look, his way of walking, a touch of his shoulder, the laying on of hands, he could subdue even the most untameable beasts—he himself found it cause for some sadness. For he regretted seeing sympathy or affection reduced to something as mechanical as this thing called "magnétisme animal," and realized that the only Chinese he had met who were lacking in gaiety were the professional "magnétiseurs."[35]

Yet, it was perhaps to this gift that he owed his earliest friendships with non humans in this land. For, while Allan remained his closest companion, other animals also came into his life, reminiscent of those of his childhood. The first was a large, foreign dog, a magnificent creature from Australia (and the terror of the whole neighborhood) who decided to live with him more than with his English masters. He waited each morning for Leger to appear in his riding clothes and accompanied him faithfully as he raced along in the open air (to the great discomfiture of the Chinese dogs in the environs).[36] Warm weather brought the arrival of another, much stranger friend—a simple mosquito. He hid all day in the binding of a small, unused dictionary and, in the evening, joined Leger at table (without, one assumes, ever stinging him). The native servants called it magic. A doctor friend could hardly believe his eyes. Yet, it was easily proved by the dot of red ink (like a Chinese actor's) with which Leger had marked the insect to identify it. He had named the little creature Ulysses.[37] A bit later, others joined the group—a small lizard who became very tame, a delightful tree frog, crickets—completing an entourage that comforted the man in his essentially solitary existence.

Thus, the first winter in Peking had passed. The year had turned. The cold receded and, with it, the sense of absence and alienation he had at first experienced. It was now the beginning of a season of heat, excitement, and explosive upheavals, a time that promised violent metamorphoses.

Summer 1917

Political unrest came to a head shortly before the summer solstice. Revolution had broken out in the provinces but had been momentarily stopped by the dissolution of the Peking parliament, on June 13, and caused a halt in the march of the provincial armies on the metropolis. A powerful leader from Manchuria decided to reinstate his dynasty. By this maneuver the storm was temporarily turned aside, and revolution aborted, at least for the time being.[38]

The next month, however, brought a coup d'état: on July 1, Gen. Tchang-Hsiun brought his savage hordes to Peking and put the emperor Siuen-tong (who was then only eleven years old) on the throne as a mere symbol of legitimacy. A large part of the population of Peking fled in terror to the provinces. The immense city remained nearly empty since the Chinese had disappeared, like insects beneath the sand. The contrast was especially striking, for only a short time ago the congestion of rickshaws and the cries of the departing had filled the streets.

The counterattack occurred promptly. The general of the Republican army bombarded Peking from dawn until the following afternoon. The short-lived dictatorship came to an end. Its leader fled, abandoning his troops. The Third Republic was proclaimed. In the smoking ruins of parts of the city there lay unburied cadavers, the bodies of wounded who had been decapitated, carcasses of horses that had died "cleanly" or been carbonized, the very small corpse of a Chinese child who had carried ammunition from trench to trench. It had been an "étonnante tourmente," for the entire upheavel had lasted only twelve days.[39]

There was, however, in the midst of this "torment," an incident that took place in the wings and that quenched the young diplomat's thirst for risk, excitement, and amusement. It was the highly entertaining mission to bring the president of the Chinese Republic and his family to a place of refuge in the inviolate Diplomatic Quarter. It seemed to Leger an adventure worthy of a Venetian courtier in the heyday of intrigue. The exploit elicited his laughter for quite some time.

He decided to send a nonoffical—and off-the-record—account of the exploit to his minister, Alexandre Conty, in Peking—using his own transposed Chinese name (Lei Hi-gnai or Thunder Beneath the Snow)[40] as well as that of his chief.

The letter recounted, in a pastiche of official language and filled with piquant details and tongue-in-cheek humor, some of the highlights of the venture: the extreme heat and the excessive chirping of crickets; the unsuspected number of President Li's concubines and the limited number of seats in the diplomatic limousine; the exodus, led by the president's wife, "un être chèvre-pieds habillé de vert bronze suivie de ses filles en tunique claire, suivies de concubines en soie prune, suivies . . . de gens de maison et d'écurie, hommes de confiance et hommes de peine, femmes de chambre et intendants, rôtisseurs et confiseurs, guérisseurs, policiers et porteurs" and, finally, high above the crowd, "demi-nu et porté à bout de bras par un géant coiffé d'un melon beige, un enfant sale aux bracelets d'argent: le dernier-né des fils du Président"; the assault of the limousine by all this throng, amid "le vacarme des cigales, des choucas, des pintades et des pies, les croassement des corbeaux, l'aboiement des chiens de race, les murmures d'un grand arbre chargé de voisins"; the voyage across Peking (among a supposedly hostile but actually indifferent crowd) during which the president's wife, from behind her fan and beneath the green bandages across her temples, for a migraine, "tint son regard fixé sur les menaces inexistantes de la mort"; the large number of odd creatures who hung on to all the outer parts of the limousine, giving the rescue operation the appearance of a kidnapping and leaving no doubt in anyone's mind that it was a matter of "une affaire galante." He ended the letter by assuring his minister that he did not know "ce qu'il convient le plus de louer dans le maintien de ses principaux acteurs: la décence de ceux qui n'eurent à maîtriser que leur peur, ou . . . la correction de ceux qui eurent à maîtriser leur rire."[41] It was quite evident that he was in the camp of the latter.

Laughter, however, was not always considered proper in the diplomatic circles where Leger moved. The letter, although personal and private, had unfortunately reached Paris with the mail of his post. Its lighthearted tone threatened to seriously affect his reputation at the Quai d'Orsay.[42] Had he not had the friendship of Conty, or the high patronage of Berthelot to protect him, the price for humor might have been extremely high. Obviously, his nonconformist nature was coming to the fore and reached the eyes of those who were least capable of appreciating this quality.

It is hard to say what his colleagues would have thought of the other activities that absorbed Leger now, whose character conformed even less to their way of life. Surely they would have thought him seriously deranged or even quite mad if they had known that of late he spent every free moment in a retreat among the hills above Peking, in a temple named Tao-Yu,[43] a kind of hermitage ("plus ascétique et nu qu'un crâne de lama"),[44] which the Taoist monks had rented to him at a very low price and with the greatest of ceremony for the entire summer.[45]

It was his "'haut lieu' chinois."[46] From there he could dominate the endless landscape. By day one saw a vast country without a name, people, or animals. The only sounds were those of the river that flowed below and of the small stone drums struck by those who wished to be ferried across. After dark, one was face to face with the immense nocturnal void. It was an experience such as he had never before encountered—a kind of "frénésie," in which one felt "l'insistance extrême du vide et de l'absence, ouverts au songe"; a visionary state, a glimpse of the beyond through "l'oeil sans paupière, ou la paupière sans cils, du dormeur éveillé." He sat and listened, hearing "tout autour . . . cet étrange persiflage du rien, où l'âme chinoise se rit de ne pas être une âme et le Tao lui-même se dévore la queue."[47]

At dawn, in the distance, appeared the vistas of the West, where the Mongol lands and Sinkiang lay, where the legendary caravan trails began. Beyond, "plus loin, enfin, l'absence, l'ir-réel, et l'horizon terrestre barré du seul regard intemporel . . . toute l'Asie bouddhique, lamaïque et tantrique."[48] He murmured: "Je m'en irai moi-même un jour par là, je le sais—."[49]

It was in this "high place" that he began to think, once more, of poetry. It had been a long time—in another life, almost—since he had written anything. So much had intervened; so much action, so many worlds had claimed his attention for the past few years. But now the time seemed ripe, the place right, for turning toward "le songe" once more, that other pole that was an integral part of his being. "La paix ici est grande pour l'esprit, la marge incommensurable . . . on entendrait se consumer le temps," he wrote. "Transpositions et transgressions ici sont telles," he continued, "que j'y serais parfois tenté de prendre la plume, contre toutes mes vieilles résolutions."[50]

And he indeed took up his pen once more. And the end of that summer of violence and metamorphoses would—among its harvests—produce a great poem. It was in this Taoist temple, in a landscape of timelessness and solitude, that "Anabase" was created, in the space of a few weeks.[51]

It was work of far greater scope than anything he had written before—commensurate with the incommensurable nature of this land. In form, it corresponded to a dream he had had, long ago it seemed, of writing a vast poem, a kind of epic that went beyond those "brèves indulgences du passé,"[52] something reflecting expanses such as he had now encountered. How strange that he had known over half a dozen years ago what he must one day do. He remembered his conversation with Claudel, beneath the

Elbe, when he had reiterated his wish to encounter a work that
he could conduct, like an "anabase"; and thought also how frequently Claudel had mused—and spoken—about the resuscita-
tion of the long poem in the epic vein, filled with the immense
riches that history, science, and social law offered.[53]

Perhaps it was the confluence of such reflections that underlay
the shape that "Anabase" had taken. But surely these were only
minor factors in its creation. Other, more mysterious forces were
instrumental in its fecundation, determined its gestation,
prompted its birth. They were inextricably linked to the place
where the poem was conceived.

It was not set in any particular location, far from it—and far
from any recognizable locality. It took place in what appeared to
be a mythical domain:[54] in pastures immemorial, where years
were without links and without days; outside all limitations of
time and space; beyond the confines of life, in a realm of absence
and unreality, where the gaze encountered endless domains,
"toute l'Asie bouddhique, lamaïque et tantrique."[55] The fruit of
transpositions and transgressions, it had been forged in silence,
solitude, and confrontation with the void. One could only imagine one possible point of orientation: the infinite vistas of the
West, "le Couchant . . . la vraie patrie de tous les hommes de
désir . . . celle du Bouddha Maitreya, vers laquelle se mit un
jour en route le fabuleux Laotzeu."[56]

The journey of which it spoke, that "anabase" or "descente
vers la Mer, la commune Mer,"[57] was thus not a particular expedition but the quintessence of all journeys, the sum of all
dreams, the vision seen by "l'oeil sans paupière, ou la paupière
sans cils du dormeur éveillé"—or the dreamer-poet. And the
"Stranger" who traveled through the pages of the poem traveled
the paths of the entire world—and otherworld. Living among
the living, yet not one of them, reviving the dead and standing
guard before death's door, he was "L'Etranger qui passait . . .
L'Etranger qui riait . . . [le]Voyageur dans le vent jaune . . . le
Conteur."[58] Chieftain of a vast people of nomadic tribes, hierophant in strange archaic rituals, the brother of the Poet (or his
double), he was far more than a projection of personal glory, or a

self-portrait of the poet. A hero of epic, even cosmic proportions, he symbolized the sum of everything that the visions in this "terre arable du songe"[59] had produced in the creator of this poem.

Yet the work, with all its endless perspectives and mythical dimensions, was filled with things from that "monde entier des choses" that the poet never ceased to honor—and with details that only Leger's life in China could have produced: the warlike ambiance that pervaded the poem; the birth of a colt, at the outset of the opening "Chanson"; the image of a horse under a tree filled with doves, at the end of the "Chanson" that concluded the work; the "pays fréquentés [où] sont les plus grandes silences," "ces terres jaunes, notre délice," where there were children "triste comme la mort des singes," "mangeurs d'insectes, de fruits d'eau . . . acupuncteur[s] et saunier[s]," "grands oiseaux de terre, naviguant en Ouest [qui] sont de bons mimes de nos oiseaux de mer."[60] While all of these were aggrandized by the nobility of tone, the splendor of the language, the immensity of the vision, they transcended—but never denied—their worldly origin—just as the poet himself did not remain in the domain of the timeless, the otherworldly, but descended from the heights where creation had taken place and plunged back again into the populous city, to dwell in the world of living things that he had celebrated in his poem: "Choses vivantes, ô choses excellentes . . . beaucoup de choses sur la terre à entendre et à voir."[61]

Winter 1917–Summer 1918

There was indeed much to hear and to see. Life took on a great variety of forms now. Periods of creation and destruction followed each other in cyclical fashion—solitude alternated with gregariousness, asceticism with license, silence with loquacity, purity with contamination, and living with dying.

The great stillness of the Asian plains gave way (although it never vanished) to the multifarious movement of the metropolis. And the world of dreams was balanced by that of action.

Leger evidently functioned well in both spheres. For, despite his nonconformist attitudes (and secret poetic ventures) he was promoted consistently in his diplomatic work and now held three positions at the same time: secretary of the Diplomatic Corps, secretary of the Allied Ministers, and first secretary of the French Legation.[62] Conty had been replaced by a new minister (Boppe), after being deposed by what Leger considered perfidious means.[63] He found Conty's departure regrettable, having had much liking for the man. His own situation, however, was much improved, since he was now able to discontinue living in the mansion of the minister and move into a house of his own. This gave him far greater freedom, officially, as well as in his private life,[64] where he had often felt benevolently spied upon by his superior.[65]

He was, as ever, extremely discreet (almost stealthy) about his personal life. Women, for whom he quite evidently had strong positive feelings and sensual appreciation as well as a non-puritanical attitude, where never openly alluded to. References to them could be found only in his writings, where the erotic erupted with great intensity and concreteness from the very first,[66] and in a few rare remarks of an oblique nature, scattered throughout his correspondence in the past few years: one brief mention (somewhat cryptic in character) of "great happiness" in London, contained in a letter to his friend, Larbaud,[67] which, if linked with a short statement to his mother some years later,[68] might point to a liaison that had begun in England and continued to interest and preoccupy Leger in China; one might add to this a long letter, written to a mysterious woman, referred to only as "une dame d'Europe" but full of personal details and hints of passion,[69] which leads one to suspect that it concerns the same person and indicates a long-lived liaison that survived distance and absence.

As far as Leger's exploits with women during his sojourn in China are concerned, very little direct evidence is available. One finds remarks here and there, such as the one (in a letter to Conrad) about "la faune cosmopolite de Shanghaï" among which there were "de belles aventurières . . . d'Amérique et de Russie blanche"[70] that, when linked to an earlier one about Leger's stopover in Hong Kong (during the journey to China) where he described the women who came aboard, as "de grandes aventurières de Shanghaï, qui viennent chercher loin le voyageur comme des pilotes de haute mer,"[71] lead one to suspect a predilection on his part for such female explorers. But all further traces of Leger's activities with women have been carefully effaced or concealed, and one can only conjecture about the equilibrium he surely achieved between the ascetic and the sensual.

The surest insights regarding such matters can be gleaned from a reexamination of his poetry of this period, namely "Anabase." There, sexuality is strongly manifest. It appears in numerous images that range from the explicit[72] to the evocative,[73] from the incantatory[74] to the ritual,[75] and it pervades the entire poem, culminating in Section IX, the penultimate sequence of the poem.[76] It is evident that the persona of the nomad-chieftain-poet is endowed with an intense awareness and appreciation of the erotic, and it does not seem likely that his creator was any less gifted in this domain.

He was much less taciturn about balancing his penchant for stillness with movement, or creation with destruction. The teeming life of China evidently solicited his interest, and he involved himself in all aspects of the country, its customs, its rituals, its mores—down to the minutest, and most curious details. His curiosity was insatiable. Observation alone did not suffice; he sought the company of specialists of renown and spent long evenings in discussion with them at his home. Such men as Pelliot, Granet, Staël-Holstein, as well as Bacot, Toussaint, and Lévy-Bruhl,[77] by their expertise added to his own ever growing knowledge. He also traveled extensively to various parts of the Orient whenever his diplomatic duties left him free time. Every opportunity and every form of locomotion appealed to him: he went on horseback, by ship, by automobile to Indochina, Manchuria, Korea.

Movement continued to draw him in whatever shape or circumstances, whether it took the form of historical upheavals,[78] windstorms,[79] or the play of nature's forces.[80] As he himself admitted, he always hoped for a "bonne petite rupture d'équilibre . . . j'aime en tout, et d'instinct, le jeu des forces naturelles, le mouvement que crée leur active intervention."[81] This was so even if these forces took the awful shape of the plague: an outbreak of the dread disease occurred in the north of China in the early spring of 1918 and threatened to spread to Peking. Leger was charged with directing the campaign to protect the Diplomatic Quarter from its ravages. As discreetly as possible, to avoid panic, but also with utmost efficiency, he prepared everything necessary for such an emergency: hospitals and barracks of all kinds, isolation wards, camps for quarantine and disinfection, a medical staff, pharmaceutical supplies, and masks. Outside the quarter, he had assured himself the cooperation of the Commission Chinoise de Défense contre la Peste that would allow him, if necessary, to close railway lines, quarantine homes, order medical inspections of isolation camps, and the like. But the epidemic had nevertheless reached Peking, taking its toll in the Diplomatic Quarter and even claiming the lives of several of Leger's own friends.[82]

He felt grief at their loss but balanced his pain with admiration—for the attitude of the Chinese, whose supposed fatalism was based on the belief that "la nature devait être libre de régler comme il convient le problème démographique. . . . [par] des lois supérieures d'harmonie naturelle."[83] Moreover, by his own admission, he had experienced the entire catastrophe with unusual intensity (an attitude that had been his ever since childhood, when the great cycles of destruction and creation had been revealed to him). Right after the epidemic he wrote:

J'ai vraiment aimé toute cette bataille de la peste. Je l'ai passionnément vécue, comme une grande aventure et qui rompait pour moi beaucoup de platitude ambiante. Faut-il aller plus loin dans l'inavouable? Je ne puis, je n'ai jamais pu m'empêcher d'aimer, en toute époque et en tout lieu, ces jeux des grandes forces naturelles: inondations,

typhons, épidémies, et soulévements divers—toutes ruptures d'équilibre tendant à renouveler l'élan vital du grand mouvement en cours
par le monde. (Il ne fallait pas, Mère très chrétienne, confier mon
enfance antillaise aux mains païennes d'une trop belle servante hin-
doue, disciple secrète du dieu Civa.)[84]

It was a fascinating admission, whose latter portion, especially,
revealed the secret springboard of so many of his deepest penchants.

Autumn 1918–Spring 1920

He threw himself with all his being into life in China now. Its
politics—constantly confused and problematic, in a continual
state of flux and therefore fascinating—absorbed him utterly. He
formed a close friendship with one of the Republican generals,
Toan Tsi-joui,[85] which further involved him in the country's political world. He saw new cabinets formed, new presidents
elected, and witnessed the continuing imbroglio of the nation's
government. The changes and complexities suited his temperament. He realized that he often knew "instinctively" how to deal
with difficult situations, that he understood the spirit of the
Chinese, the rhythms of their actions, their sense of time (so
different from that of the Occident); and he was fascinated by
"cette Chine nouvelle et . . . son évolution future . . . préférant
aussi de beaucoup cette vie d'action en Chine à celle des bu-
reaux du Quai d'Orsay ou des grandes Ambassades d'Europe."[86]

So absorbed was he with China that, when World War I ended
in November of that year, he hardly seemed to notice it.

His personal way of life had also become much more adapted
to the ways of the country: he now had a house of his own, rather
large for a man who lived alone, with two floors, numerous
rooms, and a retinue of servants. Yet, the whole establishment
was quite simple for someone of his rank, for he did not particularly demand, or relish, comfort or luxury. (The nomad in him
seemed to require a lack of "settled" accommodations.) He
heated only the rooms he needed, with four great Russian

stoves, and, when dining alone, took his meals in a small winter garden adjoining the parlor and dining room. It was his favorite spot in the house—full of light, warmth, plants, and animals (the tame lizard, the delightful tree frog, a variety of insects). The extent of his "domesticity" was limited by a relatively small number of servants: a chief "boy," a cook and his assistant, a coolie for heavy housework and another for errands in town, but no gardener or laundress, nor a groom for his stables. He rented rickshaws, had his clothes washed by an old woman who came in occasionally, and his horses cared for by a stable boy from the legation. When he had dinner guests, he hired extra servants. He also entertained sometimes at the local club.[87]

Living in his own quarters gave him far greater independence; a choice of people he wished to frequent; and the possibility of solitude, which he continued to crave.

He wrote to almost no one,[88] least of all to writer friends from Europe. When letters from them came, he found that he had no desire to reply. From some of them, such as Jammes, he felt quite estranged; others, such as Claudel, Gide, and Rivière, left him indifferent. He no longer wanted to know anything of European literary life.[89] Only Valéry had moved him, for an instant, when his new poem, *La Jeune Parque*, arrived;[90] but that was only because he knew the personal drama behind it and remembered their last conversation, shortly before his departure for China, on a bench of the Champs-Elysées, in July, when Paris was totally deserted, during which they had confided a great deal to each other, both humanly and intellectually. He profoundly admired Valéry's poem and was overjoyed at the latter's reentry into literary life.[91] But the French publishing scene seemed light-years away, small and vain compared with what he was now experiencing.

The only European writer with whom he felt he could share his thoughts and feelings was Conrad. He asked for his latest books, remembered their conversations, and wrote an extraordinary letter to him in which he spoke of his most intense experiences in China. It was, oddly enough, to this man, whom Leger considered "le seul poète de la mer," to whom he could write of this "pays le moins fait pour un homme de mer." In his letter, Leger spoke of Conrad's recitation of "The Jumblies" of Lear, his own passion for Dostoevski and his dislike of Turgenev—but most of all, of his obsession with the sea. "La mer est pour moi chose élémentaire, comme mêlée à mon sang même, et qui a fini . . . par me tout envahir," he wrote. "Rien dans tout cela de métaphysique," he went on, "très jeune encore, entendant une grande personne affirmer péremptoirement que la femme était le cinquième élément, je ripostait crûment que c'était la mer, distincte pour moi de l'eau." And he continued to muse: "La Chine . . . n'est que poussière, un Océan de poussière au vent . . . la Chine intérieure exerce pour moi la même aliénation que crée . . . l'étrange anonymat de certaines mers."[92] And, he concluded (in wonderfully paradoxical fashion): "Ainsi la Chine terrestre, sans paradoxe, m'aura fait plus conscient de ma hantise de mer, qui tend ici à l'obsession. Jamais je n'ai si bien compris, loin du site de la mer, combien la mer est en nous-mêmes."[93]

(The letter came from such deep recesses of his being that in this last phrase lies the key to a vast poem, one of the most magnificent that he would write, almost forty years hence— *Amers*[94] in which "la mer en nous" is celebrated.)

There was, however, another writer with whom Leger might have shared as much as with Conrad, had they but met. Their paths crossed in China, but they passed each other by as two ships might, in midocean, who do not recognize each other's flags: Victor Segalen, poet, seafarer, horseman, plague fighter, dramatist,[95] novelist,[96] deeply involved with Chinese culture and Taoism, as evidenced in many of his works,[97] whose masterpiece, *Stèles*,[98] especially showed the profundity of his encounter with the Orient.[99] It seems certain that if the two men had known each other a companionship of major import would have resulted. But it was one of those ironies of fate that, although they had friends and acquaintances in common,[100] shared numerous experiences, and were on the same soil at a particular moment in time, they did not establish contact. Perhaps Leger had encountered Segalen's work during his stay in China (*Stèles* was published in Peking in 1912 and thus may have caught his eye), but there is no evidence of this to be found. And Segalen would not have known of Leger's activities as a poet, for the latter continued to be clandestine about his writing, and few, if any, of those who knew him suspected that the young diplomat had another, secret side.[101]

It was probably mostly with Chinese writers that Leger shared this part of his existence—with Lou Tseng-tsiang, a great man of letters and translator of French authors,[102] and with Liang Ki-chao, admired for his work in numerous literary genres and active in the political sphere. This "Prince of Intellectuals" and "brilliant writer"—according to Leger—motivated by civic concern and patriotism, had momentarily abandoned writing for action in the hope of achieving the unification and rebirth of his nation. He used his pen as would a social activist, reformer, economist, and jurist, something like "the French writers of the XVIIIth century."[103] It was a choice that Leger greatly admired. (One could suggest that this admiration for Liang Ki-chao and the use to which he put his talent is a key to Leger's own actions in the future. Both men, however, provide insights to the kind of companions that he now appreciated, the milieu in which he moved, and of how deeply he absorbed the lessons of this land and its people.)

Indeed, China apparently fascinated Leger to such an extent that he sought ways of remaining there for many years. It pleased him greatly when the president of the Chinese Republic asked him to become his political advisor—a position created especially for him and offered under exceptional conditions.[104] He had only to convince Berthelot to allow him to accept this post. In January 1920, although greatly disappointed that Leger was remaining so long in Asia and did not heed his call to return to Paris (perhaps even regretting his pronouncement that he would stay in China for ten years, in 1916), Berthelot finally resigned himself to Leger's acceptance of the position.[105] Leger was overjoyed. He relished the prospect of being "hors cadre"— outside the confines of French diplomatic circles, yet always being able to return if he should so desire. It agreed admirably with his love of the uncircumscribed; his taste for new horizons; a certain kind of control over events; and even, eventually (by virtue of his independence), "le droit . . . à quelque insolence envers l'événement."[106]

Unfortunately, events on the world scene were against him: China's fate at the Paris Peace Conference that followed sometime after the end of the war was a disaster. It had availed it nothing to have fought on the side of the Allies. Those who met at Versailles refused to restitute the province of Shantung to China (which they had taken back from Germany), but attributed it instantly to Japan as a reward for its services in the war. Leger considered this move ignominious, as well as a political error whose consequences would be dearly paid for.[107] As a result of the action, the Chinese delegation had left the conference without signing the peace treaty. Needless to say, Leger now had to abandon his plan for becoming political advisor to the president of China. It seemed futile and even dangerous to persist. "Cela ne rime plus à rien," he wrote, "n'offre plus aucun intérét ni possibilité d'action utile, serait d'ailleurs des plus précaires, et . . . pourrait même . . . me faire soupçonner ici de parasitisme."[108]

The conclusion to be drawn was obvious. He wasted no time arriving at a decision: "J'étudie donc les conditions de ma rentrée en France. Il serait temps pour moi de quitter la Chine."[109]

Spring 1920

It was inconceivable to leave China, however, without carrying out the dream he had harbored for such a long time, the project that had haunted him ever since the beginning of his stay: an expedition into Central Asia.

Within less than a fortnight—so urgent was his desire—the plan had become a reality. His itinerary was traced, the preparations made. He would first go to Kalgan, where his journey into Outer Mongolia would begin. It would lead him across the Gobi

Desert, as far as Ourga, "capitale très fictive de ce pays de nomades, non loin de la frontière russe"; from there, he planned to go west, as far as was possible on horseback, to study the eventuality "d'un retour en Europe par les vieilles pistes du Sinkiang ou Turkestan chinois."[110] The right of passage for this trip through Mongolia had been granted him owing to the intervention of the Chinese government with Mongol authorities and the "Bouddha Vivant d'Ourga."[111] His companions in this adventure had been carefully selected and were a choice crew: two friends, Doctor Bussière (who had already made such expeditions in Iran) and Gustave-Charles Toussaint, a Tibetan specialist and "un autre grand consommateur d'espaces, rompu depuis longtemps à l'expérience des voyages solitaires en Asie centrale."[112]

His excitement grew to a fever pitch as the time for departure drew near. He wrote:

J'exulte de pouvoir enfin réaliser le rêve qui m'aura tant hanté . . . il y a longtemps que ces grandes étendues désertiques qui règnent en Ouest . . . de la Chine exercent sur ma pensée une fascination proche de l'hallucination . . . Je suis infiniment curieux des incursions d'ordre intérieur que peut amorcer en moi-même un tel engagement de l'être, avec tout l'inconnu qui peut m'en être révélé."[113]

The voyage to the interior of Asia was thus also a journey inward, into the unknown regions of the self. And both would lead, he knew intuitively, to major revelations.

The three companions set out on May 9. The trip would very likely last until the beginning of June. But time had no meaning in a venture of this kind, in the ascent toward the "hauts parages d'Asie centrale" where the atemporal reigned. It seemed only yesterday that Alexis had written to the friend who now rode at his side: "L'Asie bouddhique, lamaïque ou tantrique. . . Je m'en irai moi-même un jour par là, je le sais—et avec vous peut-être, qui aimez tout cela comme moi, infiniment." And yet, that was over three years ago.[114]

They began their trip through Mongolia on horseback. Alexis rode his Mongolian horse, Allan, who now truly proved all the admirable qualities of his race: robustness, courage, resistance to cold, singular endurance, and valor.[115] Most striking, however, was the wordless understanding and secret kinship that made them, more than ever, seem one being. Strange events began to occur in the heart of the desert. More dramatically even than before, horse and horseman stopped and, at the same instant, turned their faces inexplicably in the direction "où gît la table invisible de la mer et le site du sel."[116] As they proceeded farther among the endless sands, where no orientation seemed to have any meaning, Alexis saw an object, half buried, some distance away. It might have been a mirage, for surely there were no markers here to guide one. As he drew closer, the object took on the guise of a sign, something pointing in the direction they were to take. Allan moved toward it as if of his own accord. As his head bent forward, the object revealed its true outlines—it was the skull of a horse, swept clean by the desert sands, polished by the winds, and bleached by the sun, until it shone like old ivory. It was of such beauty and purity of line that it could have come only from the Cheval de Prjevalsky, the ancestor of the whole equine race, whom he had long dreamed of encountering. He carefully lifted it from the sand and placed it in his saddlebag, as one would a treasure of great price.

Then it seemed as if they were, mysteriously, in contact with the sea. It had begun at the moment that Alexis and Allan had intuited its presence. They now encountered camel drivers in whose eyes he saw, to his amazement, "comme un regard d'hommes de mer." Even the wagons used by the nomads of the desert were rigged with a sail, "comme en mer." The very birds there, the gulls and swallows, created the illusion of marine life.[117]

The impression grew stronger as they traveled due west. Alexis began to feel "la même aliénation que crée . . . l'anonymat de certaines mers."[118] As they penetrated ever more deeply into "la terre haute," he began to have visions that linked the land with the high seas:

La terre ici, à l'infini, est le plus beau simulacre de mer qu'on puisse imaginer: l'envers et comme le spectre de la mer. La hantise de mer s'y fait étrangement sentir . . . La contrée silencieuse fait . . . à l'oreille comme un murmure lointain de mer.[119]

The sensation increased as they advanced. It seemed that the sea was everywhere, molding the sand into waves, invading the high places, pervading even the remote monasteries that they encountered, from time to time, in their journey. It was infinitely strange to find that

dans toutes les lamaseries mongoles ou tibétains, où il n'est pas un homme qui ait jamais vu la mer, les conques de mer sont associées au culte, le corail et le nacre sont ornements d'autel, et les grandes trompes . . . sont utilisées pour entretenir, aux bas offices, le mugissement de l'océan.[120]

As they proceeded farther into the interior, the landscape became even more fantastic. They encountered vast depressions or kettles in the soil that resembled ancient "fonds de mer . . . comme l'envers même de la mer." as though the two elements sought to be joined, each longing to become the other, in a primordial form of encounter that, when it occurred and the alliance was consummated, made him exclaim, in awe: "Unité retrouvée, malaise dissipé."[121] It seemed the summation of all he had dreamed. The desert had been the quintessence of silence, serenity, anonymity. It had dwarfed the human, swallowed the steps of the caravans, effaced all earthly traces from the memory. Here, there was ineffable beauty and harmony, as though one had truly left the earth.

On the high plains the scenery became "extraplanétaire." It resembled lunar craters (or the "Mers de la Lune," as the ancient astronomers had called them) and giant "méduses" such as Alexis had never seen, except in the sky, when the aurora borealis[122] transformed the heavens into a vast phantasmagoric spectacle.

They traveled on, no longer aware of temporal or spatial limits. Sometimes it seemed as if they were not of this world at all.

At the end of their quest lay the "Tolgoït d'Ourga," the fabled capital of the land of nomads, the seat of "le Bouddha Vivant."[123] The three "compagnons" had reached their destination.

It was the time of Alexis's thirty-third birthday.[124] At this ultimate moment of culmination (as myths everywhere testify) the man born under the sign of Gemini had crossed the frontiers into the unknown and gazed at what could only be called the other side of life. He would speak of it simply, in muted tones, as though the ineffable must be preserved by a semblance of silence: "Et l'expérience . . . m'aura conduit là encore plus loin que je ne m'y attendais: aux frontières même de l'esprit . . . Le souvenir ne s'en effacera pas pour moi."[125]

As if to insure the indelible memory of the revelation, a sacred object had appeared on his path at the final stage of the journey: "une pierre de foudre de chaman ramassée près du Tolgoït d'Ourga."[126] And, in an uncanny encounter of symbols, the shaman's thunder stone coincided with the Chinese transcription of his name: Thunder beneath the Snow.

He knew then that he had arrived at the goal of his quest.

Alexis Leger's name transposed into Chinese (Lei Hi-gnai). Calligraphy by Chinese artist C. H. Chao. (In the private collection of the author).

It was time to leave Asia. He had obtained everything that he had longed for. "La Chine," he wrote, "a suffisamment élargi pour moi le champ de mon regard terrestre sur l'étroite planète."[127] And he had seen, beyond these confines, a vision far larger in scope. Never again would life appear in the same light as before.

At the moment of leave-taking, all the material objects acquired during his stay in the Orient seemed of no import. He would bring nothing away with him in the nature of earthly riches or possessions gained. Far greater wealth had come his way. The only mementos of his stay on the other side of the world—of life—were three objects: a stele with his Chinese name,[128] the horse's skull found in the Gobi Desert, and the shaman's thunder stone[129]: the symbolic sum of all that he had attained.

CHAPTER 5

EMINENCE GRISE AND THE MASKED POET
(1921–1940)

*Et qui donc m'eût surpris dans mon propos secret? gardé par le
sourire et la courtoisie; parlant, parlant langue d'aubain . . . aux
grilles effilées d'or de quelque Chancellerie. . . . le regard au loin
entre mes phrases . . .*

—Amers (OC, p. 263)

Seven ships would carry him west, from the Far East to the
shores of France.[1] His journey would begin on April 2, 1921,[2]
when he embarked at Tientsin on a small Japanese steamer
and—after crossing the Yellow Sea—explored the islets of the
Korean Strait and Japan's "Mer Intérieure." At Yokohama he was
to board the *Shinyu Maru*, which would take him to the Hawaian
Islands and dock at Honolulu. Once there he hoped to find some
tramp steamer[3] that went to Samoa, Tonga, and Fiji. From the
latter, he planned to navigate (by sail) to Tahiti and various other
South Sea islands.[4] After returning to Honolulu, he would cross
the Pacific on the S.S. *Manoa* (a British ship of the Matson Line)[5]
land in San Francisco, make his way through the North American continent, reconnoiter its East Coast from Mexico to Canada,[6] and finally board the French liner *Lorraine* (the last of the
seven ships)[7] in order to traverse the Atlantic to France. The
journey would last over three months[8] and take him to the opposite side of the world.

"Je quitte la Chine sans espoir de retour," he said, as he cast a last, lingering look at this land that had such a deep impact upon him. But he instantly continued: "Il ne faut s'accoutumer nulle part . . . courons donc nous renouveler. Passer outre est le mot d'ordre."[9] For he knew that even the profoundest experiences must give way to others, equally imperious, and no place become a permanent abode. The word "satiety" rang in his head now (dangerously akin to "stagnation"). He suddenly felt he had had "enough" of China.[10] Fulfillment could easily turn to quietus, plenitude to surfeit. After having penetrated into the heart of this land, he presently craved a watery expanse, "les tables nues de la mer."[11] Thus, this "Chevalier de l'errance"[12] hastened to wander off; to exile himself once again, to seek distance, detachment, and solitude before entering a new stage of life, the next turn in the cycle of his destiny.

The voyage out was instantly liberating. As soon as the small ship left the Chinese shore and headed toward the deep, he felt only his sharp appetite for the unknown. The past receded and flowed away with each passing wave. It was as though he sloughed off a former skin and acquired a new one at each port of call.

Only once was there a momentary setback in his thrust forward and the exhilaration it brought—when, after leaving Yokohama, he was struck down by illness on the *Shinyu Maru*. At first it seemed serious: an American doctor aboard diagnosed it as typhoid (the same disease he had had in childhood). But, now as then, he recovered with amazing speed, and (blaming his ailment on the first ship's bad fare) he attributed his cure to the sea, which had always healed him.[13]

The remaining laps of the journey were full of excitement and astounding variety. Not only a number of oceans, but island after island passed before his gaze: those that lay in the Sea of Japan, in some odd ways, resembled the landscape of Saint-Leger-les-Feuilles; Polynesia's Fiji and Samoa had scenery that vied with the beauty of the native artifacts (bark cloths painted in natural hues and geometric patterns with an amazing purity of design), and in Tonga he saw an unforgettable performance of Racine's *Esther* by some young girls who did not understand a word of French but had learned the lines by heart, "comme un texte sacré" (thus rendering the true miracle of poetry, its "pouvoir magique");[14] the South Sea islands—especially Tahiti—did not belie the splendor of Gauguin's paintings (one of which had haunted him in youth and inspired an early prose piece);[15] Hawaii's volcanic islands offered their uncanny sands and waves of legendary height—the treasures that these seas contained were seemingly without end.

It was with some regret that he saw his Pacific crossing come to a close. Even the beauty of San Francisco, at the western extremity of the American continent where they touched land, did not make up for leaving the ocean. But he had human bonds to renew here: Agnes Tobin, his old friend from the London days, was ill and now living in this region. A visit to her was imperative. Perhaps the opportunity to re-live some of the laughter they had shared at the John Donne Club would lift her spirits. He planned, however, to soon push on, stop only in Chicago, and reach Washington as quickly as possible. There, the official mail from Paris awaited him, certain to contain a message from Berthelot, who was eager for his return and had indicated that he had plans for Leger's future. Berthelot had recently been made secretary general of foreign affairs and had already intimated that they might work together.[16]

But, before leaving this continent, whose immense spaces and grandiose natural phenomena fascinated him, he wished to navigate along its eastern shore and view its coastline from the sea— from Mexico to the Canadian border. When he had done so, he would embark for Europe from New York, a city he found extraordinary: queen among "les hautes villes de pierre ponce forées d'insectes lumineux."[17]

He felt that he had stepped on French soil, the moment he boarded the *Lorraine,* which would take him on the final lap of his journey. The sailors, the stewards, even his fellow travelers brought back an ambience almost forgotten, so long had he been away. The Atlantic seemed its ever changing, unchanging self. But how different this crossing appeared to him from the one he had made as a boy, over twenty years ago! Since then, worlds upon worlds had opened to him; great losses and gains had swept through his life. Yet, in some ways, it was also the same. The road to France seemed perilous again. He realized that he found it "pénible de reprendre cette route,"[18] not because he was arriving as a novice, but because he sensed that his existence would become somewhat circumscribed. On the other hand, it was a challenge to think of the fresh combat that awaited him there. He had gained a great deal, personally, since his departure from Europe. "Je connais maintenant le marché des hommes et la vie m'a durci," he said, "[et] ma plus grande force est dans mon détachement et dans mon manque total d'ambition."[19] It was part of the legacy of China that he had brought back with him—its lessons of detachment, its great vistas (far beyond the confines of mere individuals, above the puny concerns of men with circumscribed horizons). His long journey from the other side of the world, all that he had seen and experienced, had given him a strength born of adventure—as if a new armature sustained his being. "Je rentrerai . . . après m'être refait assez d'os et d'écorce pour présenter au Quai d'Orsay l'actualité d'un homme et non d'un spectre,"[20] he mused—ready and armed against all those who might relegate him to the Orient as though it were a kingdom of shades.

It was exceedingly strange, however, when he actually found himself in France again. His absence of five years suddenly seemed tantamount to centuries, or located in an entirely different dimension of time. It was as if every cell in his body had changed and his senses were attuned to another life. He saw the country with a stranger's eyes; its customs seemed as unusual as those of the remotest islands he had visited; his ear was no longer used to its sounds. The veil of habit had not yet descended on his perceptions, and he saw everything in its raw, unadorned form.

As the train from Le Havre rolled through the farmlands of Normandy, he wondered how his meeting with those who were closest to him would seem. The longing to see his mother and sisters had grown with every stage of his journey. But, now that it was imminent, he shrank back and preferred to keep his emotions at bay. It had been wise to ask only his brother-in-law to meet him when the boat train pulled into the Gare St. Lazare in Paris, to give him "homme à homme" the first news of his family.[21] When they all finally met, there were no words to express his feelings; he pressed the women to him as though they had been separated by far more than distance alone. So deeply moving was the encounter that he was glad there was no time for lengthy effusions. Paris awaited him almost immediately after his arrival.

Already there was talk of new responsibilities, of meetings with Berthelot, of being shortly sent to America again. Besides, there were Gide and Claudel whom he wished to see.[22] What he learned, when he met these and other writer friends, was rather astonishing. During (and despite) the long years of silence and absence, removed from this world as though it were a dead planet, his renown as a poet had grown in France—unknown to him and in the most disconcerting fashion. He was told that *Eloges* (published in such a small edition by Gide) still elicited the interest of the literary world; *Images à Crusoé* had been set to music by Louis Durey (a member of the avant-garde "Groupe des Six"); Darius Milhaud had done the same for one of the poems from *Eloges;* Guillaume Apollinaire had mentioned him in a lecture on "L'Esprit nouveau et les poètes"; and Marcel Proust had expressed admiration for his work in a passage of *Sodome et Gomorrhe.*[23] It was as if one of his prophecies had come true, for he remembered writing to his mother shortly before leaving China; "La vie me comblera toujours, malgré moi, de ce que je ne lui demande pas."[24] For he had certainly not asked for such attentions to be showered upon him.

It was also despite his wishes, and not at all what he desired, when a number of his literary friends—Fargue and Larbaud, in particular—expressed their curiosity about what he had written during his years in the Far East. Although he had brought back an entire trunk filled with manuscripts, he kept them carefully hidden from view. But they pursued the matter. Their insistence grew more forceful each day, and there seemed no way to avert their urgings. Finally, tired of refusing, and mostly to have done with their pleas, he dipped into the sea chest and pulled out a large sheaf of paper. The title it bore was—of course— "Anabase."[25]

The incident made him shy away from other such advances, but they were sure to follow. He wondered how to insure his predilection for distance and secrecy. The best course might be to leave France again. The old yearning for faraway places came back, and he began to think of ways to still it by traveling. It was thus not unwelcome news at all when he learned, at the end of that summer, that he would once more cross the sea from which he had just come: he was requested to join the French delegation to the International Conference on Disarmament in Washington as a political expert in Asian affairs.[26] It mattered little to him that his leave (earned by long service in China) had not yet come to an end. He hastened to accept this opportunity to absent himself from the Paris scene.

He had spent only a few months on French soil when he embarked on a ship that would take him across the Atlantic once again.

The conference was scheduled to begin on November 21. The *La Fayette*, which was bringing the French legation to America, would have to brave the autumn seas. Leger delighted in the rough weather, the height of the waves, the cutting wind, and the fact that a number of the diplomats on board ship did not have his sea legs. The decks were frequently deserted; each day there were fewer and fewer passengers in the dining room. He could once more savor the silence of this interim between two populous cities and recover from Paris before reaching Washington.

He relished the idea of returning to the latter in a quite different capacity than on his last visit, just a short while ago. With amusement, he remembered his reception there in June when the French ambassador, Jusserand (disconcerted by his meanderings on the way back from China and the clandestine way in which he chose to travel), had shouted, upon seeing him: "—Leger! Vous voilà enfin! Ah! c'est du joli! Vous avez déjà coûté cent cinquante francs de télégrammes à l'Etat. De mon temps, un jeune diplomate donnait toujours son addresse."[27] He wondered, laughingly, how the ambassador would take his most recent change in address. True, his position had altered. He was no longer an itinerant government employee floating somewhere between the Orient and Europe but an expert in Asian affairs, traveling in the company of such luminaries as Philippe Berthelot and Aristide Briand.

Berthelot was, of course, a friend and mentor. Briand, the head of government and the minister of foreign affairs, was a complex figure who intrigued Leger for a number of reasons. He admired this man they called the "Apôtre de la paix,"[28] who, to put his dream of peace into action, had put all his diplomatic artistry at the service of the League of Nations right after the armistice.[29] He felt an affinity with this Breton (for reasons of origin)[30] who had a profound—and poetic—rapport with the sea: a mariner by birth and predilection, he spent every free moment in its company and considered it" [son] éducatrice, sa confidante de toujours, l'amie à laquelle il sera resté fidèle."[31] Most of all, however, Leger was struck by Briand's tales, to which the travelers on board this ship listened spellbound. The latter spoke of storms, of night fishing, of the strange marvels of the sea. One of these tales was particularly evocative; the images remained for a long time in one's mind, ages after the teller's voice had fallen silent:

Une nuit, en Bretagne, au moment des marées de septembre . . . il faisait clair de lune et nous naviguions dans un banc de méduses phosphorescentes . . . nos filets, cette nuit-là, faisaient penser à d'immen-

ses toiles d'araignées en argent . . . le plus curieux, c'est qu'une de ces
méduses était pleine de petits poissons, d'éperlans nains bien vivants
. . . un véritable vivier à poissons qu'éclairaient les rayons de la lune.[32]

Definitely, Leger decided, Briand was a man of great imagination and "complexité, sensible et nuancé."[33] It would be most
interesting to know him better. He noticed that his interest was
reciprocated. For during the voyage, when the two men were
frequently the only ones on deck, Briand wandered over to the
young diplomat and engaged him in conversation. Leger was not
certain whether this was (as rumor had it) because Briand was
eager to have him as a collaborator or whether it was due simply
to the latter's lively curiosity about human beings in general.
The first of these conjectures seemed the more likely, because
the elder statesman often spoke of possible posts that Leger
might occupy. Once, facing him squarely, Briand said: "Deman-
dez-moi ce que vous voulez." Leger retorted, with a playful
smile: "Monsieur le Président, nommez-moi en Afghanistan, un
endroit où je pourrai arriver à mon bureau en bottes de
cheval."[34] The answer evidently intrigued Briand, for throughout the journey he continued to offer Leger a post in his government. But the latter evaded any such commitment and
continued to shake his head each time another suggestion of this
kind was made.

The conference in Washington lasted for weeks. Leger was
extremely occupied. He spoke with conviction (and passion)
about the Far East, basing his statements on his political experience in China; and he spent hours in consultation with
Berthelot, who was equally expert in these matters and had a
great deal to say in his capacity as secretary general of foreign
affairs. At various times, Leger noticed that Briand was observing him closely, as official receptions alternated with meetings,
and banquets with grueling sessions at the conference table. He
wended his way through this welter of diplomatic encounters,
suave, decisive, very much in control on the surface, but waver-
ing inwardly and torn by conflict. He felt divided between the
lure of travel, the independence that distance from Paris pro-

vided, and the equally alluring prospect of working with a man such as Briand with whom he felt many deep affinities.

One small incident almost tipped the scales, for it produced the kind of encounter between these two that occurs only at moments of the most privileged kind. It happened during an official cruise along the Potomac River. Someone had just suggested to the head of the French government that he write his memoirs. Briand did not answer and looked, as if questioning, at Leger. "Un livre, c'est la mort d'un arbre," the latter murmured, as if speaking to himself. He noted that Briand, upon hearing these words, began to muse. "[Il] regardait défiler sur la rive les érables rouges avec l'air d'être si loin, si loin!"[35] It was as if the splendor of these luminous trees, with all their autumnal foliage ablaze, had set him dreaming, and the death of one of them could never be justified by the recording of a man's history. Legend has it that the words pronounced by Leger secured his fortune and launched him on the path to diplomatic fame.[36] It seems just as likely that Briand's reaction, confirming his double nature of dreamer and man of action, convinced Leger that he had encountered a man fit for the kind of "compagnonnage" he valued.

It was not until many years later (after Briand's death and his own exile) that Saint-John Perse would sum up all Briand's fundamental traits and say of him:

Une large humanité jointe à l'individualisme de tous les créateurs; un sens égal de la solitude et de la foule; un mélange de rêverie et d'action . . . toutes les richesses intuitives passées au filtre de la raison . . . toute l'aristocratie d'un être de haute frondaison, nourri aux fortes racines de l'arbre populaire. Tel fut essentiellement Briand . . . curieux homme, au service de la paix.[37]

Now he intuited some of them, but he was mostly preoccupied with the split between his need for the unknown, the haunting call of distant places, the constant inward cry of "s'en aller!" and the magnetism that this kindred spirit exerted over him. For Briand was also Paris, and commitment of a particular kind; at the opposite pole lay absence, distance, and detachment. The conflict between them was great. No matter how much he weighed the alternatives, he could arrive at no resolution.

Then, strangely enough, it was all resolved in a lightning flash. It happened on the day the French delegation left the conference, and Leger stood on the deck of the ship which would take Briand back to France, saying farewell to him. The latter once more asked his question, once more beckoned Leger to his side. In an intuitive move—sprung from what source he could not say—the no he had reiterated for so many weeks suddenly turned into a yes. Briand wasted no time. With astounding impulsiveness (which Leger would long remember), Briand ordered that his passage be instantly arranged. "Il m'a empêché de redescendre," Leger recalled. "et je suis resté à bord, sans un pyjama ni une brosse à dents."[38] It was almost as though he had to be shanghaied—to fame.

The die was cast. Leger's career as a statesman had begun.

1922–1925

"Suivit la grande césure. Longtemps le poète parut avoir renoncé à toute littérature."[39]

The great schism had taken place. From this time on, it was the diplomat Alexis Leger who occupied the foreground; the poet would exist only as his shadow, a hidden double, a masked figure standing in the wings. Yet, in the years that followed, both ascended equally on the road to fame: the first, quite consciously and using all the means that a political career implied; the second, almost despite himself, as though pushed along each rung of the ladder of renown by forces that he had not willed and felt it necessary to curtail.

Leger's diplomatic career in France began as soon as he reached Paris (after his third Atlantic crossing in the space of half a year). He had become part of the Central Administration at the Quai d'Orsay where he assumed the directorship of political and commercial affairs and was second in command in matters concerning Asia and Oceania.[40] It was a first important step, and he had hoped that the latter of his functions would bring with it the close collaboration of his friend Berthelot. They had left Washington together, with Briand and a third of the French delegation,[41] but misfortune had struck Berthelot, with sudden force, on December 30, 1921. He was suddenly no longer able to exercise his functions, suspended from duty as a result of his having been accused of participation in a fraudulent affair involving the Industrial Bank of China.[42] It was a blow of major proportions and, while some attributed the scandalous imputation to Poincaré (known to be Berthelot's enemy and eager to have him removed),[43] an investigation that might result in disciplinary action was soon under way—and would result in the latter's being "mis en disponibilité"[44] less than a year later. Berthelot, with his characteristic reserve and dignity, refused to make any comment or stoop to counteraccusations. Leger, however, bore witness in favor of Berthelot's diplomatic action in this affair and personally took charge of the files; he collected documentation for the minister's own use and for presentation before the House.[45] It is very likely that his fidelity and the courageous action in behalf of his friend were instrumental in the eventual amnesty and reinstatement of Berthelot. But that would not take place until 1925, when Briand recalled him to his post as secretary general of foreign affairs.[46] At this moment, just when he made his entry into the Central Administration, Leger found himself alone, and without the friend with whom he shared most. He admired Berthelot's detachment and hauteur in this affair, but he also became more than ever aware of the dangers inherent in this career where a man could rise or fall, advance or be eliminated with the ease of a figure in a chess game.

His own advance was rapid. He had already been appointed "Secrétaire d'Ambassade de 2e classe" (aside from his other posts) on December 9, 1921.[47] And his rise in rank would be both swift and continuous. Only a few years later, Edouard Herriot, when the success of the "Cartel des Gauches" had made him minister, expressed his friendship for, and confidence in, Leger. By 1925 Briand would call upon the latter to become the director of his cabinet.[48] It was quite evident that Leger's star as diplomat was rising.

Meanwhile, the poet was not exactly dormant. He had, secretly, as it were, returned to the world of literature. Renewed contact with writer friends like Valéry, Gide, Larbaud, Fargue, and Gaston Gallimard, was evidently as necessary for Saint-Leger Leger as sessions at the Quai were for Leger. The friends he encountered anew spoke to him of the continued interest his work aroused in avant-garde circles of music and literature, as well as among members of an interesting new movement: Surrealism. Two of its members (Crevel and Vitrac) paid him a visit;[49] two others, much more famous (Breton and Aragon), were so deeply affected by his poetry that they would still speak of its impact many years later. Breton would say:

De ce côté de la voix humaine pour quoi on se découvre vers vingt ans un penchant vertigineux comme pour une femme et, le sort en est jeté, on ne risque pas de se déprendre, je suis de ceux qui aimèrent *Eloges* comme on aime alors. . . . Il s'agissait—bonheur—d'une oeuvre non encore consacrée, sa lueur était nouvelle, elle entrait toute nue dans mon buisson . . . telle étreinte ne se desserre plus.[50]

Aragon would state:

Je ne savais rien de cet homme quand les feuillets épars d'*Eloges* . . . tombèrent sous les vingt ans de mes yeux . . . plus que toute profession, m'éclairait un poète cette grande rumeur rimbaldienne de ses mots. . . . Je n'ai rien à faire avec l'homme du sourire et de la courtoisie. . . . Je l'ai aperçu un soir des années 20, dans une maison de la rue Laurent-Pichot, comme une ombre entre les verres et les rires: je n'aurai pas rêvé de lui parler. . . . J'avais dialogue avec un autre, celui qui est caché derrière ce sourire et cette courtoisie. C'était pour moi *un homme qui est parti:* mystérieux comme cet Arthur Rimbaud.[51]

Hidden behind smiles and acts of courtesy, the man with whom Aragon could hold dialogue wore his mask well in the circles where his political career was at stake. Only among those who spoke the language of poets could he, as with conspirators, reveal his other face. Even there, however, he proceeded with caution—allowing, for instance, the "Chansons" that opened and closed "Anabase" to be published only without a signature (the first in *La Nouvelle Revue Française,* the second in a magazine called *Intentions*),[52] almost as though they were clandestine tracts. And when Marguerite de Bassiano, the Princess Caetani (née Chapin), decided to found a new magazine with Larbaud, Fargue, Valéry, and Leger, named *Commerce* (which took its title from a line in "Anabase"—"ce pur commerce de mon âme"[53] and thus indicated his presence to initiates of his poetry), he would only agree to do so anonymously.[54]

His behavior may have been motivated by his innate sense of secrecy, the belief that art was essentially anonymous, the love of masks and duality; it could also have been determined by caution, a realistic attitude toward his new career—and the example of Claudel. He had observed the latter's double life and the conflicts that arose therefrom. Claudel, the statesman, continued to pursue a distinguished career; Claudel, the poet, had often feared the suspicion and disapproval his works might arouse, and considered (and practiced) anonymity and/or renunciation. Leger remembered the former's utterances to Gide, especially those that concerned *Partage de midi* and *L'Otage.* When Claudel had forbidden the performance of the former, he had written: "Je ne suis nullement sûr que cette représentation plairait au Ministère . . . Je ne puis ainsi compromettre ma position pour un peu de gloire . . . Consul, poète et dévot, c'est trop à la fois."[55] As for the latter, Claudel considered suspending its publication and finally opted for anonymity, explaining that no government official could sign *L'Otage,* for he would lay himself open to denunciation and could always be confronted with the order that forbids all officials of the ministry to publish anything without authorization—he preferred therefore to sign the work simply "Paul C."[56]

Not that Leger himself was a "dévot" or held the majestic position of consul, but he had as much—or more—at stake than Claudel, being at the start of his career and without the support of Berthelot now (who had been a potent protector of Claudel during the most precarious years).[57] He decided, for all these reasons, to proceed in continually clandestine fashion and—since Gide, Larbaud, and Gallimard had begun to urge the publication of "Anabase"—to adopt a pseudonym that was much further removed from "Leger" than the "Saint-Leger Leger" or "Saintleger Leger" of the past.[58]

The game of choosing a pseudonym was a fascinating one. He toyed with various possibilities. "Archibald Perse"—so far removed from anything resembling his patronym that it seemed a total denial of anything that might be connected with his former (or official) self—pleased him for a short while, perhaps for its humorous sound. But then one day, mysteriously, arising from some unknown reaches of his being, another name appeared—and imposed itself, by its rhythms, its sonorities. He knew it was the one that the poet in him now must bear: "Saint-John Perse."[59]

The secret self that had just been born, the new creature duly named, made his activities in diplomatic circles seem like part of a juggling act at which he excelled, except that only one half of his pins were visible. The artistry consisted of keeping double their number in motion while seemingly playing a single game. He delighted in the private nature of this feat, in the mask he wore without anyone's knowing. And in the idea that he had become two men whom no one (or almost no one) suspected of such an ambiguous character. At the Quai he was the efficient, suave, and promising young statesman who seemed to desire nothing in life but to serve his government with all his capacities; among writers, he was the poet of *Images à Crusoé* and *Eloges*, already an idol of some and the peer of others whom he himself recognized as men of genius.

Among the latter was a man called James Joyce. A book of his, *Ulysses*, had recently come out (on February 2, 1922, his fortieth birthday); and Larbaud, who had befriended Joyce and thought very highly of his work, gave a lecture and reading at Adrienne Monnier's celebrated bookshop, La Maison des Amis des Livres, in his capacity as the most respected critic of foreign literature in Paris, in December of that year. There were also plans to have the first translated fragments (gotten ready with the help of Larbaud and Fargue) appear in one of the early issues of *Commerce*.[60]

There was much to interest Leger in Joyce: his ability for "manipulating a continuous parallel between contemporaneity and antiquity" that the poet T. S. Eliot had praised;[61] his fascination with Vico's use of etymology and mythology, as well as the latter's division of history into recurring cycles;[62] the fact that, as one critic had seen, "Joyce remonte à l'origine de tout, c'est à dire à l'homme."[63] But perhaps, more than any of these, the predilections they shared—for figures that were more than personal entities, indeed a blend of all men, spoke with a universal voice, were characterized by a constantly changing presence[64]— allowed them to become friends.[65] They met mostly at Marguerite de Bassiano's house in Versailles where such luminaries of the literary world as Valéry, Larbaud, Fargue, and Adrienne Monnier assembled,[66] and spoke most probably of Ireland, which Leger had visited in his youth, and very likely of Joyce's new "work in progress" (to become *Finnegans Wake*) that would be a "night book" as *Ulysses* had been a "day book," and that Joyce had begun to write as soon as the latter was finished.[67] Leger could not know that his name would appear in *Finnegans Wake* (as "Sant Legerleger riding lapsaddlelonglegs"),[68] but he undoubtedly enjoyed the verbal inventions and delightful humor of this man who had the simplicity and strange radiance of genius.

Another of such stature was Rainer-Maria Rilke, now in his greatest period of creation, for he had recently finished the *Duineser Elegien* (*Duino Elegies*) and, the following year, had completed *Die Soneten an Orpheus* (*Sonnets to Orpheus*),[69] the first emphasizing the succession of struggle, death, and resurrection; the second accentuating joy, affirmation, and praise. It was during this period, when his own work reached its finest and most mature point, that Rilke had decided to undertake the

German translation of *Images à Crusoé,* no small tribute, since it meant devoting his talent (and, to an extent, abdicating some of his powers) to the work of another poet. Despite this, Leger hesitated, protesting that he wished to have no contact with the literary scene and, even less, to have such an early work brought to light again by publication.[70] Nevertheless, Leger must have realized that his affinities with Rilke were profound—if only by virtue of the *Sonnets to Orpheus,* that series of brilliant and exuberantly affirmative songs. And that their encounter was located at the level of both their central vision,

ce "Raum der Rührung" cher à Rilke, cet espace de la célébration où le réel, jamais déficitaire, tend vers un surplus d'être, où toute chose participe au suprême, parce que rien ne tombe sous la malédiction de l'interchangeable, source de la négation et du cynisme.[71]

But Leger was more involved with his own work now, and a major step in his career as a poet, one that would launch him— although he surely did not know it—into worldwide fame: the publication of *Anabase.*

It was in 1924. In January of that year, the poem appeared in *La Nouvelle Revue Française* and, shortly afterward, in two different editions printed by Gallimard—all signed with his new pseudonym St.-J. Perse. The second of these was an "édition grand luxe, grand format" (printed in Dijon by Maurice Darantière,[72] the same printer who had done the first edition of Joyce's *Ulysses* for Sylvia Beach of Shakespeare and Company).[73] Then followed a private printing by Adrienne Monnier, to whom the author graciously made a gift of his manuscript—which she had clamored for in a most delightful (and persuasive) way:

J'aimais votre manuscrit, il faudra me le donner—Oui, j'ose dire une chose pareille, si vous ne me le donnez pas, vous aurez des remords constants et des cauchemars horribles. Car *Anabase* aura sûrement des adorateurs, mais personne ne pourra jamais l'aimer autant que moi. . . . Un poème comme le vôtre, cela transporte, cela console de tout, cela abîme de plaisir.[74]

Larbaud's enthusiasm (as with *Eloges,* over a decade ago) had been the first to greet it. As soon as he received the opening

"Chanson" of "Anabase" (before it even appeared in *La Nouvelle Revue Française* at the same time as his article on James Joyce), he exclaimed:

Reçu . . . votre petit flacon de *Nuit de Mongolie* . . . J'en suis tout impregné, et la ritournelle m'accompagne partout. . . . Mais quelle nostalgie m'ont donné vos Provinces! Où sont-elles? Dans quel empire démesuré, capable de faire une telle dépense d'espace, de plaines, de montagnes, et d'immenses golfes de terre?[75]

When he had read the entire manuscript of "Anabase" (as yet unsigned) he wrote to Saint-Leger Leger in terms that were even more laudatory:

La poésie française a une grande oeuvre de plus. Quelle magnifique montée! Et ces feuilles qui sont comme des dessins admirables, des dessins à cent mille personnages, avec tant de détails si nets. . . . J'y ai passé des heures; et des heures de grande joie.[76]

More than simply expressing his admiration, though, and with his usual (unusual) generosity and self-effacement, Larbaud would become passionately involved in the publication of "Anabase." He personally assumed the responsibility of correcting the proofs, with utmost scrupulousness[77] (the same scrupulousness with which he participated in the translation of Joyce's *Ulysses* and saw that this difficult undertaking was perfectly carried out)[78] before allowing parts of it to appear in the first issue of *Commerce,* in the summer of 1924,[79] at the same time as *Amitié du Prince.*[80]

By a strange series of coincidences, Joyce and St.-J. Perse (as he now signed his work) were destined to appear side by side, in both *La Nouvelle Revue Française* and *Commerce*—due, for the most part, to the perceptiveness of the man who had recognized their genius and put his ardor at their servive: Larbaud.

Nor would Larbaud be content with seeing *Anabase* appear in France (bringing in its wake the publication of various other works by its author: a new edition of *Eloges* by Gallimard in May 1925 that included "Pour fêter une enfance," "Eloges," "Images à Crusoé," "Amitié du Prince").[81] He also personally encouraged and contributed to the first translations of *Anabase*—the Russian

one by Adamovitch and Ivanoff, published in Paris in 1926 by
J. Povolozky, for which he wrote the preface—and the English
one by T. S. Eliot, published in London in 1930.[82]

In all this, Larbaud was certainly not in any way aided by the
author of the poems; quite on the contrary. For events on the
Alexis Leger side of his life were developing with equal
rapidity[83] as those which concerned St.-J. Perse. The ascent of
the poet was no less swift than that of the diplomat, which promised to be an expedition under the leadership of great and powerful chiefs—an "anabase" not to be underestimated.

1925–1932

The year 1925 was a milestone in the diplomatic life of Alexis
Leger: he was promoted to "Conseiller d' Ambassade"; most
important of all, Briand nominated him head of his cabinet
(which meant that he would be in charge of directing the diplomacy of that branch of the government). Moreover, Berthelot
was recalled to office by Briand and was once more his secretary
general of foreign affairs.[84] Thus, the two men with whom Leger
was linked both by affinity and personal friendship would be the
leaders with whom he was associated from now on.

It seemed to him that his choices had been right—that leaving
China when he did, and acquiescing to Briand in Washington,
had been moves that (in some intuitive way) had brought him to
this fateful turn in his destiny. Here was adventure of a different
kind, suited to his restless spirit, his need for strong doses of the
unknown. Perhaps that is what he had foreseen when he wrote to
a woman (who evidently shared many of his feelings) just before
leaving China: "Je pars parce que je ne suis encore en paix avec
l'odeur sauvage de ce monde, qui est une grande et sombre et
forte chose."[85] It appeared to him now that one way of exploring
this savage, grand, and powerful world was by taking the high-
roads of politics.

The first encounter of this kind in which he participated was
the Locarno agreement in the same year. Briand, whose confi-

dence in Leger was rapidly growing, called upon him to prepare and negotiate this important meeting. Both men agreed that one of the major political issues at this time was to improve the system of collective security for France, deprived (by the insufficiency of the Versailles treaty and international actions that had followed) of territorial safeguards, exposed to danger due to the insufficient powers of the League of Nations (without an army or ways to impose sanctions) as well as the absence of America and any guarantee of British solidarity against Germany. In order to correct this hazardous situation, a pact of security would be the aim of the meeting at Locarno, which would insure the safety of the Rhine region by a free contractual agreement with Germany and, at the same time, an alliance with Britain, which had been sought by France for some time.[86]

Leger worked in close accord with Briand on every step of this important enterprise: from its inception to its outcome; from the writing of the agreement to the diplomatic arrangements necessary for the meeting—all the way to the final maneuvers that resulted in the tête-à-tête (in a discreetly chosen garden of a little country inn on the outskirts of Locarno), the first of its kind, between the French minister and the German chancelor, Luther. So great, apparently, was Briand's confidence in Leger that he was the only person allowed to be present at this historic encounter.[87]

Almost immediately afterward, Leger was called upon to turn his attention to the other side of the world. Events in Asia had come to a head: the Chinese Nationalist crisis of 1925–26 demanded his expertise. He was designated to personally determine the direction of French diplomatic action in the Far East.[88]

The claims made on Leger were certainly great. Yet, those that involved St.-J. Perse were no less demanding. Rilke pursued his project of translating *Images à Crusoé,* and the latter had finally responded favorably to the former's third request, feeling it incumbent upon him, however, to revise the poem somewhat and to add this altered version to the new edition of *Eloges* about to appear in France. Not that Leger could judge whether these changes had been made or indeed any of the German version executed by Rilke (having no knowledge of German himself, and being too busy to go in to the matter because of the demands of the Quai d'Orsay). Besides, he felt that he would never allow himself to comment on an undertaking by a poet of Rilke's stature and shortly lost track of both the translation and its translator.[89] Rilke, on the other hand, continued to say that "l'oeuvre . . . est de celles qu'on n'oublie point"[90] and even considered translating the other poems of *Eloges*. Finally, though, he would abandon this project, admitting that there were limits to translation and also to devoting his talent to the work of another poet. "C'est un magnifique empire," he wrote to Princess Caetani (the founder of *Commerce*), "mais je ne saurais pas jeter la conquête de son image dans la profondeur transparente d'une autre langue. Si je vénère bien d'autres, je ne saurais cependant bien servir que mes propres dieux."[91]

Even though Rilke had stepped out of the fray, the new French edition of *Eloges* appeared at the Editions de la Librairie Gallimard in May 1925, and a deluxe edition of *Anabase* followed in the same year.[92] Moreover, foreign translations were already under way. Decidedly, the poet was threatening to come to the fore. Despite all the attempts at anonymity, the publications devoid of the author's name, the new pseudonym he had devised, it suddenly seemed to Leger that he had not taken sufficient precautions and that the literary half of his self risked the danger of discovery. Disguises evidently did not suffice. The part of him that he wished to keep totally secret, at this time, must be cast off—or amputated.

He therefore imposed more drastic measures than before: he forbade any publication of his work in France and henceforth allowed only foreign translations of *Anabase* to appear. To all intents and purposes, the poet St.-J. Perse had fallen silent. The only time his voice was momentarily heard was when, deeply moved by the death of his old friend, Rivière, he allowed a homage to the latter to be published in a memorial issue of *La Nouvelle Revue Française* (April 1925).[93] But even there, aside from signing A. Saint-Leger Leger, he began his tribute by saying: "Mon nom n'appartient pas aux lettres,"[94] specifying that he would speak solely of Rivière, the man; he proceeded also to contrast the "catacombes de la communauté litteraire" with "la dignité d'une vie d'homme . . . cette pure histoire" and concluded with a statement by Rivière that showed his distance from the literary world.[95]

Leger's own distance from this world was growing steadily, as he immersed himself in his life at the Ministry of Foreign Affairs. True, he could not be indifferent to the fidelity and passionate involvement of Larbaud, who had just written a splendid foreword for the Russian translation of *Anabase* (published in *La Nouvelle Revue Française* in January 1926)[96] in which he prophesied that, of the poems written in that era, mainly those of Claudel, Valéry, and Saint-John Perse would survive, and affirmed that *Anabase* surpassed other poetic masterpieces of the ages, being a "monument poétique planétaire."[97]

But Leger had other—if not planetary, then worldwide—concerns now. After the crisis in China, Europe and further imperious demands there preoccupied Briand and thus, him also. He had begun to work on a pact that was to result in an international renunciation of war as an instrument of national politics. Conceived and carried out by Leger, as the head of Briand's cabinet,[98] it would result in the Pacte de Paris (or the Briand-Kellog Pact), an audacious document that prepared the way for a collective organization of nations even more audacious—such as a Federal Union of Europe.

Briand, whose greatest dream always centered on peace, saw with intense satisfaction the paths along which his young collaborator's imagination and political vision moved. He entrusted more and more responsibilities to Leger, knowing that they worked in perfect accord;[99] and the latter, fired on by such confidence and thriving on the liberty with which his superior allowed him to proceed, worked passionately at his projects. He prepared the necessary outlines, arranged diplomatic approaches and official discussions of a preliminary nature, and wrote the text of the pact as well as the speech of presentation that Briand would read on the day of its signature.[100] In writing this text, Leger found not only that he could make use of the legal training and the political experience he had gained in the past but that he could also express many of the ideas that were an integral part of his being and formed the fundamental vision he had of life and human existence. Beginning with the affirmation that the event here celebrated marked "une date nouvelle dans l'histoire de l'humanité," since those assembled would sign a "véritable traité de concorde" and take part in an "esprit nouveau,"[101] he went on to define this new spirit (in words of skillful oratory):

Pour la première fois, à la face du monde . . . la guerre est répudiée sans réserve en tant qu' instrument de politique nationale, c'est à dire, dans la forme la plus spécifique et la plus redoutable: celle de la guerre égoïste et volontaire . . . une telle guerre est enfin destituée juridiquement de ce qui constituait son plus grave danger: la légitimité. Frappée désormais d'illégalité . . . d'une véritable mise hors la loi . . . c'est l'institution même de la guerre qui se trouve ainsi attaquée directement, dans son essence propre. . . . A cette heure mémorable, la conscience des peuples, épurée de tout égoïsme national, s'efforce sincèrement vers des régions sereines où la fraternité humaine puisse s'exprimer dans le battement d'un même coeur.[102]

It was a moment of profound gratification when Leger heard his words pronounced before the representatives of fifteen great nations,[103] assembled in Paris to sign this pact, which combined dream and action, a far-reaching vision, and realistic terms—an equation to which he so profoundly subscribed. The political arena had acquired all the exhilarating qualities that he had thought possible only in other realms.

And yet, as he sat in his office at the Quai d'Orsay, surrounded by all the trappings of diplomatic life that had begun to come his way, he inwardly yearned for the other side of his being. Secretely—at night, and during the leaves he could now and then take—he turned once more to poetry. A small notebook (quickly stored in a side pocket or stowed away in an inaccessible drawer of his desk) began to be part of his accoutrements. Those who knew him well saw that he frequently withdrew this object from its hiding place, to make notations if a word struck him or a detail in his surroundings elicited his interest. But that was only among intimates.[104] At the Quai (as formerly, in China) almost no one suspected that there was a literary side to this suave and successful diplomat.[105]

Sometimes, however, during the hours that could be salvaged from official activities—which some thought were rather numerous[106]—he gave in to the desire to see some of his former literary friends, many of whom had begun to accuse him of having become "invisible" and "unattainable."[107] He longed especially to see Fargue and Larbaud. The best place to find them, he knew, was at Adrienne Monnier's bookstore, La Maison des Amis des Livres, at 7, rue de l'Odéon. Fargue had lately made his headquarters there, and

one could see him any afternoon . . . telling stories to a circle of delighted listeners, "les Potassons," as he called his friends. . . . His verbal inventions were unimagineably obscene, and so were the gestures which accompanied them. And all this in a library where nice mothers of families and their *jeunes filles* were choosing books from the shelves. Larbaud was one of his most appreciative listeners. He would blush, chuckle, and say "Oh!" in his Larbaldian manner.[108]

Perse, among the listeners, most probably did not blush or seem scandalized, but surely delighted in the contrast between Fargue's tales and the clients of La Maison des Amis des Livres. Most of all, he must have appreciated the former's verbal pyrotechnics, for "Fargue was almost as good a word inventor as Joyce—he was a word maniac"[109] (a quality Perse would have been the first to appreciate).

Across the street, at Sylvia Beach's bookstore, Shakespeare and Company, to and from which there was a constant ebb and flow, there was another group of writers who interested Perse: Archibald MacLeish (also a friend of Joyce) who had arrived in Paris recently;[110] Allen Tate;[111] E. E. Cummings, parts of whose *The Enormous Room* Adrienne Monnier had just published in translation;[112] Ezra Pound, who was the godfather of Sylvia

Beach's establishment;[113] also T. S. Eliot, who had already expressed his interest in translating *Anabase*[114] and whose *The Hollow Men* Perse would translate in turn;[115] and, of course, James Joyce, who was now deep into *Finnegans Wake*.

Both groups, and many other artists in various fields, met also at the home of Princess Caetani in Paris and Versailles, where conversation turned about all new developments in music, painting, and literature. She very likely spoke to Perse of the various poets who were so taken with *Anabase* that they aspired to (or despaired of) the possibility of translating it: MacLeish, who said that he considered it one of those rare works that a writer encounters sometimes in his life, that are akin to mountaintops from which one suddenly sees the world with new eyes;[116] Rilke, who had thought of translating *Anabase* but had to admit that "en face de ce poète subtil, je suis réduit au rôle d'auditeur, de spectateur, je suis *dans la salle* évidemment, mais pas *là* où la pièce se joue";[117] Giuseppe Ungaretti, who wrote from Rome: "Je travaille avec passion à l'*Anabase* . . . ce poème m'a entr'ouvert un monde. J'y découvre à chaque pas des stupeurs nouvelles. . . . Cette poésie m'a bouleversé et entièrement pris";[118] T. S. Eliot, who had said: "Le poème me semble un des plus grands et des plus singuliers des temps modernes, et si je peux parvenir à faire une traduction qui soit presque digne d'un tel chef-d'oeuvre, je serai tout à fait content"[119] and was preparing—in his Preface to the English edition to appear in 1930—to compare *Anabase* with Joyce's Anna Livia Plurabelle section of *Finnegans Wake* in greatness.[120]

As filled with exhilaration (and laughter, too) as this world of artists was, as welcome a contrast it provided with life at the Quai d'Orsay, he found that he needed other ways of finding relief from pacts and oratory, stuffy offices and banquets with diplomats. Just as he had to escape from Peking to the endless sands of the desert, so he now fled from Paris to the high seas to seek renewal in their vast reaches: silence to still the din of voices, battles against the elements instead of clauses in peace agreements, and words that came from reaches deeper than the prose in which he dealt every day. He began to take his vacations at sea, exploring the Atlantic by sailboat all the way to the Aran Islands or along the route to Newfoundland.[121] He traveled alone at these times or, at most, with a crew of two, for he valued solitude[122] that was so rarely his. It was during these journeys that he wrote; a new cycle of works had already begun to take form. Mountains, a Taoist temple, or the sea (sites far from the tumult of men, where the eye encountered immense vistas and timelessness prevailed) were as necessary to him for creation as the deep earth is for the growth of giant trees.

He returned from these voyages with a dreamlike gaze (which he had to swiftly dissemble) and a contraband treasure in his seafarer's gear (which he stored away in a secret cache). He could let nothing show of his other face or any of his work as a poet appear while he moved in the sphere of politics. Only much later, at the time of his "libération" (as the age of retirement was called in this milieu), was he planning to allow it to come to the fore.[123]

Now, however, he had other concerns. The diurnal world in which he moved was fraught with jealousies and a variety of other pitfalls. Even the possible envy of one's friends could be dangerous. He had seen that some compared him favorably with Berthelot, his immediate superior, whose favorite, hope, and perhaps heir he was usually considered. One observer was especially outspoken:

Tout descendait vers le sol chez Berthelot. . . . Tout montait du sol chez Leger. Il semblait tout juste toucher terre pour y puiser l'élan naturel comme un geyser d'énergie vers la poitrine forte, les épaules éffacées, le visage grave et droit et qu'éclairaient des yeux inoublia-bles. Je rêvais au lumineux Vulcain de *La Forge* de Velasquez. . . . "Ceci tuera cela," me disais-je, les regardant l'un et l'autre, placés par le hasard comme deux cariatides aux deux bouts d'un long manteau de cheminée, dans un bureau du Quai.[124]

It would not do to have Berthelot suspect such thoughts, especially when the former's advancing age made him vulnerable to the latter's youth.[125] It was imperative for him not to feel surpassed by the younger man—not even in a game of cards. Berthelot often measured himself against his assistants at such play. One evening, when all the others had been rapidly eliminated, Leger remained his only adversary in the tournament. It was a most delicate situation and one that called for all of the latter's training (and presence of mind):

Le combat fut long et rude, tenace aussi. Les deux hommes mirent toute leur intelligence, toute leur malice aussi, à contribution. La partie dura longtemps . . . Philippe Berthelot, qui n'eut pas de chance et même risqua des coups plus audacieux que son vis-à-vis . . . [vit] qu'il était fatal qu'il perdût. Furieux, bien que cela n'ait en somme aucune importance, il tira sa montre et s'aperçut, opportunément, qu'il était déjà tard. "Il faut nous arrêter," dit-il, "il est plus que temps de rentrer au Quai d'Orsay." M. Leger acquiesça et, sentant celui qui était alors son patron irrité d'avoir été inférieur, eut un *magnifique mot de diplomate:* "C'est ennuyeux, car on ne saura jamais lequel de nous aurait gagné."[126]

Fortunately, there was no such rivalry with Aristide Briand. The two men worked harmoniously together, at games far greater in scope—involving the maneuvering of nations, and complex moves worthy of giant chessboards—in which the stakes were war or peace, the preservation or destruction of the European continent, indeed the world.

The project they were now involved in was the organization of a "Union fédérale européenne," an enterprise of unusual initiative and rare courage, in these times of economic crisis, characteristic of Briand's constructive course of thought and one that Leger fully subscribed to. As the head of Briand's cabinet, Leger was personally in charge of studying the procedures necessary for its realization and the actions needed to carry it out. He was also entirely responsible for drawing up the memorandum that would be presented for the consideration of the twenty-seven European members of the League of Nations, outlining all the aspects[127] of this novel and audacious plan.[128]

The first meeting, called by Leger, took place on September 9, 1929, in Geneva. Twenty-seven European nations, all of whom were members of the League of Nations, were asked to consider

Alexis Leger at the Quai d'Orsay ca. 1930, at the time of his project for a "Union fédérale européenne." (Photo Harlingue-Viollet).

the advantages of a federal bond between European countries that would establish a system of continual solidarity between them, and the possibility of studying and solving problems of common interest to them. The response was unanimously favorable, and all the representatives promised to submit the plan to their governments for further study. They also asked the French representative (Leger) to prepare a memorandum in which all points proposed were elucidated, to gather and to record the various governments' reactions, to draw conclusions from this survey, and to prepare a report to be submitted to a European conference in Geneva at the next meeting of the Assembly of the League of Nations.[129]

The memorandum submitted by Leger, as the representative of the French government before the League of Nations (in 1930), contained the following major points: The need for a general pact that would establish the moral principle of a United Europe and solemnly consecrate the solidarity between European nations; the necessity for creating a mechanism to insure that the Union of European States had the means indispensable to its task; the need to establish, in advance, the essential directions that would determine the general conceptions of the European Committee and guide its work of establishing a program for organizing Europe; the possibility of reserving the study of all questions of a specific nature (such as economic cooperation, finance, communications and transport, labor problems, health organizations, intellectual cooperation and exchanges, etc.), either for the next European conference or for the European Committee to be created in the future.[130] He concluded the memorandum by an appeal to the nations of Europe that bore the stamp of his fundamental convictions (and the ring of his powerful writing style):

L'heure n'a jamais été plus propice ni plus pressante pour l'inauguration d'une oeuvre constructive en Europe. . . . Heure décisive, où l'Europe attentive peut disposer elle-même de son propre destin. S'unir pour vivre et prospérer : telle est la stricte nécessité devant laquelle se trouvent désormais les Nations d'Europe. . . . Aux gouvernements d'assumer aujourd'hui leurs responsabilités . . . le groupement de forces matérielles et morales dont il leur appartient de garder la maîtrise collective, au bénéfice de la communauté europénne autant que de l'humanité.[131]

As he delivered these words, it was the statesman in him who predominated, and seemed to claim every fiber of his being. The poet had moved—for the moment—into the shadows. It mattered less that *Anabase* had, or was about to be, a major literary event in England, Italy, and Germany[132] than to have these same countries become involved in his dream of a United Europe.

That dream, however, was never to be realized. The forces of destruction were already gathering. They would tear Europe asunder, and although he would try—one last time—to take up the thread of a collective organization of European nations (in 1935), the odds against him were too great for him to be able to succeed. As far as Briand was concerned, it would have taken more than the lifetime of one man to carry out the plan for a Union of Europe, and his life was about to end.

The "vieillard chargé d'humanité"[133] had begun to ail. With the last vestiges of his strength, he tried to let his "grande voix pathétique" be heard once more[134] while the storm clouds of war were gathering. Soon, however, just as peace in Europe, so Briand was also on the point of dying.

In the winter of 1932 Leger was at his bedside standing vigil (as he had done for his father years ago). The night was cold and long. What he saw before him was more than the death agony of one man:

Le vent d'hiver qui soufflait cette nuit-là semblait chanter aux hommes la limite de l'effort humain. Un grand tourment soulevait l'âme du vieux lutteur à bout de souffle. Et par trois fois on l'entendit délirer. . . . L'Europe hantait cette agonie, l'Europe hantait cette chambre close, moins comme un mot que comme une vision douloureuse, angoissante.[135]

One would have sworn it was an omen for the future, ominous, tragic.

When Briand was buried, the hope of peace went with him to the grave. His death marked the end of an era. Gone were the grand designs for international harmony and the hope for their realization. Gone, for Leger, were seven years of companionship in dream and action.[136] The loss he felt was for both the man and all that they had striven for together.

Berthelot also was gone from the political scene.[137] The friend from the earliest days in this world had moved into the shadows of retirement. Leger now stood alone. He carried on his shoulders a heritage that might prove increasingly fragile in this era where violence had begun to rear its head. He wondered how he could proceed—unaided—as its executor.

As he crossed the threshold of another epoch, he had the dread premonition that, after the glorious anabasis, a catabasis was about to begin.

1933–1940

And yet, the next seven years began with a personal triumph that appeared to belie this prophecy: Leger was promoted to ambassador and became secretary general of foreign affairs on February 28, 1933,[138] inheriting Berthelot's post and occupying what was considered *the* key position in the French government. He dominated the diplomatic chessboard, for the *éminence grise* (behind the throne of the Ministry of Foreign Affairs) was really the secretary general. And although the official star of the Quai d'Orsay was Joseph Paul-Boncour at this time, he reigned but did not govern. "Le vrai ministre s'appelle Leger," one observer noted.[139] For this man, whom another compared with "le comte Mosca dans *La Chartreuse de Parmes*,"[140] was at the top of the pyramid that constituted "le Saint des Saints. . . . la *sous-direction d'Europe*"[141] and stood in the reflected glory of the

grandes ombres du passé . . . surtout celle d'Aristide Briand. Non seulement en bas-relief, accolé à la grille d'honneur, y commémorait "l'apôtre de la paix," mais ses disciples et admirateurs . . . y occupaient des positions clefs, avec, au-dessus les autres, Alexis Leger, le secrétaire général.[142]

It appeared at first that he might succeed in administering the legacy with which he had been entrusted, for Paul-Boncour was, without a doubt, the most faithful and brilliant of Briand's disciples,[143] and harmony reigned between the two men. Leger worked tirelessly at his tasks. It was fortunate that the rigorous training to which he had always submitted his body gave him the stamina required to maintain the grueling pace. Many others had exhausted their physical and emotional strength at this job. From dawn until late at night, one was under continual pressure: interviews, discussions, receptions, policy decisions, attention to all details,[144] visits by journalists and dignitaries (such as Pertinax, Elie Bois, Geneviève Tabouis, André de Fels, "Secrétaire Général de l'Alliance démocratique"—who were among Leger's most frequent callers).[145]

He found it almost impossible now to see any of his former friends. The charges of "invisibility" and "distance" multiplied. But, as he would assure one journalist, that was part of the diplomat's lot. Seated at the table that Berthelot had occupied, he said with a slight smile: "Nous travaillons tous ici dans l'anonymat. Laissez-nous au doigt l'anneau de Gygès. C'est notre luxe. Et ne cherchez pas trop de mérite dans ce goût de l'invisiblité: vous risquerez peut-être d'y trouver plus de fierté que de modestie."[146] But, despite this taste for hidden power, he managed to help Larbaud and Valéry precisely because of what it allowed him to do.[147]

Poets and poetry, however, had to be relegated to the background during these years. Constant vigilance was now required, and he bore the burden of the watch on security. On the foreign scene, the times were beginning to be out of joint. In Germany (where danger signals could already be detected in 1930, and he had lately been noticing a "mentality of prewar imperialist" character) the Nazi party had begun its rise to power. He was convinced (and said so) that the French and British must unite to face this menace, make no more concessions to that government—in essence, say: "Thus far and no further."[148]

But, despite his sharp insight and vast power, Leger was doomed to become the defender of lost causes. The Locarno treaty (upon which he and Briand had based such high hopes), although it maintained sufficient power to stem Hitler's war tide for a while, could not resist it indefinitely. It had been written at a time when one could still believe that the age-old conflict between France and Germany could be resolved. Now there was no longer any chance of agreement with the masters of the Reich; the problem had become one of containment.[149]

That, at least, was how Leger saw it. Unfortunately for him, he would have to serve under a succession of foreign ministers, during the years 1933 to 1940, that ranged from Paul-Boncour, to Barthou, Laval, Flandin, Delbos, Bonnet, Delbos, Daladier, and Reynaud (a list that speaks for itself) and, with the exception of Barthou (who was rapidly assassinated), some feel, "never had a minister who combined the vision and the will to carry on the great rules of French diplomacy."[150] Despite his high ideals, the fundamental liberalism that characterized his political philosophy,[151] he would have to—as a servant of the state—agree to do many things that went against his convictions. Especially since he was never able to have his resignation accepted, he was bound to support the policies of the Quai d'Orsay no matter how deeply he disagreed with them.

One of the most important of these disagreements arose in 1935. It concerned negotiations with Italy (and Mussolini), a country that had proposed a four-way pact in 1933 but that had found France (and Leger) suspicious of such an entente and successful in rendering this agreement inoffensive by limiting the changes in clauses suggested by Italy. Now, however, negotiations with Italy were once again under way—this time, with Laval as minister of foreign affairs. The Quai d'Orsay (under Leger's guidance) had worked assiduously to put an end to Italy's claims to North Africa, but Leger saw that his minister was less interested in the substance of this contract than in making a prestigious voyage to Rome. Laval, on the other hand, put credence in the rumor that Leger had a phobia about Italy and was ready to sabotage any entente with that nation. The dissent between the two men reached such proportions that Leger threatened to resign. Laval (concerned about the consequences that the departure of the secretary general might have on his negotiations with Mussolini) refused to have Leger leave.

There was no choice but to continue. Despite the fact that Leger knew that his reputation for utter integrity might be used to cover up maneuvers he would not have condoned;[152] despite his awareness that Laval liked neither the League of Nations nor the "briandistes" of the Quai d'Orsay and, most notably, Alexis Leger.[153]

The Conference of Stresa (April 11–14, 1935) brought together Laval, Leger, Ramsay MacDonald, John Simon, Sir Robert Vansittart, and Mussolini.[154] Leger spent a great deal of time observing the Italian dictator. What most interested him was that Mussolini "poursuivait une démonstration avec un esprit logique absolu, en ligne droite"[155]—perhaps because it was the polar opposite of his own penchant for flexibility, ambiguity, and paradox—which some, such as Paul-Boncour, even considered "souple à l'excès";[156] probably also because he feared that Laval would make concessions to Mussolini and that, as a result, France would come away from the meeting as an ally of Italy.[157]

Only a month later he would have the opportunity to observe Stalin. From May 13 to May 15, Laval met with Stalin in Moscow, and once again Leger was called upon to participate in the conference.[158] It would be as difficult for him, since he was no more ready to submit to pressures from the Left than from the Right, and just as little inclined to a Communist as to a Fascist orientation in matters of foreign relations. Besides, he considered this prestige journey of Laval to Moscow, shortly after his trip to Rome, nothing but "'un voyage de cabotin,' a stage on the circuit of the strolling player."[159] Laval, on the other hand, said to Leger (who wanted time for longer preparations for the meeting): "Vous couchez avec les affaires."[160] Actually, it was not political lovemaking but a plan that would have resembled a Locarno of the East that Leger had been devoting his nights to.

Although this dream was not realized, the meeting nevertheless resulted in the Franco-Russian Pact, a treaty of mutual assistance between the two countries whose most important result was to turn Russia aside from the old notion of a military alliance with Germany.[161] Aside from such vital maneuvers of international politics, what Leger brought away from his meeting with Stalin were some interesting observations. He was the only dictator whom Leger had ever seen laugh.[162] And not only was "ce pur Asiate non dénué d'humour", but he also found that "personne aujourd'hui parle un français plus sûr de ses nuances, plus naturellement mémorable."[163] (These were observations perhaps more private than official, proof of the poet more than the statesman.)

The third dictator he would meet—being one of the rare diplomats to have approached all three personally[164]—was shortly afterward on French soil. On March 7, 1936, Hitler reoccupied the French left bank of the Rhine. Leger disagreed again with his minister (Flandin, this time), who did not accept his interpretation of the Locarno Pact, as allowing—even demanding— immediate action by France (even though it might stand alone and act before the League of Nations had considered the matter) against Germany's violation of the agreement. He offered to resign. But once again, this action was in vain. Leger had to remain at his post, and Flandin went (without him) to London to negotiate.[165]

The acceptance of the German occupation of the Rhineland, which was the outcome, signaled to Leger the downfall of everything Briand and he had worked so hard to construct, the entire edifice of collective security meant to insure peace in Europe. After the "end of Locarno," he knew that the struggle was lost. "C'est à la Conférence de Londres de mars 1936, non à Munich, que gît la véritable responsabilité du débordement hitlérien," Leger would one day say, when evoking the memory of Briand.[166] Never would that fighter for humanity have allowed this to happen; but he was gone and, at that time, seemingly forgotten.

At times such as these, diplomatic life (which claimed so much of his time now) appeared somber and quite unrewarding. He would gladly have called his shadowy double—the poet—to come to the fore. How long ago, it seemed, he had dwelt in those regions. A great yearning seized him, as he stood among the powerful of this earth, at the gilded portals of chancellories, before conference tables laden with words of an official nature. His gaze became distant. He seemed to listen to other sounds: to the roar of the sea and the call of migratory birds, to words that named but did not bind, opened unknown domains rather than defined territories. But he knew that he must not allow his faraway look to be noticed and that he must shield the poet's face from view. The mask of the diplomat instantly concealed his other features if anyone approached. In these days of strife, the warrior's armor must prevail.

The only moments that could be said to constitute "le repos du guerrier"[167] for Leger were those he spent with the woman who had, for some time, shared his existence (although not bound to hm by ties of legality). She was Comtesse Marthe de Fels, with whom he shared matters other than those of state. Her beauty and intelligence, the friendship that linked both of them to Briand and Claudel, their mutual interest in literature[168] all contributed to their relationship. But perhaps most of all, it was that with her that Alexis could dream of sea voyages, carve a small boat from a piece of wood,[169] walk through the countryside with their dog (a beautiful white creature—which he would one day immortalize in a poem),[170] and delight in other than diplomatic encounters.

But the world of dream and the joys of the senses had to give way, much of the time, to claims by matters of state. In 1936 there seemed to appear a light amid the somber events on the political scene: the Front Populaire had come to power and with it, Léon Blum, a man for whom Leger had both respect and personal friendship.[171] Going to London with him was quite a different matter than making the voyage with Flandin. Yet, the relationship with the new French government was also somewhat problematic. Leger had always considered himself to be politically on the Left, but although now his enemies referred to him as "ce 'rouge' du Quai d'Orsay,"[172] he felt that it was absolutely necessary to maintain his judgment as a diplomat above all his political sympathies.

This was especially difficult now that civil war had broken out in Spain. Despite his personal sympathies (which undoubtedly lay with the Republicans), he realized that, because there was danger of Communist terrorism on the other side of the Channel, it was absolutely necessary to insure British neutrality by a guarantee of nonintervention from France. He proceeded to convince Blum of this point of view, despite the fact that such a decision exposed Leger to the fire of his own supporters and made himself the scapegoat of the Communist Left in France (while being attacked by the Fascist Right for other reasons).[173] He stood his ground and maintained his position, considering it essential for France's foreign policy. But the enemies he made, by this and other decisions—motivated by integrity and intransigence—would be at the root of his ultimate downfall, as would the fact that some thought "il croyait excessivement aux vertus de la 'pactomanie,' aux traités compliqués . . . [et] avait introduit l'ambiguité dans la politique française."[174]

It was primarily his intransigence that would make him a thorn in the side of figures more powerful than any faction in France: the new master of the Third Reich. Leger had already aroused his anger by taking action against German aggression in Spanish Morocco, thus convincing the Nazis that a firm hand was steering French diplomacy—a most unwelcome discovery.[175] But, in the year that followed, Germany had more than individual hatreds in mind (or worrying about the man it considered a public enemy of the Reich): the Anschluss of Austria (in March 1938) and the matter of the Sudeten.

Leger would again have to travel in unwelcome company: to the Munich Conference, with Daladier. Despite Leger's fierce opposition to the policy of "appeasement" and Hitler's well-known hostility toward him, he was forced to attend, as the representative of the Quai d'Orsay, for ministers of foreign affairs (Bonnet, in France) were not called to this meeting of heads of state.[176] They left Paris on September 28, 1938, with Leger as the designated negotiator.

At Munich, Daladier refused to start proceedings without him. "Where is Leger?" he queried. "I won't begin if Leger is not here. He knows all the tricks of the trade."[177] Leger indeed attempted to use all his "tricks" (or expertise) to strengthen Daladier's arguments. As Paul Schmidt (Hitler's interpreter) remembered, Leger sat at Daladier's side during the entire meeting, prompting him to ask questions and to object to the demands Hitler was making.[178] At one point, Leger himself shot a question at Hitler—arrowlike in its directness—demanding to know whether Hitler was for or against the survival of Czechoslovakia.[179] He watched the effect it produced. It was something like a seizure. Leger had been observing their adversary for

Alexis Leger (appearing at the extreme right) at the signing of the Franco-German agreement in December 1938 by Georges Bonnet and Joachim von Ribbentrop (Photo Collection Viollet).

some time, with fascination—and horror. It was mostly Hitler's eyes that struck him.[180] But his entire behavior was something he could never forget. He would describe it with a pathologist's accuracy:

Quant à Hitler, je me souvenais en face de lui de mes années d'études de médecine, lorsque le praticien provoque un état second chez un malade par un signal ou un bruit. . . . Chez Hitler, ce qui déclenchait l'état second, c'était l'introduction dans le débat d'un argument logique implacable. A ce moment précis, Hitler se retirait, s'éloignait, s'enveloppait dans un tonnerre de mots. Beaucoup de gens ont décrit ses yeux, ont cru les voir sombres. En réalité, il avait des yeux clairs, glauques, des yeux de poisson mort.[181]

Despite the maniacal shrieks and the hideous eyes fixed upon him, Leger continued to probe, to attack, and to use all his considerable skill to fight in order to achieve some status for Czechoslovakia (a country he respected and whose president, Beneš, had been a friend ever since the days of Berthelot) that would justify international intervention on its behalf.

The disastrous outcome of the Munich Conference is well known in world history. Its results were even more devastating when, not long afterward the International Commission of Ambassadors gave in to Hitler's most inadmissible demands for the transfer of the disputed Czech zones. Leger insisted strongly on the guarantee given that country by the Four Powers, but to no avail. When the Germans entered Prague in March 1939, he demanded that—at least—the French ambassador (Coulandre) be recalled from Berlin to mark the gravity of the situation, but again nothing was done. He complained to Daladier of the government's posture of weakness and hesitation. But the only answer he received to this was that the minister of foreign affairs left for London, four days later, without him.[182]

These were dark days. Despite all his energy and basic optimism, Leger began to feel that he was fighting for lost causes. Gone was the exhilaration he had voiced only a few years ago when he had considered that "la complexité d'une situation internationale est . . . un excellent stimulant. . . . La véritable preuve de la diplomatie . . . est la complexité des événements, leur multiplicité et leur rapidité."[183] Now neither the knotty problems of diplomacy nor their diversity and rapidity were a source of excitement and fervor. It was simply a question of retarding an awful tide, or salvaging whatever possible from a cataclysm sure to strike.

Crisis followed crisis. First was the one in Poland that (contrary to his expectations) did result in a formal promise from England to stand by that country; attempts to detach Italy from the Axis (which resulted in many errors in French foreign policy for which Leger himself would be blamed—although some historians think it was thanks to his actions that Italy remained neutral until after France's defeat);[184] the worsening of the Polish crisis in the summer of 1939. It all led up to the outbreak of World War II on September 1 of that year.

It was the end of all the dreams of peace. The edifice whose cornerstone had been Locarno (West or East) had been totally shattered. It seemed to him that it was in another age that these visions had seemed possible. Now all was devastation and inhumanity of man to man. True, he had seen death and destruction occur in a number of ways (and on both sides of the globe)— earthquakes, epidemics, revolutions. But this cataclysm had a character quite different from anything he had known. It was in no way an expression of the cyclical forces of nature, or an upheaval founded on a need for renewal, but a mechanical plan of strictly human fabrication to dehumanize the world. Indeed, it seemed as though the world was about to founder by its own devices.

In the midst of all this, personal misfortune seemed a relatively puny matter. One man's downfall was but the displacement of a grain of sand in this gigantic avalanche. As often in times of disaster, scapegoats were rampant and victims for sacrifice abounded. The only mark that distinguished pathos from tragedy was the dignity with which a man assumed the role he must play.

That was what made Leger's fall from power an event worthy of note in all this global devastation. It happened shortly after the outbreak of the war. The government had changed several times. Daladier had become minister of foreign affairs and attempted to gain time to arm France by pretending to make peaceful proposals to Hitler: in March 1940 he had had to resign in favor of Reynaud. Things had gone very badly for England and France in the spring of 1940. The Germans had broken through the French frontier (after their attack on Holland and Belgium) and were advancing toward the Channel.

On May 16 Paris was in a state of total panic. The arrival of the Germans was expected from hour to hour. Reynaud also was behaving like a terror-stricken animal at bay. Some of his advisors urged him to "liquider la guerre";[185] he himself declared to the Chamber of Deputies that day: "Nous aurons peut-être à changer les méthodes et les hommes";[186] and, in the vain hope of regaining the confidence of the people, he called in Pétain and

Weygand and decided to reorganize his cabinet (taking charge himself of the Ministry of National Defense and having Daladier replace him at his post in the Ministry of Foreign Affairs).[187] Moreover, as is so often the case when hysteria takes hold, blind moves are easily oriented toward those whose presence is perceived as a threat (or even provokes uneasiness).

To Reynaud (despite the ironic fact that they essentially agreed on many matters—resistance to the Germans included), Leger was such a man. It was inherent in Leger's personality and in his most valuable qualities. "Leger's tireless search for an expression precise and pure of the banal, his refusal to compromise his integrity—all, in the end, acted as intolerable goads to politicians who found him an uneasy presence."[188] Reynaud was certainly affected in this manner, for he is reported to have said about Leger: "We haven't the same kind of mind. I don't know how to deal with his infernal Socratic method."[189] Even Leger's courtesy, which was famous, was not always comfortable for others: "most of all, the worldly and the ambitious were made uneasy by his aloofness, the subtleties of his language, and the sinuous progressions of his thoughts."[190]

But there was more to it than that. Leger had alienated those who were closest to Reynaud—chief among them, Comtesse Hélène de Portes, Reynaud's mistress, who governed not only his affections but also his political moves—by his quite correct refusal to speak of confidential matters with Reynaud in the presence of his friends.[191] The hatred that sprang from such slights would result in an actual conspiracy against Leger with, at its center, Baudouin, the secretary of Reynaud's War Cabinet, and the Comtesse de Portes, who now undertook a real campaign to unseat Leger.[192] Pressure exerted on Reynaud to put Baudouin in his place was the first step. But, in order to do so, another post had to be found for Leger, preferably one that would be sure to discredit him by assigning him an impossible task. The most astute suggested sending the latter as ambassador to Washington, with the special mission of convincing the United States to enter the war. Since he would surely not succeed, his enemies would win out twice: his mission would be a failure and he would have been gotten rid of.[193] And Mme de Portes would triumph since she had vowed she would have "la peau de Leger."[194]

On the night of May 18 the conspirators got Reynaud to sign the decree of Leger's replacement. But now there was the problem of who would have the courage to inform him of this blow. Actually, it should have been Reynaud himself, in a frank conversation. But, either out of fear that Leger, with his "infernal Socratic method," would wind rings around his arguments, or cause him to feel shame for his unjust action (seeing that there had been no political disagreements between them to warrant his removal), or out of sheer cowardice, Reynaud preferred to pass the unpleasant task on to Daladier.

Leger had had no inkling of what was brewing. When Daladier informed him of Reynaud's plans, he was completely taken by surprise. All his self-control and mastery of feelings came to the fore. Instantly, a mask of stoical indifference covered his features, as though the visor of a helmet had been lowered. "Son visage mat ne se colora pas. Ses cils ne se baissèrent point. Sa voix unie se borna à protester que, le jour où l'on disposerait de son poste, il ne consentirait à en occuper aucun autre."[195] He then proceeded, point by point, to refute every aspect of Reynaud's plan to send him as ambassador to America, with all the diplomatic skills he had acquired and with the implacable logic he had learned how to use,[196] knowing full well that he had been placed in a trap, and fighting with the last means at his disposal against its closing jaws.

Leger spent the night at his office in the Quai. On the morning of May 19, one of the members of his staff brought the announcement of his removal to the attic room[197] (some say with tears in his eyes) and handed Leger *L'Officiel* containing the decree signed by Reynaud during the night that sealed the latter's "disgrace."[198]

Very few moves in this endgame were now left to him to play. He would refrain from accusing those who had betrayed him—

not only out of innate dignity, but also because the grave danger
to France demanded his silence (being sufficiently wracked by
chaos not to be able to tolerate further upheaval in the government)—and take the only course that his character and circumstances dictated: refusing to accept the post of ambassador to
Washington, he stated that it was inadmissible to send Roosevelt
a diplomat whose reputation had, by irregular measures, been
defiled; insisting on his "mise en disponibilité."[199] Only his final
words, as he presented the decree to Daladier for his signature,
were as full of rage as of memorable hauteur: "J'ai droit à toute
l'injustice."[200]

It was the end of the man known as Leger: the demise of the
éminence grise, that powerful figure who had reigned so discreetly, almost invisibly, in French foreign affairs during the
most crucial years between world wars, had dreamed and acted,
won and lost, risen and fallen in the game played on this
chessboard as large as the world.

It was also—though he did not yet know it—the destruction of
the masked poet, St.-J. Perse. As soon as the Germans entered
Paris, the Gestapo ransacked his apartment on the avenue Ca-
moens, where he had left all his unpublished manuscripts.
Thinking that they were aiming at the diplomat, they struck at
the poet. All his papers were pillaged, and the writings accumulated during so many years would be carried off across Germany,
to the castles of Wartheland; they would later be removed by the
Russians when they conquered that region and would disappear.
No trace of them would ever be found.[201] Almost beyond a
doubt, everything the poet had written during these two decades was lost, irremediably.

As Alexis Leger/St.-J. Perse stood ready to leave French soil
on June 16, 1940, he was a man divested of every glory that the
years since his return from China had heaped upon him. Both
the diplomat and the poet were now empty-handed. It was as
though the past years had been effaced from his life and there
was nothing left except a tabula rasa, as bare as "les tables nues

de la mer" that he had yearned for (at the threshold of another departure) long, long ago.[202]

A ship (now, as then) waited to take him away. In the estuary of the Gironde, a British freighter prepared to take him to the far side of the Channel; another would carry him to a distant continent.[203]

The future was a total unknown. The past was gone. War was tearing asunder the Europe he had once hoped to unify. Violence threatened to destroy those dearest to him whom he must leave behind. He was certain that he would never see his aged, ailing mother again.[204] As he clasped her, for the last time, in his arms, he knew that the point of no return had truly been reached.

Thus, at the age of fifty-three, this man, who had ascended to such great heights, had reached the lowest point in his life. A great abyss yawned before him. Absence, distance, silence had never seemed so inexorable.

Exile, in its quintessence, was his now.

CHAPTER 6

EXILE AND OTHER KINGDOMS
(1940–1957)

Portes ouvertes sur les sables, portes ouvertes sur l'exil . . .

Exil (OC, p. 123)

L'homme libre de son ombre, à la limite de son bien.

—*Amers (OC,* p. 385)

1940–1941

During the long sleepless night of July 14,[1] he stood at the window and looked at the city below. From the high corner room (something like the prow of an immobile ship) in a vast, impersonal hotel on the island of Manhattan,[2] New York now seemed a harsh and lonely place to the alien he had become—as if resolved to repulse one by the sheer starkness of its physical traits: juttings of steel and stone, glaring glass surfaces, lurid neon lights, the graphlike linearity of its nameless streets, skyscrapers miming lusterless stalagmites, identical dwellings rising like headstones in an untended cemetery.

Even the climate added to the city's hostile presence. Summer exuded violence here. He had not encountered such oppressive heat before; it bore no resemblance to the torrid languor of tropical islands but attacked every fiber of one's body. It was due, it seemed, not to the sun's rays, but to some vicious force that erupted from the asphalt streets. One could almost smell blood in the air. Even the night brought no relief. It was filled with sounds of creatures on the prowl—not animals but unseen humans hunting for unknown prey.

When dawn came, it was not renewal or a source of fresh strength. A haze hung over the city. It bleached the sky until it was colorless and dull as the endless roofs that stretched to a horizon obscured by stagnant smoke. He wandered through the hotel corridors, past rooms that numbered into the thousands and had an interminable sameness that lulled the mind, into the dining room where limp figures sat, too wilted to speak or eat. He passed as a stranger and had lost almost all sense of speech. No one addressed him, and he did not attempt to communicate. A heavy coat of silence had descended on him; his tongue seemed thick and loath to move—not that there were any words he wished to utter nor anyone he would have desired to share his insularity.

The weeks passed. August stretched out in deadly torpor. He lived on this populous, overpopulated island as though shipwrecked there. Now and then a message reached him from Europe, as though it had miraculously been washed ashore. But the news that came took the form of repeated blows. In the period that followed, he learned that the Vichy government had deprived him of his nationality, confiscated his possessions, eradicated his Legion of Honor; a member of his family was threatened with arrest in Paris; a press campaign raged against him, incited by the government in power; his apartment had been ransacked by the Germans and had undergone further seizures by the French authorities.[3] It was a bitter harvest which the end of that summer brought. He himself had sunk into a morass of isolation, muteness, and immobility. Each time another blow struck, he fell further into its depths.

Finally, however, autumn came. With it came a movement in the air, change in the trees, the beginning of that almost forgotten splendor he had experienced—it seemed eons ago—when he and Briand had floated on the Potomac and seen the blaze of foliage glide by. His forces slowly started to return. It was not that the bitterness was gone, the anguish over the fate of those whom he had had to leave behind, but his innate life drive could not long remain dammed up. Among the first signs was that words came back to him once more—stiffly, awkwardly, not spoken but written. He communicated by letter with the sister of an old friend, in Washington, relaying a message but not yet attempting a meeting.[4]

When he did speak, it was during quite another type of meeting, almost foisted upon him by reporters from France who were now also on foreign soil and wished to hear of the events that had led to his exile and have his views on the world situation in these times of war. He felt some of the suppressed anger, so long contained, well up in him and decided to acquiesce to their request. As he spoke, all his former training returned—the control learned as a diplomat and the objectivity in assessing a situation. It was a test of his powers, for every move he made was carefully observed. Apparently he succeeded, for one of the journalists noted:

Il parlait sans élever la voix, mais avec une rage concentrée et surmontée. Et je fus frappé par la hauteur qu' il prenait, comme sans y prendre garde, avec les événements. Il était amer, déçu au plus profond, mais dès qu'il parlait de ce qui s'était passé, il ne pouvait s'empêcher de juger les choses avec le détachement de qui connaît le fond de la politique.[5]

What this observer could not have known was that his detachment came from a source far deeper than that of political training. It was the distance achieved by a man who had, in the heat of summer, begun to undergo a profound metamorphosis. Alexis Leger was vanishing. A new figure—of far greater dimensions—would, one day, appear; not like the phoenix (in a blinding flash, emerging unscathed from the ashes), but through a slow painful trial by fire. Only thus could the dross of the worldly courtier be burned away, in this rural crucible, and the poet emerge in the future.

The first steps in the alchemical process were halting, almost clumsy, and fraught with detours. Roads were indicated and rejected. Some were unthinkable, mostly because they would have led to a low form of compromise: several publishers had suggested that he write his political memoirs—a proposal that many would have considered opportune and would have been willing to accept but that he instantly refused.[6] Others were intolerable, since they had an aura of charity and would have robbed him of the last possession he clung to, his pride.

In the final analysis, the route that was the most natural, and therefore most fecund, was that of simple human contact. But it was only with great hesitation that he advanced in that direction. As an alien, one stepped somehat gingerly into friendships with those who were natives here, even though they had been described as having rare qualities. Thus he accepted, with some trepidation, the first meeting with such a being: Mrs. Francis Biddle (the wife of the attorney general), critic, dramatist, poet, and the sister of Marguerite de Bassiano,[7] whom he had known so well in Paris. She came to New York especially to make his acquaintance and to assure him of the welcome that awaited him in Washington.[8] It was an encounter that touched him deeply. The letter he wrote afterward expressed the warmth of human presence he had felt and how it affected him: "Il y avait tant de bienveillance et de délicatesse dans votre accueil, que j'ai senti, pour la première fois, se détendre en moi cette dureté que je m'efforce de maintenir dans ma solitude d'exilé."[9]

But the exile in him also drew back easily into his solitude. A step forward was usually followed by an opposite move and a period of silence. Almost two months passed before he wrote to her again. The interim was explained by the assertion that he had lost all sense of time in the desert in which he lived and where speech seemed incongruous: "J'émerge à peine de ce Gobi où le mutisme me paraissait mon premier devoir social."[10] Lest his situation appear unique or subject to self-pity, however, he instantly qualified and expanded the notion of his personal exile to human beings in general—and to animals:

Quant à l'exil lui-même, n'est-il pas partout, à commencer par le coeur de la femme? Je le trouve, en tout cas, dans l'oeil du petit noir qui me cire les chaussures, dans l'oeil du cheval de police qui me refuse chaque nuit, avec la même douceur, mon morceau de sucre sur la voie publique.[11]

He would even, a short time afterward, be able to see his own role with something resembling irony. For he spoke of his muteness as an "armure d'exilé, qui ressemble un peu trop à l'habit du scaphandrier,"[12] aware of the rigidity, the heaviness, and the insulation it provided while impairing the freedom of movement. Movement, always an integral part of his life, now began once again to occupy his mind. He considered ways to change his life, occupy his time, alter his habitat. To remain where he was had little appeal: being a navigator or a nomad horseman exploring the desert had its excitement; being a transient in a New York hotel was quite another matter. He started to listen to various proposals—a possible move to Argentina (where friends urged him to come)[13] but also one to Washington. The latter had been suggested by a fellow poet, Archibald MacLeish (who had already admired *Anabase* in Paris in the 1920s but had been discreet enough never to request a meeting with the man whose diplomatic functions demanded the greatest discretion when it came to literature), director of the Library of Congress since 1939. MacLeish now saw an opportunity to provide the exile with a position that was both honorable and (he hoped) interesting, as well as furnishing him with a modest means of livelihood: to become a literary consultant at the prestigious library.[14] The presence of the poet Allen Tate[15] and Katherine Biddle (who was the poetry consultant) seemed to MacLeish an added inducement, or at least an argument in favor of Leger's acceptance.

Leger hesitated before answering MacLeish's letters. When he did, it was with some caution, probably for a number of reasons: the ones cited were of a moral (and legal) order and had to do with accepting the salary provided by a national institution of a land where he was not a citizen[16] (and even classified as an "alien"); the others, not voiced, might easily have been related to his old dislike of libraries, the disgust for books, and the prospect of being shut up in such surroundings. The question of his salary was soon settled: the funds would come from private donations and take the form of a grant (such as the one that had been awarded Thomas Mann).[17] The other was outweighed by the human qualities of MacLeish: his offer was so carefully prepared and made with such tact and delicacy that it could not help but touch one.

Leger decided to accept and to make his move to Washington at the beginning of 1941. MacLeish, in his enthusiasm, made other friendly plans as well: for Leger to give lectures at various institutions in the United States. But these Leger rebuffed, politely but with firmness. "J'aspire de tout mon être, à sauvegarder encore dans ma retraite, le maximum de solitude, de silence et de repli sur moi," he wrote[18], as though someone had invaded the island on which he still needed to remain alone. Apparently, although isolation and muteness at times appeared to be an abyss into which he was plunged,[19] it was not yet time for him to emerge, and he needed an interim of distance and anonymity.

The streets of Manhattan were the perfect place for this. He spent many hours walking there, invisible in the crowds, seeing yet unseen.[20] The very vastness of the city spelled exile also, for nothing was scaled down to human size. One could disappear easily and escape from one's own species. He began to frequent the company of animals—the squirrels whose friendship he cultivated in Central Park, the gulls he watched flying over the East River.[21] And he began to spend a great deal of time also in the vicinity of the port area where ships moved to and fro and of the sea, which evoked so many memories.

True, they were bitter memories as harsh as the winter that caused sheets of ice to nearly block the estuary. In December the news from France overwhelmed him with anguish once more. It was the fate of the women he loved that he found hardest to bear, for, as he said:

Il est facile, pour un homme, d'accepter l'épreuve personnelle, de lui souhaiter même la bienvenue comme à l'étranger qui franchit notre seuil; mais comment supporter, à distance, l'épreuve de ceux qui nous sont chers et pour qui l'on ne peut rien? La pire souffrance virile, n'est-elle pas pour un homme, de faire défaut à d'autres êtres?[22]

His cry echoed an anguish felt long ago, after his father's death, when he had exclaimed: "Je ne peux rien pour ces quatre coeurs de femmes que de me tenir près d'elles."[23] But now he could not be near them or any that he held dear. A bitter sense of failure and impotence assailed him, stronger than any he had felt before.

The year 1940 ended on this cruel note, a winter solstice far darker than the one had experienced, in Peking, a generation ago.

The new year, however, brought fresh movement into his life. Only a month after it had begun, he arrived in Washington. The city seemed to be half botanical garden and half crossroad. Built next to a rich forest many of whose giant oaks had been preserved, filled with rare and varied vegetation, it seemed a series of green islands; but it was also a place where all the paths of the world met, where people from every point of the globe gathered and dispersed, and the revolving doors of the imposing edifices swallowed or disgorged a constant flow of passers-through.[24]

He had found a small lodging in this city that appeared to be another "geometrical locus"[25] of the world. It was located on an abstract street of this abstract city, with an address defined only by a number and a letter in the alphabet: 3120 A Street, N.W.[26] In a large building with numerous dwellings on each floor, the one and a half rooms were sparsely furnished. His mode of life also was spartan: an erratic cleaning lady did the household chores a few hours a week; unused to dealing with material details, he depended for sustenance on a small Chinese restaurant, the corner drugstore, the eggs he sometimes attempted to cook on an improvised stove, the hospitality of a few friends.[27] His suitcases always remained half packed, ready for instant departure,[28] or indicating that this nomad had not settled here for good.

But there was also a more sedentary side to his life now. His work at the Library of Congress had begun. From morning to evening, he sat among the dusty books, feeling that he must honor the task he had undertaken, prove his usefulness, pay his homage to hospitality. He started to research and prepare a complex reference work for the library: "A Selection of Works for an

Understanding of World Affairs since 1914,"[29] a subject that must have (not always pleasantly) recalled many of his experiences of the past decades.

The surroundings in which he worked were also far from pleasing. Isolated in his own "petite cellule vitrée,"[30] evoking solitary confinement, he worked for hours on end. But if his quarters seemed prisonlike, the main reading areas of the library were even more objectionable: "Là-même où furent, par milliers, les livres tristes sur laies comme servantes et filles de louage."[31] It was a sight that made his gorge rise, with the same intensity as long ago, enough to make him want to spew forth all this fetid matter. One day he would write (but could now only think silently):

Les livres tristes, innombrables, sur leur tranche de craie pâle . . . tout ce talc d'usure et de sagesse, et tout cet attouchement des poudres du savoir . . . dépôt d'abîmes sur leur fèces, limons et lies à bout d'avilissement—cendres et squames de l'esprit.[32]

Once in a while an event occurred that made his laughter break forth and ring through the hushed atmosphere. One such incident upset and mystified the officials of the library: each day, a fresh deposit of excrement was found on the dome that crowned the venerable edifice. The police, called in, suspected that it was the handiwork of vicious jokers. Then it was discovered that the "jokers" were none other than an enterprising pair of vultures who lived, during the day, at the Washington Zoo and had decided to establish their night quarters at the highest point of the Victorian structure.[33] But the "Ange de l'Absurde"[34] did not for long brush the library with its wings. Once the mystery was solved, everything sank back again into its stifling routine. Then only his imagination (and the humor recently reawakened) could provide the diversion he craved. He began to make observations—often of a zoological nature—of the creatures who came to inhabit the library. One of his most delighted (and delightful) discoveries concerned nothing more unusual than the drinking fountains in the hallways, where he saw:

l'eau très pure et consolante qui, dans les petites vasques des couloirs, comme dans les serres et volières des jardins d'acclimatation, continue d'être prodiguée aux gorges de colombes des dactylographes, aux gorges de lézardes des étudiantes chinoises, aux gorges de tortues des vieux "Scholars."[35]

Inventions such as these helped the days pass, as did conversations with MacLeish, who had become a friend. After work, he walked across the green expanse of Washington, the verdant slopes of this white city that floated above the ground like a light summer mist,[36] to return to his spartan quarters and essentially solitary life. "Jamais exil ne fut assumé dans plus de simplicité et d'honneur,"[37] one of his old friends thought. To him, it was simpler than that. He sensed the need to reduce everything to basics at this juncture in time.

Perhaps that is why he spent so much of his free time at the zoo. The animals there were more exiled than he but assumed their state with more patience and dignity than humans. He was deeply moved when he found the "Cheval de Prjevalsky" among them.[38] All his life in China came rushing back, the journey on horseback across the Gobi Desert, and *Anabase*—written so long ago—"poème de la solitude dans l'action."[39]

Was it then that he dimly realized that his own exile was not only circumstantial, nor even the universal state of exile that is human fate, but also due to the part of himself that he had so long exiled from his life and that was clamoring to return? Now that the diplomat had been annihilated, the poet demanded to be heard. Perhaps that is why he had, almost rudely, rebuffed MacLeish's suggestion—after his arrival in Washington—that he begin to write again and had protested that this would never occur.[40] Yet, as the year turned and spring made its insistent incursions everywhere, he found that the urge toward words mounted as steadily as the sap in the bark, ready to break out with the same force as shoots and leaves.

When, at the start of summer, his friends Katherine and Francis Biddle offered him the use of their house at the edge of the sea, he acquiesced—with a strange sort of trepidation and an excitement that spoke of stirrings in some deep recess of his being.

Summer, 1941, Long Beach Island[41]

It was a naked place: nothing but sea, stretches of sand, sparse vegetation, and isolation. Everything was reduced here, pared to the core. Only essentials prevailed. It suited his needs—absolutely.

During the early part of his sojourn, time became nil; he let the nothingness invade him, reaching a state close to nonbeing. Sometimes, as he lay flat on the sand, it seemed that he had come to the lowest level of life possible, that to go further would be entry into the void. His bodily functions nearly ceased: breathing slowed almost to nonexistence; his extremities seemed endlessly far away: he felt he had become transparent and could hardly feel his pulse beat or blood coursing through his veins.

For a long time, he remained thus. Level with the sea, the sand. On the verge of nullity. Then, slowly, there was a turning back. He started to become aware of the faintest of sounds, a slight touch of air, a glimmer of light on the sea, a blade of grass. His hand moved, without his volition it seemed, to encounter a small object—a pebble or beach glass; the cry of a gull pierced the silence that had descended on him; the odor of brine forced its way into his nostrils.

One after the other all his senses returned. And they were present with a new keenness. It was as though he had been born again. It seemed to this new being that he encountered words for the first time, in all their freshness and nascent splendor. Words came rushing forth, with a power gained from the death they had conquered, the silence in which they had for so long been entombed. A work was forming within him, pouring out with such imperious force that it left him humble before its onslaught. He knew what it was to be in labor, to bear what was no longer a stillbirth. And he also knew that the work would be greater than anything he had created before: "un grand poème né de rien, un grand poème fait de rien."[42]

The poem would speak of a return to life's origin, of birth and rebirth, of naming and being named, of claiming a birthright: "Les mains plus nues qu'à ma naissance et la lèvre plus libre. . . . Me voici restitué à ma rive natale."[43] "J'habiterai mon nom,"[44] the poet would exclaim, and chant, exultantly: "Ma gloire est sur les sables! ma gloire est sur les sables! . . . J'ai fondé sur l'abîme et l'embrun et la fumée des sables."[45]

But he would also cast a longing look backward and let the poem remember what the exile had left behind. It lingered, with tenderness, on the women loved (and lost)—two among them, most of all: "ô mère du Proscrit . . . Et toi . . . compagne de sa force et faiblesse de sa force, toi dont le souffle au sien fut à jamais mêlé."[46] Tenderness that it must tenderly chide in order to vanquish; the backward glance that must be refused if new passions were to arise. The poet who would assume his place among the "princes de l'exil"[47] must utter a cry that cut away the past and move toward future illuminations:

Tais-toi, faiblesse, et toi, parfum d'épouse dans la nuit comme l'amande même de la nuit. . . . Tais-toi douceur, et toi présence gréée d'ailes . . . Je reprendrai ma course de Numide, longeant la mer inaliénable. . . . Ceux qui flairent l'idée neuve aux fraîcheurs de l'abîme . . . savent qu'aux sables de l'exil sifflent les hautes passions lovées sous le fouet de l'éclair.[48]

As he wrote the last words of his poem, he knew that he had reached a turning point. A new phase in the cycle of death and rebirth had opened. A fateful moment had arrived: "Et c'est l'heure, ô Poète, de décliner ton nom, ta naissance, et ta race."[49]

When he left the island, at the end of that summer of summers, the poem "Exil" had been born. Alexis Leger was gone. Saint-John Perse had come to life.

1941–1948

Years of intense creativity now followed for the poet. One after the other, like flashes of lightning, the works appeared annually—once *Exil* had opened the way: *Poème à l'Etrangère*,

Pluies, Neiges, Vents.[50] It was as though a dam had broken and
all that had been harbored in darkness and in silence came rushing forth. The phase of his greatest productivity had begun.

Saint-John Perse (as he now signed his work, having arrived at
the fullness of his name) emerged victorious from the shadows.
Having stated his name, his birth, and his race,[51] he proceeded
to render them illustrious. Past poems were brought back into
the light; *Eloges* would be published in a bilingual edition, with
an introduction by MacLeish, by Norton: *Anabase*, especially
thanks to T. S. Eliot's translation, which had appeared in England and America, and Octavio Barreda's Spanish translation
published in Mexico, had established the reputation of Perse on
this continent[52] and prepared the way for further works he
wrote. The newest poem, *Exil*, dedicated to MacLeish (and presented as a gift, to him, in manuscript form), appeared almost
instantly—in French—in *Poetry* magazine (Chicago, March
1942), was reproduced, first, by the *Cahiers du Sud* (Marseille,
May 1942), then at the Editions des Lettres Françaises (Buenos
Aires, July 1942), and by La Baconnière (Neuchâtel, October
1942), and finally in Paris, clandestinely, by Gallimard (in a private edition, signed only "S. J. P." and "N. R. F.," on October 15,
1942).[53] A young Irish poet, Denis Devlin, began to undertake
the translation of the poem into English.[54]

It was the beginning of a new, joyous "compagnonnage." The
two men usually walked up the hilly green streets (which reminded Devlin of his native Ireland) after lunch, to Perse's apartment in Georgetown, to work on the translation. They spoke of
poetry, unaware of their surroundings, already totally absorbed
in the task that awaited them. Devlin was struck by Perse's extraordinary impersonality when discussing his own work—pro-
ceeding as though they had a Latin text before them, in whose
composition he had had no part, or—even more so—some fragment preserved from one of those mysterious civilizations that
his poetry touched upon. Meanings were explored and explained
almost entirely through grammar and linguistics; the very matter
of poetry became, first and foremost, language. The poet, as

master and guardian of language—it seemed to Devlin—the figure that Perse incarnated, appeared to officiate with words newborn, like a priest of an ancient and secret sect. His insistence on
the purity of sound, and the importance he attached to rhythm,
added to the charm of their discussions. Perse, as a poet, was
fundamentally convinced of the impossibility of transposing a
work into another language and preserving its integrity (which,
Devlin agreed, was indeed impossible) and sometimes reduced
his translator to the most comical despair. But the latter de-
fended his territory with valor, standing his ground, and even
winning at times—if he could show deviations from the Latin
root or the impossibility of the same cadence for analogous
polysyllables in both languages. They worked for long hours
together, in this form of friendly combat, until evening fell
softly over the city, and the voice of a black man in the streets
underlined, for an instant, the color of a rhythm. Then they put
down their various dictionaries, and it all ended in a burst of
laughter.[55]

There arose also, at that time, another sort of "compagnonnage" that joined the poet to a mysterious woman. She was a
stranger, just as he, "l'Alienne" whom he would identify only as
having "le sang vert des Castilles" flowing in her veins,[56] and
became a companion in exile. He would address her, with his
usual reserve, but also with tenderness and understanding, in
the work that emerged in 1942: *Poème à l'Etrangère*.[57] The poem
would carry no dedication (in contrast to the other works of this
period), and its author would say only that it was written "en
hommage à une amie étrangère qui connut aussi l'exil en Amérique,"[58] with characteristic discretion or desire for secrecy (that
surrounded all his relationships with women). But it hardly matters if we shall never learn the name or identity of the unknown
"amie" (that word which has such delightfully ambiguous meanings); the poem itself reveals much more than any description
could provide:

Its epigraph, "Alien Registration Act," instantly establishes
the link between the two aliens whose dialogue will follow—
"L'Etrangère" (or "L'Alienne") and "[l] homme de France,"

whom the former exhorts: "Vous qui chantez . . . vous qui chantez tous banissements au monde, ne me chanterez-vous pas un chant du soir à la mesure de mon mal? . . . un chant de grâce pour l'attente . . . ?"[59]

The poet will comply, first with attempts at consolation by pointing out the charms of animals (a red bird, dressed like a "prince de l'Eglise," that is, a "cardinal"; a squirrel on the veranda; a pair of eagles that hold the city under its spell—perhaps a euphemistic version of the vultures on the roof the Library of Congress). But these attempts will fail, and the plaintive voice of "la veuve," as "l'Etrangère" is also called, will counter with: "Oui tout cela . . . pèse moins qu'à mes mains nues de femme une clé d'Europe teinte de sang."[60]

The poet's exhortations continue to counteract the woman's mourning with examples of the splendor of nature, "grandes roses d'équinoxe comme aux verrières des Absides," "le fruit du mûrier [qui fait] . . . de si belles tâches de vin mûr," and culminating in the exclamation: "l'abîme enfante ses merveilles: lucioles!"[61] But, suddenly arrested in midspeech by the grandeur of her suffering, he will exclaim (as if he had seen the true face of tragedy):

Poème à l'Etrangère! Poème à l'Emigrée! . . . Chaussée de crêpe ou d'amarante entre vos hautes malles inécloses! O grande par le coeur et par le cri de votre race! . . . L'Europe saigne à vos flancs comme la Vierge du Toril.[62]

The Poet then, having bowed before his companion's pain, joins her in sorrow: "Sur le tambour voilé des lampes à midi, nous mènerons encore plus d'un deuil, chantant l'hier, chantant l'ailleurs, chantant le mal à sa naissance"; but, significantly, he adds: "et la splendeur de vivre."[63] Having affirmed the profound paradox of existence (which a young man, named Alexis, had discovered long ago), the equilibrium between pain and joy, mourning and splendor, the Stranger begins his wanderings anew. His path is both a thrust forward and a return, freedom from memory and memory reclaimed; and his chant transcends the human and is most poignantly human:

je m'en vais, ô mémoire! à mon pas d'homme libre, sans horde ni tribu, parmi le chant des sabliers, et, le front nu, lauré d'abeilles de phosphore . . . sifflant mon peuple de Sybilles, sifflant mon peuple d'incrédules, je flatte encore en songe, de la main, parmi tant d'êtres invisibles, ma chienne d'Europe qui fut blanche et, plus que moi, poète.[64]

Thus, in the years that had elapsed since *Exil*, with its stark and solitary splendor, a road had opened that led the alien into the human world once more—a realm of friendships, new tenderness, and contact with his fellowmen. And even the bitterness of the diplomat, the need to efface this side of his life, yielded to the urgency of humanistic concerns. The voice of Leger made itself heard once more (although in the wings): he expressed his solidarity with the French resistance movement and wrote at length to Churchill analyzing its inner workings; he aided the representives of La France Libre (despite his wish not to become involved with the military and political aspects of the organization and declining de Gaulle's invitation to join him in London); published a message to Frenchmen in America (on July 14, 1942) in *France-Amérique;* pronounced a speech in memory of Briand in the same year.[65] All affirmed the belief that every man must measure "la souffrance humaine sur la terre"[66] and fulfill his human obligation. Perhaps more than any of his other actions, it was his commemoration of Briand that expressed his deepest feelings. He remembered his mentor and companion in all his complexity but honored most of all Briand's dream of international peace—and his humanity.[67]

A flow of feeling had begun to fructify the arid soil of isolation. In the third year of exile, it began to inundate his poetry, changing absence to presence, drought to flood tide. For it can be no accident that the great work that then poured forth was a celebration of that force whose fecundating role is as ancient as the world (and as the human imagination): rain.

The actual composition of *Pluies* (*Rains*)[68] supposedly occurred on a trip to the South (which coincided with nascent emotions that had slowly accumulated). It was a joint venture with friends—Katherine and Francis Biddle, in particular—and took the voyagers to South Carolina and Georgia.[69] As they progressed in a southward direction, the changes in vegetation produced a strange sensation in him. It was as though they journied not only through space but also in time. For the flora of his childhood appeared once more, and familiar surroundings gave him a feeling of déjà vu that was almost uncanny. It increased when they stopped at Beaufort (still filled with signs of Franco-Hispanic history) and stayed at Tidalhome, a grand old colonial dwelling surrounded by magnificent green oaks draped in Spanish moss, and visited the plantations of the environs, the ruins of chapels, and cemeteries with the tombs of aristocrats.[70] Added to all these evocative sites were the laughing faces of black children in the Penn School whose natural outburst of hilarity (when he addressed them in French)[71] charmed him—being so reminiscent of the "rires dans du soleil"[72] that had brightened his early days.

They moved farther south, stopping at Sapelo Island in Georgia where one of his ancestors (a former officer in the Royal Army who had emigrated there during the French Revolution) had lived and died in exile. Nothing was left now except a few vestiges of the eighteenth-century habitation, and even his tomb had been washed into the sea.[73] The "Man of the Atlantic" had long been reclaimed by the ocean, but his descendant was reminded of his birth and his race.

They traveled on. Nature itself now seemed to underscore their voyage with its phenomena. Adding to the recall of the past, the gathering of memories, a heavy pressure made itself felt in the air. After a long period of drought that had scorched the soil and rendered it sterile, an autumn storm was brewing. A strange sense of expectation hovered over the land, as though it waited to be delivered from its torpor. The voyagers themselves were in state of unusual excitation, as if on the brink of a momentous event.

Almost immediately after they had arrived at their hotel in Savannah, the dam of the sky broke. A torrential downpour came down on the earth. Vast bolts of lightning tore through the clouds. A long sigh of deliverance seemed to fill the world.

He rose and left his friends. At the window of his room, facing south, he sat and watched the rains pour down all night. At dawn he went to his table and began to write.

When he rejoined them in the morning, his face showed the traces of the sleepless night; it seemed as if his gaze was still filled with shadows. Although he tried to resume the gay, bantering tone of conversation that had enlivened their voyage, they sensed that something momentous had intervened. Only later, so great was his discretion when it came to writing, did they discover that he had brought back from this journey—in the small looseleaf notebook they sometimes had seen him take furtively from his pocket—the first draft of his long poem, *Pluies*.[74]

The final version of the work revealed all these experiences—and much more: it was dated Savannah, 1943, and dedicated to Katherine and Francis Biddle;[75] the opening and penultimate sequence of *Pluies* framed the poem with a striking image, "le banyan de la pluie"[76] (that establishes and releases its hold on the City, as the storm breaks and subsides), linked past and present, memory and purgation of memory. The nine sections of the work (a number ever significant for Perse) proceeded to trace the purification and liberation effected by rain(s) through a variety of means: those of female warriors and dancers;[77] lightning in its most erotic guise, which vivifies desire and resuscitates fertility;[78] most of all, laughter (of almost olympian proportions, a dreadful and joyous divinity: "Seigneur terrible de mon rire," evoked repeatedly in the poem).[79] And to celebrate the great tasks accomplished by the rains—ablution, epuration, lustration, absolution—with their ability to cleanse everything in the world, laving the face of the dead and the living, the strong and the violent, those afflicted with doubt and prudence, smugness, culture, and knowledge.[80]

In the long litany addressed to the Rains, the Poet finally asks them to purify poetry itself, thus evoking their powers, not only to purge all dross, but also to consecrate man's highest achievements:

O Pluies! lavez au coeur de l'homme les plus beaux dits de l'homme!
les plus belles sentences, les plus belles séquences, les phrases les
mieux faites, les pages les mieux nées . . . lavez, lavez la literie du
songe et la litière du savoir: au coeur de l'homme sans refus, au coeur
de l'homme sans dégoût, lavez, lavez, ô Pluies! les plus beaux dons de
l'homme.[81]

But the work goes even further; acknowledging that epuration
verges on the Void, that language cannot render the ineffable,
the poem advances the belief that the true celebration of the
Rains takes place in silence, in that "poème, ô Pluies! qui ne fut
pas écrit!"[82] by a poet who remains, awed and mute, at the
threshold of creation.

The deepest understanding of such a poem came, naturally,
from a kindred spirit: Conrad Aiken, the great American poet
(who had also been among the first to welcome Saint-John Perse
in this country).[83] He would speak of *Pluies* as a litany of litanies
that related and incarnated the sad and rich, terrible and glorious history of humankind, a poem from which one emerged
metamorphosed, having been led—as if ritually—to the true
knowledge of being and, after being freed from enslavement and
shame, able to proceed onward. And he concluded by judging it
to be one of the most beautiful poems of the century.[84]

To be thus welcomed, humanly and poetically, by such fellow
poets as Aiken and MacLeish meant a great deal. It even made
the return to less privileged realms bearable. The latter had
lightened the stay at the Library of Congress by his presence.
Another poet would render that institution a meeting ground by
his companionship: Tate, the most brilliant representative of the
southern school of poets, the Fugitives.[85] The two men met in
the autumn of 1943, shortly after Perse's return from the South,
and instantly became friends. Tate never forgot the unusual courtesy, patience, and dignity of Perse—nor his spontaneity[86]—and
rejoiced in the exchange that came so naturally to them, given
his own sensitivity to French poetry and Perse's vast and exact
knowledge of English verse.[87] Perse, on the other hand, valued
not only Tate's human qualities but also his work, especially
Seasons of the Soul, in which he saw "L'élégance de 'l'âme' la

cruauté envers soi et le refus de toute complaisance sont ici tels,
que la nudité y semble poussée jusqu'à l'invisibilité"[88]—
qualities that encountered his own. It was thus with great joy
that he accepted the offer made by Tate, who edited the *Sewanee
Review,* to publish *Pluies* (a task that Tate undertook with infinite, and touching, care).[89]

There can be little doubt that contacts with men of poetry such
as these, coupled with the liberating force that had now been
unleashed by his own writing, caused Perse to move forward
with great strides now. His works emerged in rapid succession
during this period: *Neiges* in 1944, *Vents* in 1945.

The first of these, however, arose during a time of deep dis-
tress. Written in the dead of winter, in New York where he
stayed once more in the lonely heights of a hotel room, it was to
be a gift for his mother,[90] a gift born of anguish, regret, and pity.
He had recently had the most distressing news of her from
France, where aged, alone, and in captivity, she lived far from
her son. Once again, the torment of knowing that he had failed
those he loved assailed him, coupled with the added guilt of
learning that his very name caused part of their woes[91] (since the
enmity it had attracted at the end of his diplomatic career now
surely fell on his family). He spent endless hours looking for
ways to aid them; his thoughts turned as if in a cage, finding no
solution. "Je me cogne la tête à tous les murs, à la recherche de
vaines formules,"[92] he exclaimed, feeling more harshly than ever
the gulf that separated them, the distance that had kept them
apart for so many years of their lives, the closeness of death that
was inevitably drawing near, given her great age.[93]

All this, and winter with its further power to isolate, assailed
him. As he looked out at the impersonal expanse of the city
below, snow began to fall—silent, secret, covering footsteps and
effacing paths, enveloping the world as in a shroud. All his longing, regret, and pity gathered and culminated in a poem.

The "vaines formules" he had turned about in his mind before
were transformed into lines of such purity and beauty that inca-
pacity and absence became powerful presence, empty-handed-
ness a gift of rare price, the accursed name that of a great poet.

It was an intimate offering he made to his mother, in the form of *Neiges*, as gentle and subtle as snow, filled with familial details (which had not appeared since *Pour fêter une enface*, written when she was first widowed), where she appeared, whitened by age, bowed with sorrow, and waiting, but endowed with pure grace and mute understanding, evoked by the poet—full of melancholy and infinite tenderness—amid the mysterious and dreamlike fragility, the marvel of the snows. Bridging the vast expanse, crossing the war-torn seas, breaking captivity and loneliness, his cry resounded: "Et il y a un si long temps que veille en moi cette affre de douceur," and (as if she had answered without speaking): "et il y a un si long temps que veille en nous cette affre de douceur."[94] Regret mingled with smiles; muteness became wordless communion; pity turned to grandeur; language attained its most ancient strata and moved, finally, into the realm of the unnameable, where pure silence reigned. "Qu'on nous laisse tous deux à ce langage sans paroles dont vous avez l'usage, ô vous toute présence, ô vous toute patience!"[95] he chanted, entering into a domain of the most profound union, that which precedes birth—but also that of poetry. "Désormais cette page où plus rien ne s'inscrit"[96] were the last words of this offering beyond words.

(*Neiges* would be published and sold for the benefit of the Comité français de secours aux victimes de la guerre.[97] The name "Leger" would be vindicated when the poet's nationality and full rights as a citizen were restored and he was reinstated as ambassador "en disponibilité," shortly afterwards at the liberation of France.[98] It was as though the poem, in some strange way, furnished the aid he had despaired of providing and removed the stigma and threat from his name.)

The spring of 1945 brought other auspicious signs. The war that had devastated such a large part of the world (and would claim the hideous sum of 36 million victims by the time it was over) was drawing to an end. The last, fierce battles raged, but it seemed that the downfall of Germany was certain. On May 8 the Wehrmacht capitulated in Berlin.

It was as though a heavy weight had been lifted. Peace was once again possible. The seas would be open once more. The barrier of war no longer shut Europe off from this side of the world. As if in response to this liberating sensation, he began to travel more widely than before: south, west, and north, in a movement that embraced a large part of the continent. He visited the Sea Islands off the coast of Georgia, stopping at Cumberland (a large private island, where wild horses and marine eagles had their habitat); went to Texas and Arizona (exploring craters formed by comets and the flora and fauna of the Painted Desert); continued to the Grand Canyon and the gorges of Colorado (to make geological observations); then navigated along the Maine coast and in the gulf of the Saint-Laurent in Canada.[99]

In the summer, however, he returned to a place that had become a favorite retreat several years ago: Seven Hundred Acre Island, near Dark Harbor (Maine). It was a wonderfully savage place, more isolated than ever, due to the war, which had closed villas on neighboring islands, drafted fishermen, forbidden navigation at certain hours, and added to the mystery of this place— closed in upon itself "comme une âme forte et silencieuse et sûre d'elle-même et dont l'intimité . . . est chaque jour une révélation nouvelle."[100] It belonged to Beatrice Chanler, "une vieille amie de France," full of "affectueuse sollicitude,"[101] a fascinating woman whom he had met in Paris long ago, seen when he visited Washington as a young diplomat, and found again when he came as an exile to New York, who did her utmost to "alléger les premières épreuves de sa solitude."[102]

He had already spent a month at this island in the summer of 1942, living the life of an explorer, woodcutter, and poacher; examining shipwrecks; swimming in the icy waters; and resuming with passion his studies in entomology, botany, and geology. As his only companions, he had a large Irish setter and two strange young women who did the housework, the daughters of a Penobscot Indian and a Danish sailor, who taught him the name of the "simples" of the region and some of their ancestral rites (never to pull a plant out of the earth without returning something—if possible, a bit of tobacco—in exchange), as well as watching for any unusual happenings in the night sky and awakening him at the first signs of an aurora borealis. Among his visitors he counted some ospreys, a blue heron, a solitary old seal that accompanied him as he swam or followed along the shore as he walked, as well as swarms of cormorants and loons.[103] It was a place and form of life that suited him wonderfully, joining action and dream—an infallible combination, as far as he was concerned. "Je devrai beaucoup à cette île, où j'ai consommé déjà tant de solitude, et marché, de jour en jour, dans des songes plus riches,"[104] he had written three years ago.

It was to this island where he now returned, to complete the greatest work he had undertaken to date. A poem more vast in scope and vision than any he had written before, the sum of many experiences and deep drives, the unleashing of his own (and the universe's) greatest powers, "Vents" he knew would crown his achievements as a poet.[105] And yet, this "homme parlant dans l'équivoque,"[106] at the time of its completion, wrote one of his most enigmatic pronouncements concerning his role as a poet, to a friend:

Vous me retrouverez . . . un tout autre homme—car c'est une oeuvre assez étrange que je suis venue cette fois achever ici dans la solitude: destruction en moi du poète . . . il est plus difficile de détruire que de bâtir. L'île un peu sombre et très nordique où je m'attarde pour cette besogne m'y aura grandement aidé par la sévérité de ses eaux froides. . . . Sachez seulement, que ce n'est pas par plaisir, loin de là, ni par affectation, que j'ai eu à étrangler en moi le seul être qui me soit au fond naturel, et que j'ai déjà eu à combattre toute ma vie.[107]

Evidently (and most fortunately, for poetry) the strangulation attempt did not succeed. Paradoxically, the work that emerged was infused with an enormous breath that sweeps through the entire universe: respiration as vital (and as intimate) as human breathing, but also divine afflatus that rules the motion of the cosmos and is the harbinger of destruction and creation.

The Winds that reign in "Vents" triumph over all "hommes de paille, en l'an de paille,"[108] over all that is worn or dry, as they

liberate singing desire, its face burning with love and violence.[109]

Their gusts shake the great tree of language. The "Narrator,"
their companion, will—like a shaman—proclaim (with sacrificial
rites) the birth of fresh life, as he chants: "Se hâter, se hâter!
Parole de vivant!"[110] And, as the Winds increase in force, the
divinity of the Storm appears, full of license and awesome
power: it awakens the virulence of the spirit in the salt flats, and
the fresh scent of the erotic in the forests; seed and sap swell, life
bursts forth to vanquish all that was formerly sere, dead, hollow.
It disperses all barriers and means of orientation, divides the
wheat from the chaff, dead works from living, and awakens "les
écritures nouvelles encloses dans les grandes schistes à venir."[111]
"Tout à reprendre. Tout à redire. Et la faux du regard sur tout
l'avoir menée!"[112] the poet exclaims and proceeds to renew all
experience—through laughter, as violent as the Storm: the first
cut of the scythe mows down the "Basilique du Livre,"[113] altars
without meaning, all that is lukewarm, fetid, festering. And his
cry resounds in the wind: "S'en aller! s'en aller! Parole de vivant!"[114]

Celebrating the god of the abyss with sacrificial rites and hierogamy,[115] he then arises—free, unpredictable, assailed by the
god, drunk on new wine, and as if pierced by lightning[116] —to
move to the very frontiers of the human, now that all seals have
been broken. And the Poet, his face in the wind, sings to the
accompaniment of the typhoon, the glory of the storm, of desire,
of movement beyond all limits.[117]

This movement is ever westward. The poet-voyager, led by the
Wind (his "Maître du chant," "Maître de camp"),[118] moves toward the splendor of the West, place of death and rebirth ("où
vont les hommes vers leurs tombes," "là-bas mûrissent les purs
ferments d'une ombre prénatale"),[119] the true homeland of all
men of desire, as Claudel would say.[120] New Lands, new waters,
new women, new years, new worlds, new texts appear. And a
new being arises—hard, stripped to the bone, reduced to skeletal purity, as is the shaman[121]—who reaches summits never attained before: the Poet who speaks as would an oracle, in a

double tongue ("versions données sur deux versants! . . . Toi-même stèle et pierre d'angle")[122] and is addressed thus by the poet:

O Poète, ô bilingue, entre toutes choses bisaiguës, et toi-même litige entre toutes choses litigeuses—homme assailli du dieux! homme parlant dans l'équivoque! . . . ah! comme un homme fourvoyé dans une mêlée d'ailes et de ronces, parmi les noces de busaigles![123]

Having reached the zenith, illuminated by his vision but menaced by the encounter with the divine (for one does not frequent the sacred with impunity),[124] the Poet, who has attained the outermost limits in his encounter with lightning and having himself assumed the dread form of lightning,[125] must turn back. The superhuman has been rejoined. Now the cry of the human demands to be heard. And the Poet will heed it:

Mais c'est de l'homme qu'il s'agit . . .
—Quelqu'un au monde élèvera-t-il la voix?
. . . .
Se hâter! se hâter! temoignage pour l'homme![126]

Returning to the world of men, he stands among them, "avec tous hommes de patience, avec tous hommes de sourire . . . avec tous hommes de douceur . . . avec hommes d'abîme et de grand large. . . . Car c'est de l'homme qu'il s'agit et de son renouement."[127] The link with the human has been reaffirmed. The Poet, however, must never forget his vision, the "pupille ouverte sur l'abîme" that now illuminates his view of the world: "Contribution aussi de l'autre rive! Et révérence au Soleil noir d'en bas!"[128] His works will reflect the "other shore," the "black Sun of the nether regions" while celebrating the presence of the human world: "Et le Poète . . . est avec nous. . . . Son occupation parmi nous. . . . Non point l'écrit, mais la chose même. Prise en son vif et dans son tout . . . Lieu du propos: toutes grèves de ce monde."[129]

Lest life, however, with its calm and redundancy, its tenderness and prudence, engulf the Poet, the Winds must ever serve as a reminder, an irritant, a goad; and waves of devastation, floods, storms recall his revelation and the encounter with the

divine he risks forgetting among humans. Renewing the earth—
and his works—by their violence (in an endless cycle of destruction and creation), they cause the old tree of language to be
replaced by new growth, "un autre arbre de haut rang montait
déjà des grandes Indes souterraines, avec sa feuille magnétique
et son chargement de fruits nouveaux."[130]

The poem, *Vents*, was a turn of the tide, a great divide, in the
life of the man who returned from his stay on the solitary island
off the coast of Dark Harbor: he was indeed "un autre homme,"
as predicted. He had, however, not garrotted the poet, as he had
planned. Instead, he had freed his voice, allowed it to resound in
his grandest work to date. And he himself emerged from his
fierce struggle against that part of his being with the knowledge
that, from now on, his true place was among poets.[131]

Indeed, their voices now began to arise, bearing witness to his
work. The first was Claudel's who, as soon as he had read the
poems of exile (published by Gallimard in France),[132] hastened
to write: "Ça a été une grande joie pour moi de posséder désormais avec vous, au-dessus du gouffre de ces quatre abominables
années, le pont monumental qu'établissent vos QUATRE magnifi-
ques POÈMES: Le malheur a du moins révélé à la France le grand
Poète qui se cachait sous le Serviteur méconnu."[133] Aiken, in
America, published his perceptive study of *Pluies*, almost at the
same time, placing the work of Saint-John Perse foremost among
those which produced a unified vision, combining total mastery
and complete freedom.[134] And Gide would soon speak of the
concluding portion of *Vents* as "un pont jeté vers l'avenir,"[135]
Evidently, they all recognized the works that had emerged during exile—during the long years of solitude, silence, absence—
as a bridge, a link, an affirmation of presence, a triumph of life.

The life of their creator would now also be assumed more fully,
more openly. The poet came into the fore—in his actual guise. In
November 1946 Saint-John Perse terminated his functions as
"Conseiller pour la Littérature Francaise" (which he had assumed since February 1941) at the Library of Congress[136] and
signed a contract with the Bollingen Foundation[137] that included
a "grant-in-aid"[138] or an annual stipend that would, hopefully,

permit him to remain in America with some form of independence through literary activities, rather than having to resume the servitude of public life in France.[139]

It was a choice made despite the urgings of old friends and supporters in the French diplomatic realm, who now also clamored for him to join their ranks. To Blum he wrote that, while remaining faithful to his beliefs and sympathies, he considered his administrative career terminated and that, if he returned to France, it would be only as a private citizen.[140] Paul-Boncour also desired that Leger return among them and wrote: "J'estime que vous devriez bien revenir partager nos misères, nos anxiétés, et hélas! faire votre possible . . . pour éviter que nous allions au pire."[141] And Claudel would attempt to incite him to come back (by means not atypical of his methods of persuasion), saying that Leger was being "forgotten" at the Quai d'Orsay and lecturing him on the error of "sulking" or assuming the stance of a "statue que la maxime stoïcienne nous engage à faire, de l'être vivant que nous sommes, après tout!"[142]

It was no use. Neither friendship nor anxious recall to duty nor reprimands and attempts to shame him into acceptance could sway him now. His mind was made up. He would remain in America—and as a poet.

In the next few years, however, no new work of poetry by Saint-John Perse appeared. It was as if he had, for the moment, exhausted his breath through *Vents* and must wait until he could begin again, until his forces swelled into another creation. In the interim, he traveled, gathered impressions, stored up raw materials. Significantly, he spent most of his time close to the sea: he visited the Florida Keys at the outermost point of the North American continent, navigated in the Gulf of Mexico, stayed on the islands of Sanibel and Captiva, and often spent long weeks in Cape Cod.[143]

The last of these places, Bound Brook Island at Wellfleet, was a favorite haunt mostly because of its owners, his friends the Biddles. With them, it was possible to simply live on the dunes, enjoying the "perfect no use" that they shared without reproach, and to look forward "au libre rire et à la chaleur humaine d'un beau partage d'été vers l'Atlantique."[144] They, in turn, were always delighted anew by his rare capacity for human warmth and understanding and by his simplicity in all dealings with people. They observed that he most enjoyed the company of forest rangers, fishermen, farmhands, cowboys, sailors—or someone like their gardener, a rough rustic man with large, gnarled hands, bushy red hair, and simple ways with whom Alexis spent almost all his time when visiting. They cut the bushes together, dug up old grapevines, transplanted all sorts of trees. The gardener followed the poet everywhere, faithfully, attentively, apparently fascinated by this odd stranger and became more familiar in his form of address as the days went by. One day Katherine Biddle heard him say to her friend: "O.K., O.K. 'Sonny Boy'! We'll do it your way." When she protested gently: "No, really you can't let him talk to you like that!" he answered: "And why not, dear Katherine? He's the only person in the world who calls me 'Sonny Boy.'"[145]

Just as he preferred simplicity and unaffectedness in human contacts, surprising people by his predilections, so were they frequently disconcerted by his tastes, expecting loftiness in everything done by this man who traveled in the highest diplomatic and social circles and was being recognized as a prince of poets. They would never have guessed that he disliked cocktail parties, was attracted by a certain crudeness in concrete things, was bored by games, liked physical activity but not sports, did not care for the theater but was enchanted by films (especially Westerns), had a penchant for folksongs and popular music.[146] Nor would they have suspected him of having a playful sense of humor and of being capable of amusing himself at the expense of others—especially if he found them pretentious. Thus, for example, one of the "précieuses" (not infrequent in literary cirlces) of Washington had once succeeded in penetrating the natural barriers that usually kept such creatures at a safe distance, and had said (obviously quite proud of her knowledgeability): "I know that you are a poet. But I don't know if it is T. S. Eliot who translated one of your works or if it is you who are the translator of one of his most famous poems." He instantly answered: "Your second hypothesis is the correct one." And during the entire course of the dinner, they continued to speak of a poem by T. S. Eliot entitled *Anabase*.[147]

Laughter, however, ceased abruptly for him in 1948. It was a year during which he plunged into a gulf of pain, probably the deepest he had ever experienced: on October 24 his mother died[148]—far from her son, in France. He had felt, with anguish, since the beginning of that year, how distant he was from her and his most profound "attaches humaines" but had judged that he could not yet return to France for simple material reasons (no lodging of his own, a salary "de disponibilité" of which hardly anything remained after taxes, and that he put at the disposal of his mother and an unmarried sister).[149] Now she was gone without his having been able to be near her at her last hour. Words were too weak to express his grief. "Je n'en parle pas," he wrote to his close friend, MacLeish. "C'est une profonde tristesse sur laquelle se referme mon coeur, et ma solitude s'en trouve grandement accrue. A ce coeur de mère je devais tout ce que j'ai pu garder de foi dans la nature humaine."[150] Thus he payed his last—and perhaps greatest—homage to her.

So much was ended now. All links with the past were disappearing. Old friends were ailing and dying (with the notable exception of Claudel who, it seemed to him, was living "la vieillesse splendide de Sophocle")[151]: Valéry and Fargue were both dead;[152] Larbaud was so diminished by paralysis and aphasia that it was dreadful to think of his plight.[153] It was with a heavy heart that he remembered this friend of his youth, so full of adventure and laughter, and recalled the story he had been told (about Larbaud's attempt to nominate him for the Académie Mallarmé):

Incapable d'articuler même un lambeau de phrase, on m'a peint sa lutte physique, sa crispation à son fauteuil et toute une longue torture de la face, pour arriver . . . après beaucoup d'efforts, à pousser, épuisé, un seul cri: qui était mon nom. Larbaud avait été le premier à prononcer mon nom, et ce nom était peut-être le dernier prononcé par lui.[154]

It was such thoughts that filled his mind now, as he felt shrouded once more in almost total solitude. Even his wanderings suddenly seemed to him empty motions, as he stalked this continent, which had nothing but an "intérêt planétaire" and brought him "rien d'humain";[155] on the contrary, it only accentuated the great distance that separated him from everything that had meant something in his life. True, he had improved his situation somewhat when he had changed apartments a year ago. For he now had a slightly less abstract address than before—a street with a name rather than a mere letter in the alphabet or, worse still, a plain cipher—2800 Woodley Road,[156] situated close to the Zoological Park he loved. But the sparse furnishings and the half-packed trunks seemed suddenly to speak of his essential isolation.

As spring and summer came, he began to travel once again— more out of innate restlessness than of desire. Or to seek solace in nature, as always before. He went to North Carolina, Tennessee, and Kentucky this time; and he decided to live for a while in the forest of the Smokies, following on foot a part of the Appalachian Trail. To give himself an aim in these wanderings, he undertook to reconstitute the itinerary of the eighteenth-century French botanist, Michaux, searching for a plant the latter had discovered and that had been forgotten for a great length of time.[157] As he moved through the forest, pitting himself against the elements, during this quest for a humble botanical specimen, "une plante rare et sans éclat, apparantée . . . à la famille des cyclamens,"[158] it was as though he groped for a hold on the simplest things, the most elementary (and elemental) forms of existence, in a struggle to return to life once more when its tide had nearly ebbed away.

1949–1960

"Haine en toute chose de l'abandon!" he wrote, less than a year later.[159] And, indeed, he had refused to yield to any such temptation. New friendships and an interest in new poets had sprung up: he had met Max-Pol Fouchet, a fellow poet and the editor of *Fontaine* (which had published the work of Saint-John Perse in Algeria during the war) after the latter had flown over the entire American continent with *Vents* in his mind, giving meaning to this immense expanse.[160] In their correspondence, which followed, he had asked Fouchet to write him about the poets of "les nouvelles générations." "Elles m'intéressent plus que toutes, et c'est précisément de ce côté-là que je suis sans contact humain," he added, but also inquired about those whom he had already read, such as René Char whom he considered among "les meilleurs [des] pur-sang," also Georges Schehadé, whose "pure voix poétique" he had himself encouraged by his wishes, and Henri Michaux.[161]

Concerning his own poetry, Saint-John Perse was somewhat more reticent. It was not yet time for him to begin a new work. For, while he knew that a poem had for years, perhaps decades, been ripening in his mind, he waited until the propitious moment for its creation had come. In the interim, he continued to travel, storing away related impressions, collecting materials, allowing his emotions to gather momentum. Perhaps that is why he went to the Virgin Islands that year; spent a month at Cape Hatteras, at the foot of an abandoned lighthouse (collecting plants from the sea and sands);[162] and finally returned to Cape Cod and to Maine once more. There, the preliminary work might begin, although he knew that he was not ready to broach his subject, not yet having arrived at the auspicious time or, as he termed it:

J'ai beaucoup à travailler, pour mener à terme une oeuvre de longue haleine, la plus ambitieuse que j'aie en vue, mais que j'ai dû trop souvent déserter: je m'interdis en effet d'y céder tant que pèsent sur moi tristesse et soucis, car je me suis juré, en défi de notre temps, de n'y accueillir que de la joie, libre et librement donnée.[163]

He would await joy, which he knew must follow pain—as surely as the day the night—for he would not write otherwise, refusing to reconnaître à la création poétique d'autre objet que la libération de la joie, ou plus exactement du 'plaisir' dans son essence même—la plus mystérieuse, la plus inutile, et par là même la plus sacrée. D'où le refuge, pour l'agnostique, dans une révérence aveugle et comme vitale.[164]

At the moment, smaller joys came his way. He was no longer (officially) an alien, for the United States Congress had passed a special law admitting Alexis Leger, a French citizen, as a permanent resident.[165] And in France, a special issue of the *Cahiers de la Pléiade*, paying homage to Saint-John Perse, was in progress. Many of his writer friends (with the exception of Valéry, whose absence pained him)[166] would be present there: Fargue, Larbaud, Gide, Eliot, Claudel, Breton, Ungaretti and Char, Supervielle, Schehadé, Devlin, MacLeish, Spender, Fouchet, Jouve, Tate, and others[167]—speaking of his work as only they could, being his true "compagnons."

But another source of joy or, more exactly, "du 'plaisir,' dans son essence même," with all its mystery, came into his life a short time later in the form of a woman. He referred to her only as "D" in his letters to friends, but despite his reserve (or because of it) it was evident that she had become an important part of his existence. She was an American, tall, lithe and beautiful, full of nobility and grace, from an old family yet perfectly modern in her ways, a fine horsewoman and swimmer, who expressed herself with equal charm in English and French.[168] But, aside from these rare qualities—which coincided so well with his own—she was also full of adventure, vitality, and gaiety. It became evident as they raced along in her car through the New England countryside—Plymouth, New Bedford (Melville's town), Mystic (where the old whaling ships and the clipper, *Joseph Conrad*, lay)—in September 1950.[169] The wind was fresh as it blew in their faces, and their laughter resounded in the autumn air. He felt rejuvenated by her presence. Joy had come with full force into his life with the advent of "D."

Actually, her name was Dorothy Diana Russell (née Milburn), from an old American family of English origin. She had been

Photo of Saint-John Perse, Washington, during the 1950s. (Photo by Dorothy Norman).

born in New York and was brought up partly in that city and partly on her family's property in Manhasset—where social life was still modeled on that of England (fox hunting, polo, yacht-ing). Educated later at Foxcroft in Virginia, she had traveled widely in Europe with her grandparents and formed a particular attachment to France—both the country and its language (which she had spoken since childhood, having had a French governess and tutor). She was probably most influenced by her grandfather, John George Milburn, an unusual man with a great love for literature, a friend of Matthew Arnold and President Cleveland, a lawyer and the head of the New York Bar Association, who had taken a special interest in the intellectual and artistic formation of his granddaughter.[170] Obviously, the results had been everything he could have wished.

Certainly Alexis—as she soon decided to call him—thought so. For not only did she possess the physical attractions to which he always responded in women,[171] but they quite naturally shared many interests, and she also had an unusual understanding of his need to travel, to preserve his independence and solitude.[172] For he continued to wander to such distant corners of the continent as the Bay of Fundy (where some of the greatest tides in the world are to be found) and to Mississippi (at the time of the rising of its waters), as well as to Avery Island (which was not an actual island but an extraordinary accumulation of salt in the countryside of the Mississippi River Delta); he also roamed in the forests on the Canadian border, quite isolated for a number of weeks, absorbed in geological and mineralogical studies.[173]

Honors began to be heaped upon him now, as a poet (some of which he accepted, and others which he declined—such as the invitation to occupy the Charles Eliot Norton Chair of Poetry at Harvard or the election to the Académie Mallarmé)[174]: he was awarded the Grand Prize for Poetry by the American Academy and National Institute of Arts and Letters, in the form of an Award of Merit Medal (at the same time that William Faulkner received the Grand Prize for the novel), an unusual homage to a non-American writer.[175] In France an international homage to him had appeared in the *Cahiers de la Pléïade* (under the direction of Jean Paulhan), in which the beginning of his newest work in progress—"Amers"—saw the light for the first time.[176]

It was on this poem, "de longue haleine, la plus ambitieuse," which would welcome only "de la joie, libre et librement donnée,"[177] that he was working intensely now that the time had finally come to warrant such a creation. The work stretched over a number of years, quite fittingly so, for it was vaster than anything he had written before and dealt with the love of an entire lifetime: the Sea. Everything that he had experienced and was experiencing now flowed into it—all his deepest penchants, all that he had thought and dreamed and felt, all that was coming to fruition in these autumnal harvest years. In truth, it was the sum and the culmination of his whole life.

From its opening sequence, "Amers" revealed the grandeur to follow, and the profound meaning of the poem for its creator:

. . . Or il y avait un si long temps que j'avais goût de ce poème, mêlant à mes propos du jour toute cette alliance au loin, d'un grand éclat de mer—

. . . .

Car il y avait un si long temps que j'avais goût de ce poème, et ce fut un tel sourire en moi de lui garder ma prévenance: tout envahi, tout investi, tout menacé du grand poème.[178]

Thus it chanted, speaking of the slow maturation, the coming into existence in the fullness of time, when:

Les sagaies du Midi vibrent aux portes de la joie. Les tambours du néant cèdent aux fifres de la lumière.[179]

At the end of his "invocation," the poet rejoices in the task to be undertaken and asks a jubilant force to lead him in his enterprise:

Guide-moi, plaisir, sur les chemins de toute mer. . . . Le beau pays natal est à reconquérir . . . et sa défense est dans mon chant. Commande, ô fifre, l'action, et cette grâce encore d'un amour qui ne nous mette en main que les glaives de la joie![180]

Truly, it was to be a work of joy, a celebration of all the forces of life that seemed to him now to have reached the zenith. For, strangely enough, he had arrived at the point of high noon and summer solstice in the autumn of his days.

As if in accord with this state, he began to follow the sun. He spent that winter on Jupiter Island, in Hobe Sound on the east coast of Florida and navigated in the Gulf Stream and the Keys, as well as on Lake Okeechobee and in the Everglades. In the summer he sailed around the islands of the North, in Casco and Muscongus Bay.[181] Liberated from his confining stay in the Library of Congress and able to manage on the income from his writings, he could once more engage in the activities he loved (sailing, exploring, mountaineering)[182] and combine a life of action with that of the dream.

He was deep into his work on "Amers," as he journeyed ever farther on various seas in the next years: the waters of the Bahamas, with a stop at Nassau and Cat Kay; the Maine coast, with a stay on Monhegan Island (the farthest removed from the mainland of America); the Caribbean, where he halted at Tobago (to study submarine plants, coral formations, and seabirds) and visited the botanical gardens of Trinidad; Maine once more (where he frequented naval museums, indulging his passion for clippers and whaling ships); the British Antilles, with a stopover on Nevis Island (to investigate tropical flora and the last descendants of the monkeys imported in the eighteenth century by French noblemen); the waters near Newfoundland and Labrador (with Canadian fishermen), including a stay on Anticosti Island during a threatened cyclone.[183]

Thus the years were divided into summer and winter seasons on the sea—in a cyclical motion, encompassing all his desires.

His relationship with Dorothy Russell also deepened. She had even gone to Paris to meet his family, "où elle a conquis le coeur de tous les miens"[184] by the qualities that, evidently, had also had that effect upon him. And yet, he maintained many of his solitary ways. For, while she was in Europe, he spent the summer at Monhegan and Seven Hundred Acre Island where, late in the season, he said whimsically: "la sensualité n'est plus représentée . . . que par la complaisance tardive de quelques marsouins femelles . . . roulant des hanches auprès de mon ascétique esquif."[185] He added to this rueful admission: "D. nous reviendra bientôt de France"[186] (understandably preferring her charms to those of female porpoises).

More than any such indications—which appeared only in brief mentions in some letters of the period—of the nature of their relationship was the central portion of the poem "Amers" that came to fruition during these years, and it is there that the true intensity of its creator's feelings can be found.

The ninth (and thus crucial) sequence of the poem, "Etroits sont les vaisseaux," is comparable, in its passion and magnificence, to the Song of Songs. It is, without a doubt, the greatest erotic poem in French literature and, just as surely, a reflection of the poet's emotions. (He himself had said, in speaking of his latest works: "La fonction même du poète est d'intégrer la chose qu'il évoque ou de s'y intégrer, s'identifiant à cette chose jusqu'à la devenir lui-même et s'y confondre: la vivant, la mimant, l'incarnant,"[187] thus revealing the intimate link that binds the poet and the poem, its substance, its movement). Both the substance and the movement of "Etroits sont les vaisseaux" is that of the sea—and the love act. Miming, incarnating the rising and falling rhythm of the waves (and waves of desire), the central sequence of "Amers" relives the union of the lovers, from its inception in the encounter of "l'homme né de mer" and "la femme riveraine"[188] to their love play, and final consummation through coitus and/or hierogamy. For at the moment of orgasm, the lovers transcend the human, participate in a sacred rite, partake of divine revelation, indeed become themselves an incarnation of the Godhead. Their joining then is a paradigm of the union of Shiva and his consort[189] the creative force in the universe that revitalizes everything by this act, celebrated by the flash of lightning and the roar of thunder.[190]

Conducted on two levels (inextricably entwined), "Etroits sont les vaisseaux" traces coition with the beloved both in concrete, explicit, and singularly direct fashion (totally devoid of inhibition or prudery)[191] and in mythic terms of a universal nature.[192] Celebrating both the human and that which exceeds the human, the temporal and the atemporal, the mortal and the eternal, the profane and the sacred, it is the most complete statement (and celebration) concerning the act of creation—as the mirror of Creation.

It is difficult to imagine a greater tribute to the beloved or to the poet's greatest loves: of woman and of the sea, joined here into one surpassing whole.

"Amers" reached completion in 1956. With it, the summit of everything he had harbored—all during the long years of his life—seemed attained.

The Sea, his first and most enduring love, was here celebrated (and incarnated) in the scope, the movement, the endlessly rich details of the poem, but most of all in the final litany where it was revealed as the sum of all ambiguities—the *coincidentum oppositorum* of which all great mythologies speak:

Mer de Baal, Mer de Mammon; Mer de toute âge et de tout nom!
Mer utérine de nos songes et Mer hantée du songe vrai,
. . . .
O toi l'offense et toi l'éclat! toute démence et toute/aisance,
Et toi l'amour et toi la haine, l'Inexorable et l'Exorable,
O toi qui sais et ne sais pas, ô toi qui dis et ne dis pas,
. . . .
Nourrice et mère, non marâtre, amante et mère du puîné,
O Consanguine et très lointaine, ô toi l'inceste et toi/l'aînesse,
Et toi l'immense compassion de toutes choses périssables,
Mer à jamais irrépudiable, et Mer enfin inséparable![193]

As he wrote the last page of "Amers," he was indeed "l'homme libre de son ombre, à la limite de son bien," and could utter the pronouncement of the celebrant in his poem: "Nous qui mourrons peut-être un jour disons l'homme immortel au foyer de l'instant."[194]

It only remained for him now to return from exile. That took place in 1957, in the same year as the publication of *Amers* by Gallimard in France, and the first volume of his *Oeuvres complètes* (in a bilingual edition) in Germany.[195] A group of literary friends and admirers decided to facilitate his return to France by making him a gift of a house in the Midi (Provence maritime) and presented him with this property "en hommage au poète d'*Exil*, de *Vents*, et d'*Amers*."[196]

It was thus that he ended his exile of seventeen years. And took possession of a small kingdom on the edge of yet another sea.

CHAPTER 7

A ROAD OF GLOWING EMBERS
(1957–1975)

Lève la tête, homme du soir. La grande rose des ans tourne à ton front serein.

—*Chronique* (*OC*, p. 389–90)

Summer, 1957

Reaching the age of seventy did not bring with it any of the serenity that proverbially accompanies the advent of "le grand âge."[1] Quite the contrary. He was more divided than before, fraught with paradox: the long-awaited return to France (even though he avoided Paris)[2] engendered shock and sadness.[3] Emergence from exile and owning land of his own did nothing to dispel his sense of estrangement. He felt just as alien now as when he had arrived, empty-handed, on the other side of the world.

And yet, his property in Provence had certainly been chosen with care to suit all his inclinations: situated at the outermost point of a peninsula, high above the sea, it commanded a magnificient view. And, if the house did not actually lie at the edge of the water, as he might have wished,[4] it dominated the blue-green expanse of the Mediterranean, a fishing port, and some small islands in the distance. The land ended here; through the steep cliffs bordering it on one side, paths led down to the *calanques*[5] where one could plunge into the sea, undisturbed.

The house itself was all simplicity and pure outlines, its whiteness and silence accentuated by the brilliant light of the Midi. It seemed a citadel or aerie where one could dwell "fort bien défendu contre tous et contre tout, sauf contre le mistral"[6] (the famed wind that should have delighted the poet of *Vents*).

Nevertheless, as he surveyed all this, he cried out: "Mais que me voilà loin de l'Atlantique!"[7]

An odd sense of apprehension and restlessness had seized him as if he were in the power of "le démon de l'Absurde."[8] He knew that he showed ingratitude toward destiny, which had showered him with gifts. But there was no way to still his contrary impulsions. Now that he—and his abode—faced south, he constantly heard another call, "cette rumeur lointaine qui me descend toujours du Nord par l'oreille interne,"[9] to remind him of his Celtic origins. And, as he looked at the body of water below (whose very name spoke of its limitation), he found it flat, tame, and alien. He recoiled from "cette mer latine qui n'est point celle de mon enfance, ni d'aucun de mes ascendants."[10] And he found himself exclaiming, with something resembling despair: "A la Méditerranée comme mer, m'habituerai-je jamais? 'Nous qui sommes hommes d'Atlantique . . .' fut pour trois siècles une expression courante dans le langage de mes arrière-parents."[11]

It was not only the conflict between two seas, or two identities, that plagued him. The very vegetation of the region seemed unsuited to his temperament. He saw almost no trees, only a profusion of flowers—and he had never liked the latter. "Mon horreur de fleurs sera ici bien servi! Moins bien ma passion de l'arbre, de la feuille et du fruit,"[12] he said (with something approaching irony), as he beheld the fragrant countryside, full of herbs and blooms, basking in the sun, overbearing in its prodigality. It appeared to him pathetically extravagant—this land that offered itself to the stranger, almost in the guise of a supplicant.[13]

However, it was also a place of immense loneliness. In the evenings a strange silence reigned here. As he sat in the deserted drawing room, whose windows faced the now dark expanse of water, indistinguishable from the night sky, he felt totally isolated at his far outpost. "Et pas une bête encore auprès de moi," he mused, "au loin seulement la petite chouette de Pallas,"[14] whose forlorn call in the night only underscored distance. Even dawn, when the sea seemed to rise in the bay windows and flow into his study, brought with it waves of memory and yearning. He pushed them back but knew it was no use, for such tides "refluent toujours longuement, et sourdement."[15]

Night thoughts and dreams of malaise besieged him.[16] The past had come flooding back and, with it, a strange sense of unreality. He knew that he must fight his way out of this shadowy state and come back to life.

It was the "Mediterranean light"[17] that recalled him (as did the luminosity of the Pyrenees—long ago). No one could resist its intense presence. Then he began to remember the power of the sea to cure him. The first step to recovery was to plunge bodily into its waters. A short descent along the paths in the cliff was all that was needed. And he was once more in his element. "Des criques abruptes, au bas de ma falaise, me livrent assez brutalement à l'eau vive," he exclaimed, feeling the salt water revive him, the shock of life rush through his limbs; shortly, he discovered that "cette eau est d'une rare qualité, presque tropicale par sa clarté, avec plus de vivacité que sous les Tropiques."[18] He had united the remembered sea of the past with the one he encountered now and found that the present had won out.

The next move was to make contact with the earth. He began to belabor it with hoe and rake, infuse it with water, transplant wild things from the "maquis"[19] to the tamer terrain near the house. Slowly, he began to notice that there were even trees on his property—pines, bent and twisted by the sea wind, that merged so well with the landscape that he had not perceived them before, but also cypress and myrtle. The land started to take on a more appealing air.

Then came the awareness of space that was extraordinary on

this promontory. The site now revealed itself to him as a "pres-qu'île,"[20] surrounded by water on three sides but striving toward the sea. The constant play of winds made even the hot climate invigorating, and he breathed ever more freely as the days went by. All that was still needed was an exchange of "l'alizé contre le mistral"[21] (of the breezes of memory for the wind of the present). But that would come too. "C'est toujours du vent,"[22] he could already say, with a laugh.

As he began to acquiesce to this sea, this land, this wind, he also started to take possession of this house that was his now. The initial gesture would be to affix a piece of wrought iron—full of memories—from the Haute Bourgogne, inscribed with the date of his first ancestor's departure for the Iles des Vents. He planned to place it on the wall facing the land (with nothing "côté mer, car la mer est sans mémoire").[23] It was an idea that he welcomed almost as much as the prospect of his first visitor (the friend who had found and safeguarded this memento for him, besides being instrumental in the gift of this house): Mina Curtiss.[24]

Thus the first summer at Les Vigneaux [25] passed. At the end of it, he knew that his strength had returned. It was thanks to his daily contact with the sea, the wind, the blinding light, and this land that had become transformed, for him, into a "terre d'archaïsme et de mythologie"[26] (suggesting fertile soil for creation). True, he still felt some hesitation about writing.[27] But that, too, would come in due time. "Je reprendrai ici mon oeuvre de po-ète," he prophesied. "De nuit peut-être, pour ne rien perdre de la flamme du jour,"[28] as if to acknowledge this site of fire and the flame it had kindled in him once more.

When autumn came, he had reached a decision that recon-ciled his ever equivocal life-style and the cyclical motion he saw in everything: he would divide the year into two halves and spend each on a different continent[29]—six months in America, the other six in France. Thus, the nomad would balance the landowner, the Atlantic the Mediterranean, the West the East;

winter would complement summer, companionship alternate with solitude. And he would follow the round of the seasons, in a movement akin to that of migratory birds.

1957–1958

Fall was splendid in Washington. The giant oaks blazed in their ultimate foliage. Crisp weather invigorated everyone and everything. And he found a number of American friends—both old and new—to welcome him. He realized how much this country had become part of him, now that he had recovered the land on the other side of the ocean. A bridge had formed between the two. But it was as light as a spider's thread, as undulating as the tides.

Another bridge had also appeared (in May, honoring his seventieth birthday and the publication of *Amers* by Gallimard, but of which he really took cognizance only now), in the form of the *Hommage International de Combat,* where writers from both countries—such as Pierre Jean Jouve, Conrad Aiken, Jean Cassou, Pierre Emmanuel, Henry Miller, Jean Grosjean, Alain Bosquet—had joined together to speak of his work.[30] And, in America, W. H. Auden was preparing an article ("A Song of Life's Power to Renew") for the *New York Times Book Review,* to appear at the time of the publication of the bilingual edition of *Amers/Seamarks,* translated by Wallace Fowlie.[31] Auden would speak of the fact that Saint-John Perse was, to his knowledge, the only French poet whose entire work had been translated into English. But he would dwell at length on the universal scope and timeless perspectives of Perse's poetry, and its celebration of the inexhaustible power of life to renew itself, testimony to the sacredness of existence its creator ever sought to express. It was a tribute of such insight that its recipient could only be deeply moved.[32]

Even more than such literary links, however, it was the human ones he valued anew. He thought of Allen Tate and the rumors of a marriage he was about to undertake;[33] of E. E. Cummings, who had been such a delight to know over the years[34] but whose health was cause for worry lately;[35] of Archibald MacLeish, who now traveled almost constantly.[36] But most of all he thought of Dorothy Russell, whom he longed to see, and from whom distance often separated him.

Each time they met again, he was struck afresh by all the qualities that had drawn him to her initially and that were only confirmed by the passage of time: her beauty and grace (both outer and inner); her adventurous spirit and love of movement (whether she swam, rowed, rode, or raced along in her car); her capacity for laughter;[37] and, certainly not least, the ever deepening feeling between them—which some natural reserve kept both of them from declaring.

In the course of this winter, though, perhaps because of the summer's realizations, he took the full measure of her "rares qualités humaines."[38] He remembered also that she had won the heart of all those in his family, and the wish his mother had often expressed[39] (with her characteristic subtlety) to see his destiny joined to a woman of such qualities. But then the thought of his age assailed him. He suddenly felt all the weight of almost seventy-one winters.[40] It seemed unjust to attempt to bind another being to him at this late stage in life. Yet, emotions had no age, and he felt green for his years. And so he battled inwardly for months. He said nothing, but he could not help harboring recurrent dreams of a life together with this woman.

And then, one day, as mysteriously as the coming of spring, the sudden thrust of life from apparently nowhere, his doubts and reticences disappeared. He spoke, asking her quite simply to be his wife. To his great joy, she acquiesced, joyously.

They were married in Washington on Friday, April 26, 1958.[41] It was a beautiful warm day and, as if to crown it all, a thunderstorm was predicted for that night.[42]

Summer, 1958

"Une ère nouvelle va-t-elle s'ouvrir pour moi?"[43] he wondered, during those first months with her to whom he referred as

"Celle qui partage aujourd'hui ma vie,"[44] as he considered his new way of life.

Everything was certainly changed. He was now a husband, no longer an exile or a nomad but "l'homme d'un lieu"[45]—something resembling an established citizen. It was a state that might easily have spelled confinement to one who had wandered for so long, unattached, throughout the world, had he not found ways to invent imaginative solutions to this unequivocal situation.

Thus he decided that, being married, to be doubly so (not to one, but to two women): "Me voici . . . comme deux fois marié: à Dorothy d'Amérique et à Diane de France (car c'est ici pour moi son nom)"[46] by the simple and delightful expedient of gallicizing his wife's middle name (which also had the advantage of evoking "Diane chasseresse,"[47] the lithe divinity she resembled). As for his being "l'homme d'un lieu," that was solved by his being "nulle part à part entière,"[48] dividing his life between two continents and alternate domiciles—the villa at Giens and the house they now inhabited in Georgetown.[49] He concluded by summing up his reaction to this "ère nouvelle" that had arrived, in a phrase typical of the rest (being sufficiently ambiguous): "*Almost happy!*" (sic)—an inscription he had once seen beneath a self-portrait of the aged Audubon.[50]

Having settled these matters, he could begin to enjoy his sojourn. It seemed to him that the land was slowly opening its lids, to reveal its particular charms. He started to see it differently than before. No longer the lush supplicant it appeared last year, but (on the contrary) ascetic, avid, discreet, "sans graisse ni mollesse,"[51] it resembled a beautiful body with delicate joints and fine bone structure. Its dry, stony nature seduced him, as did the odor of resin, the color of yellow amber that clung to the bodies of women at evening time, even the invisible threat of fire seemingly ever present here.[52]

He was not content with mere contemplation of this land, though: he desired actual contact. It began with the trees. He had "won the friendship" of an undisciplined fig-bearing "monster" that now bowed low (due to his skills as a trainer) and delivered its fruit into the hands of Diane and his sisters.[53] He then planted others—an African pomegranate and an Egyptian avocado—in honor of the former and dreamed of trees from the West Indies, Argentina, and Brazil, as well as the genistra his mother had loved when they lived in the Antilles (and he could thus never see without being moved).[54] It was as if he aspired to a grove as universal as his peregrinations.

He also realized that the region housed fauna as international as the flora he wished to implant here: there were "Argentinian ants," large lizards that seemed to play at being iguanas, miniature turtles that repeated the proud geometry of their lovely marine relations, as well as "iules" and "gekkos" or "marbouyas" (companions of his childhood days). From the marshes of the Camargue there came birds of the Caspian Sea, sea gulls (born Celts who evoked the Atlantic), and one day he even found a mysterious little Arctic petrel (who had undoubtedly lost his way during the migratory flight).[55]

"Hybridité, hybridité en tout!"[56] he joyfully exclaimed.

He now saw an encounter of opposites in the very site where he lived. It seemed no longer a "presqu'île," but "une île encore mal reliée à l'épine continentale,"[57] almost ready to cast off. It was his kind of place—a form of juncture between elements where he could stake his claim. "A cette charnière entre terre et mer . . . j'ai dressé mon mât de pavillon,"[58] he proclaimed—as if the terrain were a ship, or he had now acquired his kingdom. Indeed, he had all the riches he could desire: "J'ai devant moi la mer entière et derrière moi la terre entière . . . et, à mes côtés, au loin, le sel . . . je fais le compte de mes biens et m'élève en ces lieux, contre toute menace . . . M'y aide aussi le Mistral . . . salutaire."[59]

If anything was lacking, it was some animals of his own (a large dog and a small Sicilian donkey—still in the planning stage). For the moment, he had to content himself with visitors: two charming foxes that came from the underbrush, a falcon, and some magpies.[60]

Literature was far removed in this place. There were few writers, "Dieu merci," in the vicinity.[61] Only some companion shades: "Stevenson et Conrad et le cher Edward Lear . . . et

Valéry enfin que j'aimerais tant pouvoir encore taquiner, en lui rappelant ici que la lumière méditerranéenne nous frappe de cécité et clôt pour nous le seuil métaphysique."[62] It was a summer when Saint-John Perse made way for the simple man who hoed and dug, built and planted. Or perhaps poetry was undergoing a salutory "fast" that, as he knew, was the best way "de 'se lover' pour l'instinct créateur,"[63] ready to spring when the time was ripe.

More than any literary problem, however, what preoccupied him now was the well, covered in rose-colored brick, that lay at the foot of his property and that he tended with great care; but even more so, the search for a second—lost—well, so that his "domaine . . . ne soit pas borgne comme Hannibal."[64] It was a quest that haunted him, not only because, as he said, "le mystère de l'eau . . . m'a toujours et partout bouleversé," but also because he had a premonition that to find that well would be a profound sort of revelation: "Par l'oeil magnétique de mon puits non couvert, j'accéderai ici au mystère, et comme au souffle même, de notre nuit terrestre," he wrote, on the ninth day of the ninth month at the end of that summer.[65].

A year would go by before he attained the goal of his quest. But the premonition was already his. When they left Les Vigneaux in the autumn, he had not only begun to make this spot on the earth his own but had taken with him the seeds of his next poem.

The second half of the year's cycle plunged them into another life, in Washington, filled with other concerns, sights, and customs. He saw *Amers* published in a bilingual edition in America; was among the first honorary members to be elected by the Modern Language Assocation (together with T. S. Eliot, Albert Camus, Jorge Guillén, and Jean-Paul Sartre);[66] received the degree of Docteur ès Lettres *honoris causa* from Yale;[67] and was fêted quite steadily now. He exchanged the rough clothes be wore in the Midi for the formal attire, de rigueur at official receptions in academe or cocktail parties (which he dodged as often as possible).[68] Although he tried to avoid interviews and all forms of personal publicity, it was difficult to remain anonymous. As soon as he could, he escaped to the Blue Ridge Mountains of Virginia[69] to still his thirst for high places and the third element in the triad of earth, sea, and sky.

All during the winter and spring, though, in the midst of crowds and the intense activity of the city, he carried within him—like a faint and haunting melody—the remembrance of the second well he sought, on the other side of the world.

Summer, 1959

As he had known intuitively, at the height of this summer the lost well was found. It was as though, then, everything had crested in his life. On September 9 (the same mysterious date as last year) he wrote: "Ma paix ici est faite, et l'alliance consommé. . . . J'ai trouvé le second puits; c'est mon anneau d'alliance,"[70] in a tone of jubilation.

And, as he had also known, the discovery of the second well had an even deeper meaning. It led him "au mystère . . . au souffle même, de notre nuit terrestre." He was now ready to write the poem that was "un chant à la terre et au temps . . . confondus dans une même notion intemporelle,"[71] where all form of alliance was finally consummated, and serenity came to "l'homme du soir"[72] in the evening of his life: "Chronique."

As the long days of summer passed, one into the other with seemingly unending fullness, he felt the past melt away. He stood in the brilliant, blinding heart of the present moment, truly free of all shadow. "Mes vieilles hantises de tristesse dansent maintenant la pyrrhique loin de moi, dans les steppes de l'oubli et les sables du passé. Les grandes ombres de l'exil n'avanceront plus sur mes terraces, ouvertes au futur," he exclaimed—and added, in the same breath, the phrase that was perhaps the key to it all: "Diane est heureuse ici et l'on y rit beaucoup."[73]

"Chronique," rooted in this happiness and this laughter, an overwhelming testimony to the human splendor of "le grand

Saint-John Perse at 'Les Vigneaux' (Presqu'île de Giens), ca. 1960. According to Gisèle Freund, the caption chosen by the poet for this photo was: "Grand âge nous voici" a line from Chronique. *(Copyright by Gisèle Freund).*

âge," came to fruition during this summer. It was living proof that, for its creator, great age was indeed a "route de braise et non de cendres"[74]:

"Grand âge nous voici. Fraîcheur du soir sur les hauteurs, souffle du large sur tous seuils, et nos fronts mis à nu pour de plus vastes cirques,"[75] it begins, establishing the freedom, vitality, loftiness, and universality of the domain of great age (man's, the earth's, but also the mythic Great Age of which sacred texts speak the world over), as well as affirming the simple human joys of its creator at this moment in time.

The Poet's voice, speaking in the plural ("nous") as if for all men of all time, then evokes the wanderings still to be undertaken, the roads without limit to be explored—roads that go beyond Death itself. It sings of the lips of women, still red with the juice of the pomegranate of Cybele, that render death's grip vain[76] and of the encounter with knowledge that can only come with great age:

Grand âge, nous voici. Rendez-vous pris, et de longtemps avec cette heure de grand sens.
. . . .
Et nous rentrons chargés de nuit, sachant de naissance et de mort plus que n'enseigne le songe de l'homme.[77]

At its center, the poem that has risen like a crescendo, or a wave to its crest, in a series of increasingly powerful swells, attains (as others before it) a visionary summit:

Rétine ouverte au plus grande cirque . . .
Voici la chose vaste en Ouest, et la fraîcheur d'abîme sur nos faces.[78]

The West, now symbol of the setting sun that irradiates the earth with its last splendor, is the place of death. It leads inevitably to the mystery glimpsed in the well ("notre nuit terrestre"): the womb-tomb from which all life arises and to which all must return, in the great round of being.

The poet turns his gaze earthward finally and chants:

O face insigne de la terre . . . dernière venue dans nos louanges . . . ô mémoire, au coeur d'homme, du royaume perdu![79]

Once having recognized and celebrated this lost/found kingdom, he can proceed to his leave-taking. His song changes in tone; his steps are now oriented toward the beyond:

Grand âge, nous voici—et nos pas d'hommes vers l'issue . . .

. . . .

. . . chant plus grave, et d'autre glaive, comme chant d'honneur, et
chant du Maître, seul au soir.
Voici les lieux que nous laissons.[80]

At the end of the poem (as if at the end of life), we see the
celebrant raise his arms, in a hieratic gesture, to present his
offering, his praise, and all that he has acquired, at the moment
of departure:

Nous élevons à bout de bras, sur le plat de nos mains, comme couvée
d'ailes naissantes, ce coeur enténébré de l'homme où fut l'avide, et fut
l'ardent, et tant d'amour irrévélé.

. . . .

Grand âge, nous voici. Prenez mesure du coeur d'homme.[81]

In this ultimate pronouncement of "Chronique" lies all the
yearning, the richness, the beauty of a human life—and a summation of everything that the poet who wrote these words has
been. No epithet could better express the proud, humble, ardent, shadowy existence of this man.

Truly, it might have been his last work and testament.

1960

But no. Just as *Chronique* belied the cry uttered in *Amers* ("Mon
dernier chant! mon dernier chant!"),[82] so this poem was not a
will nor a final farewell. Paradoxically, the year that followed was
on of the most intense in his life.

It began with the realization of a dream long harbored (as
passionately as the journey to Outer Mongolia): a visit to Pa-
tagonia, Tierra del Fuego, the Strait of Magellan, and Cape
Horn.[83] Saint-John Perse was the guest of the Argentine government, all as the result of a joking reference to this "voeu le plus
secret et le plus ancien" that had led to his being taken at his
word.[84] The trip, which was originally to have lasted twelve days,
stretched to a month and a half of glorious "vagabondage" by jet
plane and ship. He saw the Antarctic region, navigated around
Ushuya, and explored the glacial realms

de toute cette rude partie du monde . . . qui m'a toujours hanté l'esprit et dont je demeure à jamais fasciné, obsédé presque, comme par un des points les plus magnétiques du monde—l'aire seigneuriale du Vent: Je n'avais jamais connu de tel depuis mes libres chevauchées au Désert de Gobi et en Asie centrale.[85]

He also visited a fascinating woman, Victoria Ocampo, at her estates at Mar del Plata,[86] saw pure-blooded horses raised, and met Jorge Luis Borges, Marcos Victoria, and various other writers in Buenos Aires.[87]

As if such adventure were not enough, as soon as he returned from South America he indulged in other "fugues irrésistibles" and, on horseback, explored one of the isolated regions of the American Northwest[88] with the energy and curiosity of a man far less than his seventy-three years.

The summer in the south of France found him once more hard at work, building terraces, cutting away the thorny underbrush, reparing masonry, planting trees—and swimming daily in the sea.[89]

When fall came, literary glory blazed as brilliantly as the foliage: *Chronique* was in the process of publication in France and, in America, about to be translated. A fine poet (Robert Fitzgerald) had undertaken the task. Saint-John Perse was being fêted by prize after prize: he received the Grand Prix National des Lettres in France, the international Grand Prize for poetry at the Biennale of Knocke, honorary membership in the American Academy and National Institute of Arts and Letters, and a corresponding one in the Bavarian Academy. The greatest honor of all, however, came his way that winter: the Nobel Prize.[90]

He traveled to Stockholm to receive this coveted award on December 10, 1960. The speech he delivered when it was presented to him was, characteristically, a eulogy of poetry rather than the pretentious utterance of a poet laureate. Its very first sentence expressed all this, with admirable simplicity: "J'ai accepté pour la poésie l'hommage qui lui est ici rendu, et que j'ai hâte de lui restituer."[91]

In the rest of his address he went on to define this craft as "plus que mode de connaissance, la poésie est d'abord mode de vie—et de vie intégrale. Le poète existait dans l'homme des cavernes, il existera dans l'homme des âges atomiques: parce qu'il est part irréductible de l'homme."[92] He then expressed his view as to the task and place of the poet as one who "par son adhésion totale à ce qui est, tient pour nous liaison avec la permanence de l'être"[93] (thus affirming his own experiences and convictions at this time of life).

Typically of him, the speech led to the word he had always held in such high esteem, for, in conclusion, he said: "Face à l'énergie nucléaire, la lampe d'argile du poète suffira-t-elle à son propos?—Oui, si d'argile se souvient l'homme."[94]

1961–1971

The next decade was a period akin to the harvest season in the life of the man and the poet. It was a time for gathering what he had wrought in the past; for plenitude and hospitality, ripeness and serenity, but also of activity, continued vigor, creativity, and generous gifts. In all domains, he had reached the joys that old age—at its best—can bring.

Les Vigneaux had the appearance of a true home now: all the objects that had acquired meaning during a lifetime had found their place here—nautical maps; ship models; Chinese silk scrolls; an antique wood panel representing a phoenix; a Tibetan banner (brought back from Central Asia) exalting the Tantric divinities of Lamaism; a miniature Buddha carved in a meteorite;[95] a black lacquer stele on which, in characters of bronze, was inscribed his transposed Chinese name ("La Foudre sous la neige");[96] drawings of horses, in the desert and swimming in a tropical sea; a collection of swords; a Malayan kriss; engraved Chinese stirrups (one of which was also a child's toy); a long and narrow Spanish table in his workroom, "ascétique comme une page de Cervantes, cher au coeur du poète";[97] a portrait of his mother; a daguerreotype of a Spanish ancestress; a photograph of a young woman on horseback; a small sextant and naval compass; a map of L'Ile des Feuilles.[98]

Aside from objects, animals now also enlivened the dwelling. A dog roamed in the vicinity of the house; Perse was almost always to be found with a kitten in his arms.[99] And birds from everywhere came to this site, as if it were the crossroads of their migrations.

Visitors (of the human species) also came from far and wide: his sisters, Eliane, Paule, and Marguerite[100] (whom he could welcome under his own roof, finally), Pierre Guerre who would become his friend,[101] the Swiss ornithologist Hoffman, Jean-Louis Barrault and Madeleine Renaud, Romeo Lucchese, the Hungarian sculptor Andreas Beck, Marie-José (the former queen of Italy whom he had known as a young girl), Robert Penn Warren and his wife (Eleanor Clark), Louis Braquier, and many others.[102]

In Washington, on the other hand, where he still spent a part of the year, alternating with the Midi, in the charming small house in Georgetown,[103] an equally nonconformist atmosphere prevailed, but of a different kind: the colors of the living room did not give in to the uniformity that the neighborhood felt it incumbent upon it to maintain and expressed their owners' individuality. The upper story also contrasted, by the simplicity of its furnishings, with the other dwellings of this exclusive neighborhood. Everything spoke of authenticity, personal conviction, and humor. There were flowers in the vases now (for, though he still disliked them, he enjoyed seeing his wife's opposite taste and laughingly encouraged visitors to bring them[104] despite his notorious attitude).

And visitors did come, here also, from every land: Octavio Paz, Salvador de Madariaga, André Malraux, Jorge Luis Borges, Pierre Boulez, Prince Peter of Greece, the composer Boucourechliev (who would write a long composition based on *Amers*), the French ambassador Charles Lucet, and a host of others.[105]

He also continued his travels, as avidly as before: cruises to the British Antilles (with a stop in Barbados where he found images of his own childhood again) and Bermuda (where he studied the singular geological formations and the ambiguity of the vegetation); excursions in the mountains of the Haute Provence and into the Camargue (including the usually inaccessible Natural Reserve); a second visit to Cumberland Island in Georgia; a stay in the North of Italy (Florence, Verona, and Ravenna—the last of which struck his imagination most particularly) and in Rome (where he met Alberto Moravia and Ignazio Silone, as well as the daughter of Marguerite de Bassiano); navigation on the yacht, *Aspara*, to Corsica, Elba, Capraia, Giglio, and Monte Cristo (marked by a memorable storm, close to Cap Corse, in full Mediterranean light that seemed to place one "comme au foyer même de la flamme" and reconciled him to "cette mer d'azur ignorante de l'ombre");[106] a stay in Grenada, the "Spice Island" and the most tropical of the British Antilles (the closest in atmosphere to that of Guadeloupe and the ancient plantations destroyed in the cyclone of 1964, eliminating all vestiges of his past and leaving nothing of La Josephine except the eighteenth-century cemetery of the family,[107] a small piece of whose iron grill Jacqueline Kennedy brought back for him as a memento);[108] another Mediterranean cruise on the *Aspara* to Sardinia, Sicily, Panarea, Stromboli, Lipari, Vulcano, Salina, Filicudi, Alicudi, with stopovers in Naples, Capri, Ponza, entry into the Fiumicino Canal, before going on to Porto Ercole, Santa Margharita, San Remo and Antibes.[109]

His poetry, in the meanwhile, traveled as far and wide as he: His collected works were published in a new and revised edition in France in 1960, followed by an Italian bilingual edition, and one in Argentina; in the same year, *Chronique* was translated and appeared in a bilingual edition in Sweden and in Germany, as well as in a Spanish translation; in 1962, translations of *Anabase* and *Chronique* were published in India and one of *Chronique* in Argentina; in 1963 a translation of *Amers* appeared in Yugoslavia, and a film by Laure Garcin, *Etroits sont les vaisseaux*, in France; 1964 saw the publication of *Anabase* and *Exil* in Japan, of *Vents* in Germany, *Exil* in Holland, *Vents* in Bulgaria, and a *Choix d'Oeuvres* in Spain, Argentina, and Brazil; in 1965 various works appeared in Czechoslovakia; 1966 brought the appearance of *Chronique* in Italy, of *Amers* in Czechoslovakia, of *Eloges* in Finland, and of a *Choix d'Oeuvres* in Rumania and Poland; in 1967, it was the turn of *Anabase,* in a trilingual edition and of *Amers* in Italian, Czech, and Norwegian translation; 1968 brought the publication of his *Oeuvres complètes* in Italy, the United States, and Czechoslovakia, the translation of *Amers* in Hungary and of a *Choix d'Oeuvres* in Portugal; in 1969, the *Oeuvre poétique* of Saint-John Perse appeared in Italian, English, Czech, Slovak, Hungarian, Bulgarian, Rumanian, and Hebrew translations; and in 1971 his *Collected Poems* in a bilingual edition (with the translations of W. H. Auden, Hugh Chisholm, Denis Devlin, T. S. Eliot, Robert Fitzgerald, Wallace Fowlie, Richard Howard, Louise Varèse) were published in the United States.[110]

But it was not alone the works of the past, bringing world wide renown, that marked these years. For the past was, for him, not something to cling to, but to surrender. Only the present could render "l'homme immortel au foyer de l'instant."[111] It was the sole form of eternity and must be made manifest by perpetual renewal.

Albert Camus had asked him to write a play for the new theater he had been entrusted with, but he declined.[112] Another project, however—the result of a meeting with Georges Braque, a few months later[113]—fired his imagination. It was to be a joint undertaking in which each man worked, independently, on a subject of intense interest to them both: birds. The result was a fascinating book, *L'Ordre des oiseaux* (comprising a poetic text by Saint-John Perse and etchings by Georges Braque), published in 1962.[114] Not an illustrated poem, the work was an encounter, a "compagnonnage" between painter and poet, a sort of bilingual construct where each, singly and equally, by means of his particular art form, contributed to a dyptich that exceeded the sum of its strangely parallel parts.

For Saint-John Perse, it was the opportunity to fully explore and celebrate a figure (real and symbolic) that had haunted him ever since the earliest days of his life. *Oiseaux* (the poetic text that is part of, but also stands apart from, the joint venture with Braque) bears witness to this deeply rooted predilection.

"il naviguait avant le songe" (Oiseaux). *Collage by the artist Jacqueline Kiang, Paris 1983. (In the private collection of the author).*

Its epigraph is a quote from Aulus Persius Flaccus (the Latin poet whose name, it will be recalled, Perse said had *not* inspired the pseudonym he chose)[115]: ". . . *Quantum non milvus oberret.*"[116] It thus instantly establishes the vast range of the central bird image, and of the poem. Indeed, the Bird(s) of this work is a being who exceeds (but does not deny) an ornithological definition or the celebration of its nature and characteristics. From the outset, "l'oiseau" is defined as one of man's "consanguins," defined by ardor, avidity, migration, duality ("l'alternance est sa loi, l'ambiguité son règne")[117] and thence the blood brother not only of man but of the poet, this poet. Moreover, in the bird's double allegiance to air and earth, as well as by his "conformation nautique . . . son aisance en tout à mimer le navire,"[118] he is denizen of all three elements of his creator's predilection, as well as the juncture of all three ("unité recouvrée sous la diversité")[119] and unifies nature and spirit, the natural and the supernatural.[120]

The bird, who has combined all the traits and strivings of the poet, becomes, moreover, poetry itself. His flight is seen as "une poésie d'action"[121] during which he lives and consumes himself, as does the phoenix (in an endless cycle of death and rebirth); and he is comparable to the word (or Word) with its magical powers of creation:

Et bien sont-ils comme des mots sous leur
charge magique: noyaux de force et d'action,
foyers d'éclairs . . .

Et procédant comme les mots, de lointaine
ascendance, ils perdent, comme les mots,
leur sens à la limite de la félicité . . .

Ils sont, comme les mots, portés du rythme
universel; ils s'inscrivent d'eux-mêmes, et
comme d'affinité, dans la plus grande strophe
errante que l'on ait vue jamais se dérouler
au monde.[122]

More than the poet, and even poetry itself, the Bird finally becomes not only the "Maître du Songe" but even he who "naviguait avant le songe, et sa réponse est: 'Passer outre!'"[123] He thrusts onward to forever greater heights, to vaster motions, toward that mystic center where all opposites merge, where "c'est l'unité enfin renouée et le divers reconcilié,"[124] to the very source of the cosmic cycle, "où va le cours même du ciel, sur sa roue—à cette immensité de vivre et de créer."[125]

The last words of the poem complete the image of the Great Round, for they speak of the predawn of Creation[126] and that in the spring of 1962, nearly on the eve of the poet's seventy-fifth birthday.

1968–1975

Six years of silence followed the completion of *Oiseaux*. Perhaps it was a time of literary "fast," a long moment of gathering, or coiling to spring into creation. Perhaps also, the waves of inspiration came more slowly now and were of shorter duration. The end of life was approaching. The nomad who had traveled the whole earth for more than eighty years was almost done with his wanderings.

The works of his last seven years were a summing up and a gathering of embers—a farewell. But they were also a profoundly moving record of his final battles, visions, and most secret feelings. Pared down to the core, refined of everything but the quintessential, they would constitute a slim volume (scarcely twenty pages long) but of such complexity that they ranged over the entire scale of human emotions and the greatest mythic revelations.

The first poem of this group was written in 1968—a year when death claimed two close friends: Francis Biddle and Jean Paulhan.[127] "Chanté par celle qui fut là"[128] was a grave and yearning poem, full of tenderness and sorrow. Spoken by the voice of a woman, foreshadowing her bereavement,[129] it sings of love, of pain, and of memory—to the accompaniment of signs that everything is ending. All the longing, the ardor, and the last sparks of an entire lifetime are compressed into a chant lasting a sparse three pages. It is as if the poem, in its brevity, incarnates the brief span of human existence but also, as if everything could be contained in this meager space.

As the woman addresses her beloved, moving into the shadow of death (while, during the long summer night, she harkens and hears "toutes choses courir à leurs fins"),[130] she brings him solace by evoking Ceres of the gentle hands, the owl of Pallas in the cypress tree, their dwelling open to the eternal, a humble animal building its nest, and life that takes everything under its wing.[131] Solace is coupled with a burning desire to stir the last glow in the embers, to infuse the beloved with life—through a journey toward the origin, anamnesis, or the simple human harvest of memory—even if only for an instant, before the ebb tide:

Femme vous suis-je, ô mon amour, en toutes fêtes de mémoire. Ecoute, écoute, ô mon amour, le bruit que fait un grand amour au reflux de la vie.[132]

Without turning away from the sight of Death approaching in its white-lead mask,[133] she transforms the last journey into a voyage toward the region of the setting sun—the locus of ultimate adventure and divine revelation—as she evokes the vision in which "Vers les Grandes Indes de l'Ouest s'en vont les hommes d'aventure."[134]

Although the voice of love that chants here acquiesces to life and death, Orient and Occident, creation and destruction, the eternal and the ephemeral, the human cry it utters is for one more instant of fire—to gather the riches of the past (in a summation that is also an elegy):

Ah! toutes choses de mémoire, ah! toutes choses que nous sûmes, et toutes choses que nous fûmes . . . qu'il en soit fait avant le jour pillage et fête et feu de braise pour la cendre du soir![135]

At the close of the poem, the sum of all that has been ("l'avide . . . l'ardent, et tant d'amour") offered up in *Chronique*[136] is placed like a seal upon the lips of "celle qui fut là." And she becomes the guardian, the incarnation, the living repository of past, still-present, and future:

. . . le lait qu'au matin un cavalier tartare tire du flanc de sa bête, c'est à vos lèvres, ô mon amour, que j'en garde mémoire.[137]

Thus, the work (first written and placed last in the final volume of Saint-John Perse's poems) ends upon the word—long denied, but now honored—that unifies what has been and is, the mortal or temporal with the eternal or timeless: remembrance.

Three years would pass before his next poem was written.[138] The end of life was coming closer. Illness had begun to inscribe its mysterious signs upon his body. He recognized them mutely, dimly—acquiesced and raged, alternately full of furor and fervor, at this last and inmost cataclysm. He knew that the days were numbered, that mortal time was running out, despite the tender efforts at concealment that Diane made.[139]

They remained in France now, at the edge of the Mediterranean with which he had become reconciled, in the blinding light of one stormy day a few years ago.[140] He watched the migrations of birds, the trees he had planted grow tall, the cycle of the nights and days, the seasons' gentle change, the endless ebb and flow of the tides. His forces were beginning to diminish. The time had come for leave-taking—not in a slow, ever more weary waning, but with some last bursts of energy, drawn from all the remaining springs of his being.

He began the monumental task of assembling texts and documents, letters and notes, for the definitive edition of his *Oeuvres complètes* in the Pléïade edition[141] that was to contain everything he had written so far and wished to see in print. (He had left orders that, at his death, anything found still unpublished was to be destroyed.)[142] It was, in its scope and summation, a long look back over his entire life, with all its endless complexity, its trials and triumphs, a voyage into the past and a living legacy for the future.

But there was also the present—still to be lived and to the fullest, best of all in the midst of the human, and that "chaleur humaine" he so deeply valued. Friends came from every part of the globe to visit: poets from the world over, companions old and new, the famous and the unknown, the noble and the humble. He received them all with characteristic warmth and simplicity but also with his lifelong courtesy and humor intact: he raised a flag on the mast he had planted at Les Vigneaux, bearing the initials of his current visitor (as if he were the captain of a ship who honored those that came aboard). Beside it, however, a small blue banner always flew now: the signal that a ship raises when it is "en partance"[143]—ready to cast off.

There were other signs that he knew that everything he did now was a prelude to the final parting. Surely, he sensed that the works he wrote from now on would be his last. Three years after "Chanté par celle qui fut là," he wrote the poem "Chant pour un Equinoxe." Its title (which would also become that of his ultimate volume of poetry), rose from somewhere in the obscure regions of his being—with a force as mysterious and imperious as the name he had chosen, long ago, as a poet. As brief as the first work he had published over six decades ago ("Ecrit sur la porte"),[144] it compressed into a mere one and a half pages all his still awesome powers. And it revealed the key to both his life and his death.

In simplest terms, its title affirms the first/last nature of poetry as song—the earliest and most enduring form of human expression, present from time immemorial but also spanning man's life (from the tender sounds of cradle songs to the keening wail over the dead). This "Chant," however, consecrates the equinox: that juncture of opposites when day and night, the two halves of the year, the waxing and the waning seasons (and, by extension, destruction and creation) are in perfect balance—as the two platters of a scale or the uplifted palms of the celebrant in *Chronique* —at that "still point of the turning world"[145] where the end is the beginning, and the beginning the end.

As the poem opens, thunder resounds over the earth and its tombs—thunder, the harbinger of revelation, as far beyond language as the ineffable expression of the sacred. Rain begins to fall upon the poet and his beloved, and with its fructifying, purifying, and laving power, it causes love to rise once more toward its wellsprings, not only love but all things (which, in the previous poem, had seemed to move toward their end). Taking on the accents of the seer, the poet proclaims: "Je sais, j'ai vu: la vie remonte vers ses sources"[146] as he reveals that everything returns to its point of origin—thunder, the yellow pollen of the pines, the semen of the divinity rejoining the plankton in the sea—in order that all might begin again, anew.

Then snow mysteriously appears, as fresh and tender as that of "Neiges," written for his mother, now long dead. And the sky is full of stillness, the earth free of every burden—the earth of time immemorial, and of all men.

This voiceless, motionless interim marks the turn of the Great Wheel of Being and initiates the vision of rebirth—in the simple/ complex miracle that is the birth of a human child:

. . . et quelque part au monde
. . . .

un enfant naît au monde dont nul ne sait
la race,
ni le rang,
et le génie frappe à coups sûrs aux lobes d'un front pur.[147]

Affirming the endless flow of the universe, in which death
rejoins and is balanced by birth, the dying poet sees his art
invested, incarnated, and reincarnated in a new life.

As the poem draws to a close, the poet addresses himself to
the last of the elements he has recognized (and honored in
Chronique): the Earth, maternal and sepulchral, from which all
life arises and to which all life returns—the earth in which he
shall soon lie. And he chants, in conclusion, "O Terre, notre
Mère . . . la vie va son cours,"[148] without harshness or bitterness, in an acquiescence to the vast flux of existence that goes
beyond the limits of a single life—though that life be his own.

The ultimate lines sing of the great mystery that determines
the beginning and the end of poetry and its eternal renewal—at
the instant that marks the juncture of being and nonbeing:

Un chant se lève en nous qui n'a connu sa source
et qui n'aura d'estuaire dans la mort:
équinoxe d'une heure entre la Terre et l'homme.[149]

A year later he composed his penultimate poem, "Nocturne,"[150] which expressed emotions diametrically opposed to
"Chant pour un équinoxe": not a song, but a piercing cry. As its
title announces, it is a night poem written under the sign of the
black sun—full of dread, anguish, violence, and bitterness, indeed all the feelings that assail the human creature in the darkest
hours of life. A brief, sharp outcry (three stanzas and a single,
final line), it is the sole utterance of despair ever to pass the lips
of this poet.

It rails against adverse fate, its harsh, jealous, impersonal,
inexorable dictates. From its opening words, one knows that the
hour of doom is here: the fruits of a life, grown from dreams, fed
on the blood of the poet, haunting and secret and full of desire,
are now ripe and ready for gathering. But they are bitter fruit,
though regal in their tragic purple, and must submit to the

demands of imperious destiny. And he cries out in anguish at this state.

Everything celebrated in the past seems vain and void. Even the great blazing sun of noon, standing at the zenith, which (in *Amers*) had made the poet declare "l'homme immortel au foyer de l'instant"[151] is now at its nadir and denounced as a betrayer: "Soleil de l'être, trahison!"[152] The former belief in its power seems a delusion, its plenitude a lie, its alliance a mockery: "'Soleil de l'être, couvre-moi:'—parole du transfuge."[153] All things are corroded by error and flaw, fraud, desertion, and torment. In this nocturnal voyage, all roads are uncertain, the night is fathoms deep, the sacred wrenched away. Black briars and harsh blooms border the shores along which errs the shipwrecked wanderer.

Despair colors everything, now that the fruits "d'une autre rive"[154] are ripe and death approaches. The ephemeral nature of mortal existence is felt in all its pathos, for nothing seems to remain of the poet's passage on this earth—neither an identity, a dwelling place, or a heritage. His bitterest cry is addressed to that blinding light (which had once been the living symbol of plenitude and is now the very incarnation of the void): "Soleil de l'être . . . nos oeuvres sont éparses, nos tâches sans honneur et nos blés sans moisson."[155]

Yet even more terrible than this futility is the figure standing before the condemned poet: an ominous binder of sheaves who awaits him at the ebb of evening. Not the gentle Ceres, the Terra Mater, or Maïa the Intercessor, she is the dread harvester of a life devoid of meaning, sterile and vain—to whom he must offer the blood-stained fruits of his destiny.

The poem will end upon this image of death/life, this female grim reaper, indifferent, impervious to loss or gain, who moves onward and away, gathering chaff or grain: "A son pas de lieuse de gerbes s'en va la vie sans haine ni rançon."[156]

The profoundly human cry *de profundis* of "Nocturne" is as piercing as a scream of pain. The sole utterance of anguish by this poet whose entire creation has been one vast affirmation, it is all the more overwhelming for its singularity. And yet, the poem expresses not only the deepest level of despair. It is also a threshold, a turning point, a fulcrum. For, by its journey to the very end of night, "Nocturne" announces the advent of a metamorphosis. Only after the plunge to the bottom of the abyss can the passage be found that leads from death to rebirth. Thus, this night poem marks the entry into the nocturnal domain, the realm of mystic experience, where symbols are subject to reversal, images acquire their opposite meaning,[157] and destruction is revealed as creation.

This experience attains its greatest intensity in the last poem of Saint-John Perse, written only a year before his death. "Sécheresse."[158] At first glance, its title suggests aridity, sterility, withering—a wasteland, nonlife. It seems to evoke the end of the world, and of creativity. Indeed, the initial sequence of the poem describes just such a state: parched earth, white clay cemented around all springs, empires destroyed by fire, ghostlike female gadflies draining naked men of their blood, language turned to scarlet muck and refuted as utter vanity.[159]

Yet, almost instantly, the meaning of "sécheresse" changes and—as has quite rightly been suggested—reveals the eschatological function of the poem.[160] For, in order for recreation to occur, the existing world must be annihilated, totally. The end must be reached if there is to be a new beginning. The level of nothingness must be attained before a higher state of being can prevail. The poetic act itself, in conjuring up this absence, this nullity, becomes an incarnation of the sacrificial rite in which regeneration can be accomplished only by catastrophe or cataclysm. Seen in this light, the title refers to the desert, a double symbol—of sterility and nonlife but also of illumination and revelation. Both in "Exil" and "Sécheresse" (and the two notions as well as the two titles are linked), the lowest point of existence must be reached before the upward turn of the cycle can begin again. In that sense also, drought is both the dessication of all life and the purification by heat, fire, torment, which strips away all that is corrupt and corruptible in order that a new freedom and a greater reality may arise. "La terre a dépouillé ses graisses et nous lègue sa concision,"[161] the poet intones, as if the earth itself had been consumed like a burnt offering in sacrifice and he, as the hierophant, could speak now in the voice of one transformed.

Drought, from an initially negative symbol, changes into the sign that identifies the Chosen: "Sécheresse, ô faveur! honneur et luxe d'une élite! dis-nous le choix de tes élus,"[162] just as eclipse and dearth of flesh become the marks of "l'Appelé"[163] (He-who-is-called). His very trials signal his election; the torment he undergoes is proof of his calling. As in all initiatory experiences (and, most especially, that of the shaman), symbolic death and (particularly in the latter case) reduction to the skeletal state by a stripping away of the flesh until the indestructible, incorruptible essence of the bone is attained[164] is an essential part of the ritual. Moreover, as the Chosen, the poet/shaman becomes the harbinger of drought, the agent of destruction—by ire, sacred furor, heat and fire. He sets the dry earth ablaze and, from this flaming apocalypse (when all is consumed and the end of the world has come), prophesies the advent of a new beginning.

Addressing himself to Maïa (Maya), the great Hindu divinity, known as "the enchantress . . . who lures souls into multi-form all-embracing existence, into the ocean of life," "the mother of all Buddhas," who "in her eternal, loving embrace . . . in her aspect as the 'redeeming one' . . . holds Shiva who . . . is the divine representation of the attitude of the 'redeemed one'" and is also "the power of the godhead as the whirling wheel of life in its life-bringing and death-bringing totality,"[165] whom he calls "douce et sage et Mère de tous songes, conciliatrice et médiatrice,"[166] he then proclaims that rebirth is imminent: "Les temps vont revenir, qui ramèneront le rythme des saisons; les nuits vont ramener l'eau vive aux tétines de la terre"; "la vie remontera de ses abris sous terre."[167]

In the great surge of life arising anew, love (or the creative, sexual energy of the universe) drives the sap up into the stem, swells from beneath bone and horn, renews the earth's crust,

214   UNDER THE SIGN OF AMBIGUITY

brings on the rut of stags.[168] Eros vanquishes Thanatos. The seared wasteland is revitalized by rain (in the guise of a female flamenco dancer) that awakens the world by its wild, erotic beat.[169] "O mouvement vers l'Etre et renaissance de l'Etre!"[170] the poet exclaims. And he goes on to affirm in tones of fervent prophecy: "Oui, tout cela sera. Oui, les temps reviendront, qui lèvent l'interdit sur la face de la terre."[171]

At this instant, poised between end and beginning, time acquires a new meaning: "l'offrande au temps n'est plus la même."[172] Chronological, mortal time gives way to eternal, sacred Time or—as it is called in this poem—"temps de Dieu."[173] The latter, synonymous with the Great Round or the notion of eternal return, is of course not linear but cyclical and proceeds in an endless series in which annihilation is followed by regeneration.

The poet/seer addresses himself to this sacred Time in three successive incantations—each opposing the ephemeral and temporal with the enduring and eternal; the brevity and futility of human life,[174] its fragmented, fragmentary nature,[175] its harsh, bitter, furtive aspect[176] with the infinite, unifying, propitious "temps de Dieu."

As "l'Appelé," the Chosen, having faced trials, torment, and destruction (that are the signs of his election), approaches the instant of epiphany, he stands at the juncture of nadir and zenith, at the point where the union of opposites is absolute, and proclaims the ultimate paradox: "Midi l'aveugle nous éclaire."[177] Illuminated by blindness, celebrating drought as boon and passion, possessed by the spirit of the god, raving, drunk on cataclysms, the poet/shaman—at the end of his quest—comes face to face with the sacred and pronounces his final incantation:

Par les sept os soudés du front et de la face, que l'homme en Dieu s'entête et s'use jusqu'à l'os, ah! jusqu'à l'éclatement de l'os! . . . Songe de Dieu, sois-nous complice.[178]

Voicing the belief that total union with the divine follows annihilation, that the explosion of the mortal state opens the way to resurrection on a higher plane, the dream of the poet attains the dimension of a sacred vision, a dream limitless and everlasting.

Lest the poem end devoid of ambiguity, however, its last line is a virulent denunciation of the rational,[179] nonvisionary tendency that ever assails the human creature. "Singe de Dieu, trêve à tes ruses!"[180] the irate seer shouts. And, in this juxtaposition of "Songe de Dieu," and its derisive echo "Singe de Dieu," the opposition between sacred splendor and its vain aping by reason, Saint-John Perse maintains his characteristic duality almost to the last breath.

For no other words issued from his pen before he died, except for a brief reflection upon a beloved musical composition (a fragment of the andante movement of Beethoven's *Emperor Concerto*, whose score lay on his work table), written on May 31, 1975[181]—his eighty-eighth birthday, and his last. It was a moving tribute to artistic creation, infinitely revealing of his own deepest emotions, spoken in a voice overwhelming in its simplicity and humanity. Universal at the outset, intimate at its conclusion, it was a fitting testament of the artist and the man:

> Au coeur de toute création artistique il y a parfois ce don très pur d'une larme et cette visitation mystérieuse en nous comme d'une grâce souveraine: grâce . . . rédemptrice, libératrice et secourable, au plus proche de l'ineffable et de son effusion secrète, comme la résolution finale, en musique, de l'accord longuement sollicité.
>
> J'ai connu cette grâce en présence d'une page de Beethoven. . . . Les larmes que j'ai senti parfois monter en moi devant cette page sont les seules qu'ait jamais pu tirer de moi aucune oeuvre de main d'homme.[182]

Just as revealing, however, as this last "éloge," was the work Saint-John Perse undertook during the final months of his life: the arrangements of the poems written in the past seven years as he wished them to appear in the volume *Chant pour un Équinoxe*.[183] Although not instantly perceived (because silent), the task of placing the poems in their particular, and ultimate, sequence is of the greatest significance. Close scrutiny reveals that they follow, not according to the date of their composition, but in nonchronological order[184]—a fitting statement in itself, since they speak of matters outside and beyond the temporal. Seen as a group, their thematics and imagery contribute to the creation of a movement wavelike in its crests and troughs, cyclical in its evocation of abyss and summit. Divided into two pairs, they reveal juxtaposition and resolution of equal force. For in each pair ("Sécheresse" and "Chant pour un Équinoxe"; "Nocturne" and "Chanté par celle qui fut là") the first poem speaks of torment, anguish, and annihilation, while the second affirms tenderness, redemptive grace, and regeneration. Finally, the title chosen for the volume—celebrating the equinox—accentuates the encounter of opposites, discordant harmony, ultimate synthesis, that "accord longuement sollicité" (of which the text on Beethoven also speaks), absolute unity attained as the final chord resounds.

As if the choice of the title *Chant pour un Équinox* had been a prophecy, Saint-John Perse/Alexis Leger died at the time of the autumnal equinox: September 20, 1975.[185]

Surely, the great window stood open to the water as he lay dying. And his last gaze encompassed all the seas he had known: the Mediterranean, finally reconciled; the Atlantic at the west, ocean of the past and his whole lineage; the terrestrial sea trail that led to Ourga; the trackless deep he had traveled the world over; and the great "Sea within us" that he had sung as probably no other man has done.

His body was laid in the earth of the small cemetery on the Giens peninsula.[186] Winds, salt air, and flights of birds sweep over his grave in that "cimetière marin"[187] on this all-but island.

He lies buried, as he was born, at the edge of the sea.

Plaque which now marks the "rue Saint-John Perse" in Pointe-à-Pitre.
The inscription beneath his name reads:
          "Tous les Chemins du Monde
          vous mangent dans la main"
fittingly commemorating the poet. (Photo by the author).

NOTES

Prologue: The Complex Image

1. *Vents, Saint-John Perse: Oeuvres complètes*, Bibliothèque de la Pléïade (Paris: Gallimard, 1972), p. 213. Hereafter cited as *OC*.

2. Letter to M.-P. Fouchet, 27 Mar. 1948, *OC*, p. 988. [Virtually the same phrase appears in a letter to A. MacLeish, 23. Dec. 1941, OC, p. 549.]

3. E.g., "Le Donateur," "Le plus hautement libre," "Quelques raisons de louer," "Dignité du langage," "Un poète de sang bleu," "L'Etranger majestueux," "Le seul Maître," "Miracle des mots," etc., titles of articles in *Honneur à Saint-John Perse* (Paris: Gallimard, 1965) that contains over 800 pages, almost all written in a laudatory vein. Hereafter cited as *HP*.

4. E.g., letters to G.-A. Monod and J. Rivière, *OC*, pp. 646–54 and 666–70, respectively.

5. Letter to M. Curtiss, 11 Jan. 1954, *OC*, p. 1049.

6. *Amitié du Prince* (1924), signed, alternately, "Saint-John Perse" and "St.-J. Perse;" see *OC*, p. 1347.

7. See *OC*, p. 575.

8. "Petite remontée dans un nom-titre," *Microlectures* (Paris: Seuil, 1979), pp. 195–203. [Richard's study brilliantly develops a notion already put forth by Albert Thibaudet, "L'Anabase de Saint-John Perse," *L'Europe Nouvelle*, 9 Aug. 1924, pp. 19–26, concerning a link between the poet's names and titles.]

9. Daniel Racine, "La Fortune de Saint-John Perse en Amérique jusqu'en 1970," doctoral dissertation, Sorbonne (Paris IV), June 1972, p. 459.

10. The sun at the zenith (at midday or midyear) as well as sacrificial rites constitute key images in Perse's poetry. The most dramatic illustration can be found in *Amers*, but numerous other examples testify to thematic constancy.

11. "Léon-Paul Fargue," *OC*, p. 507.

12. *OC*, p. 1094. [One cannot help but see parallels between this statement and the comparison of "Léon-Paul Fargue" and "Saïnt-John Perse"—also based on rhythmic and tonal distribution—mentioned above.]

13. Pierre Mazars, "Une journée à la villa 'Les Vigneaux,' *Le Figaro Littéraire*, 5 Nov. 1960, rpt. *HP*, p. 621. [It is also possible that the name "Archibald" came to the attention of Saint-Leger Leger because of Archibald MacLeish who was in Paris in the early 1920s, at the time the former was deciding on a pseudonym.]

14. Interview with Marcos Victoria, Buenos Aires, 1960, rpt. *OC*, p. 1094.

15. For details see *OC*, pp. 814, 1240; *HP*, p. 175.

16. Pierre Guerre, "Dans la haute maison de mer: Rencontres avec Saint-John Perse," *HP*, p. 178.

17. Mazars, *HP*, p. 618.

18. I.e., "Saint-Leger," "Saint-John Perse," "A. Saint-Leger Leger," "Alexis Leger," all on p. xix (*OC*).

19. A. J. K[nodel], "Saint-John Perse," *Columbia Dictionary of Modern European Literature*, eds. Jean-Albert Bédé, William B. Edgerton, 2d ed. (New York: Columbia University Press, 1980), p. 707. Hereafter cited as *CDMEL*.

20. *OC*, pp. x, xi.

21. *OC*, p.xli. [For a discussion of the Atlantic as an "open sea," etc., see *OC*, pp. xl–xli.]

22. In 1899, 1917, 1920, 1940, respectively.

23. E.g., see *OC*, pp. 1204–12.

24. Letter to J. Rivière, 14 June 1911, *OC*, p. 695.

25. See, esp. *OC*, pp. 1208–12.

26. In the archives of the Fondation Saint-John Perse, Aix-en-Provence, France.

27. Letter to Mrs. F. Biddle, 13 Sept. 1945, *OC*, p. 907.

28. For discouragement see *OC*, p. 942, 973, 988, 990; for disparagement see *OC*, pp. 963–64.

29. *OC*, pp. ix–xliv.

30. *Le Rituel poétique de Saint-John Perse* (Paris: Gallimard, 1977).

31. *Rituel et poésie: Une lecture de Saint-John Perse* (Berne: Peter Lang, 1977).

32. Letters to Mme Amédée Saint-Leger Leger (hereafter cited as MSLL) from her son Alexis (Peking, 1918–19), *OC*, pp. 853, 861, 871–72.

33. Letter to MSLL, 4 Apr. 1917, *OC*, p. 841.

34. Letter to MSLL, 5 June 1920, *OC*, p. 881.

35. A shaman's thunder stone, found near the Tolgoït of Ourga and a horse's skull discovered in the Gobi Desert. Letter to G.-C. Toussaint, 29 Mar. 1921, *OC*, p.894. [For more details see Chapter 4.]

36. For details concerning this see Chapter 5.

37. See note 1.

38. Letter to Mrs. F. Biddle, 11 Aug. 1953, *OC*, p. 916.

39. Marriage, Apr. 1958, to Dorothy Russell, called Dorothy in the United States and Diane in France by the poet. See letters to M. Curtiss, *OC*, pp. 1058, 1063–65, and Chapter 7.

40. Guerre, *HP*, p. 180.

41. "Hommage à Saint-John Perse," *Cahiers de la Pléiade* (1950), rpt. *OC*, p. 1298.

42. Dedication in the hand of Louis Aragon, *Le Libertinage* (Paris: La Nouvelle Revue Française, 1924), in the personal library of Saint-John Perse, Fondation Saint-John Perse. Herafter cited as *PLP*.

43. *New York Times Book Review* 62, no. 30 (27 July 1958), p. 5.

44. "Saint-John Perse chez ses amis d'Amérique," *HP,* p. 298.

45. Letter to J. Rivière, 9 Sep. 1911, *HP,* p. 606.

46. "Hommage," *HP,* p. 149.

47. *New Republic,* 20 Apr. 1953, p. 27.

48. "Hommage," *HP,* p. 155.

49. "Un poème de Saint-John Perse: 'Vents,'" *La Revue de Paris* (1 Nov. 1949), p. 4. Rpt. *HP,* pp. 4–6.

50. Dedication in the hand of Anna de Noailles, *Poème de l'amour* (Paris: Fayard, 1924), *PLP.*

51. "Saint-John Perse ou le Vertige de la Plénitude," *HP,* p. 224.

52. "Eloge de Saint-John Perse," *HP,* p. 261.

53. *HP,* p. 173.

54. Heading of a letter to Alexis Leger, 3 Mar. 1936, *HP,* p. 798.

55. "Sodome et Gomorrhe," *A la Recherche du temps perdu,* Bibliothèque de la Pléiade, vol. II (Paris: Gallimard, 1966), p. 849. [The reference is to the poems of "Saint-Léger Léger" (*sic*). Since the passage in question was composed in 1922, the reference is certainly to *Eloges,* published under the name Saint-Leger Leger.]

56. "Léon-Paul Fargue," *OC*, pp. 516–17.

57. "Pour Dante" (Oration delivered in Florence), *OC*, pp. 454–59.

58. Saint-John Perse/Alexis Leger, born May 31 (1887), shares Dante's birth sign of Gemini (the Twins).

Chapter 1: Son of the Atlantic

1. Saint-John Perse/Alexis Leger first among them. See his comparison of the form of islands to the letter *O,* which links it to its homonym (*eau*) and to the birth passage, in his letter to G. Frizeau, 7 Feb. 1909, *OC*, p. 741. See also the discussion by Etienne-Alain Hubert, "A Propos de l'Animale,'" *Cahiers Saint-John Perse 5* (Paris: Gallimard, 1982), esp. p. 134.

2. *OC*, p. 1087.

3. *OC*, p. xli; also Liliane Chauleau, *La vie quotidienne aux Antilles françaises au XIXe siècle* (Paris: Hachette, 1979), p. 235; also, Lafcadio Hearn, *Two Years in the French West Indies* (New York and London: Harper & Brothers, 1890; republished, Upper Saddle River, N.J.: Literature House/Gregg Press, 1970), pp. 36, 130.

4. *OC*, p. xl; Chauleau, op cit., p. 9.

5. *OC*, pp. xl–xli. This also corroborates the notion of a birth at sea, discussed in note 1.

6. *OC*, p. xli.

7. Ibid.

8. *OC*, p. 1087.

9. (Various races): *OC*, p. ix; Chauleau, op. cit., pp. 21, 42–43; Hearn, op. cit., pp. 38, 39, 46.

10. (His mother's hostility toward the sea), *OC*, pp. 841, 853 (letters to MSLL).

11. Chauleau, op, cit., p. 95.

12. Chauleau, op. cit., p. 227; Hearn, op, cit., pp. 34–35.

13. Chauleau, op. cit.,p. 96.

14. Chauleau, op. cit., p. 98; Hearn, op. cit., pp. 240–44.

15. Chauleau, op. cit., pp. 98–99; Hearn, op, cit., pp. 104–5.

16. (History of the emancipation of slaves in the French Antilles), Chauleau, op. cit., pp. 36–39, 176.

17. Chauleau, op. cit., p. 107.

18. Chauleau, op. cit., p. 108.

19. Chauleau, op. cit., p. 109.

20. Chauleau, op. cit., p. 121.

21. Chauleau, op. cit., pp. 121–22; Hearn, op. cit., pp. 44–46.

22. Chauleau, op. cit., p. 123.

23. Chauleau, op. cit.; Hearn, op. cit., pp. 40–42.

24. Chauleau, op. cit., p. 107.

25. *OC*, pp. x, xiv; "Notes," *OC*, pp. 1088–90.

26. *OC*, p. x.

27. *OC*, p. xiv; P.-M. Raymond, "Humanité de Saint-John Perse," *HP*, p. 111.

28. *OC*, p. x.

29. For references to the pious nature of his mother see letters to MSLL, *OC*, pp. 853, 859; also, *Neiges* (dedicated to her), *OC*, pp. 156–63.

30. *OC*, p. ix.

31. *OC*, pp. ix, 74; "Notes," pp. 1099–1100; for typical plantations in Guadeloupe in the nineteenth century see Chauleau, op. cit., pp. 133–35, 158, 162.

32. *OC*, p. 1100; also, *Pour fêter une enfance*, *OC*, p. 23.

33. *Eloges*, *OC*, p. 37.

34. (General landscape): Chauleau, op. cit., pp. 10–12. (Trees of the region): Chauleau, op. cit., p. 129; also, Hearn, op. cit., pp. 52–56.

35. "Cases à vent/à ouragon" ("wind/hurricane huts"): Chauleau, op. cit., pp. 14, 236. [Chauleau specifies that these huts, found on all plantations, had one small opening that faced west. Openness, wind, and the West, important motifs in the poetry of Saint-John Perse, thus appear as part of his childhood landscape and can be seen to have their origin there.]

36. "Ma bonne . . . sa bouche avait le goût des pommes-rose." *Eloges*, *OC*, p. 26.

37. Ibid., p. 48.

38. For a description of the life of upper-class white children see Chauleau, op. cit., pp. 245–46; for a contrasting view [black children] see Simone Schwarz-Bart, *Pluie et vent sur Télumée Miracle* (Paris: Seuil, 1972).

39. Letter to MSLL, 10 Jan. 1917, *OC*, p. 832.

40. "Et un nuage violet et jaune . . . s'arrêtait soudain à couronner le volcan d'or." *Pour fêter une enfance*, *OC*, p. 25.

41. Léon Le Boucher, *La Guadeloupe pittoresque* (Paris: Société d'Editions Géographiques, Maritimes et Coloniales, 1931), p. 187.

42. *Eloges*, *OC*, p. 36.

43. Ibid., p. 40.

44. *OC*, p. ix.

45. Letters to MSLL (Peking), 2 Feb. 1918, *OC*, p. 854; Feb. 1919, *OC*, p. 871.

46. Ibid., p. 872.

47. Letter to MSLL, 10 Jan. 1917, *OC*, pp. 829–30. [Air and space would become extremely important elements in the thematics of Saint-John Perse's poetry.]

48. Letter to MSLL, 9 Apr. 1918, *OC*, p. 859.

49. Chauleau, op. cit., p. 16.

50. *OC*, p. 872.

51. Chauleau, op. cit., p. 264; *OC*, p. 740.

52. Cited in a letter to MSLL, 17 May 1921, *OC*, p. 883.

53. *OC*, p. xi; also, descriptions in *Eloges*, *OC*, p. 34 (horse); ibid., pp. 39–40 (boat); letter to G. Frizeau, 7 Feb. 1909, *OC*, p. 741 (telescope).

54. *OC*, p. x; *Eloges*, *OC*, p. 41.

55. Letter to MSLL, Feb. 1919, *OC*, p. 868.

56. *Eloges*, *OC*, p. 34.

57. *OC*, p. xi; *Eloges*, *OC*, p. 24.

58. Alexis's paternal and maternal grandfathers had died in 1888 and 1890, respectively; *OC*, p. x.

59. (Cat) *Eloges*, *OC*, p. 45 (dog); ibid., p. 36.

60. For an account of this initiation see Raymond, *HP*, p. 111. A reference to this important incident can also be found in a letter to MSLL, written about twenty years later (9 Apr. 1918): *OC*, p. 859. For descriptions of Hindu women and Indian temples in the Antilles see Hearn, op. cit., pp. 76–77, 84–86.

61. For Shiva and his cult see Joseph Campbell, *The Masks of God: Oriental Mythology* (London: Penguin Books, 1979), pp. 169, 351, 365; Veronica Ions, *Indian Mythology* (London: Paul Hamlyn, 1967), pp. 36, 42, 116; Philip Rawson, *Erotic Art of the East* (New York: Putman's Sons, 1969), pp. 33, 39–40, 57, 164.

62. Ions, op. cit., pp. 12, 38, 42, 116; Rawson, op. cit., pp. 33, 38, 40, 165–66; also, O. E. Cirlot, *A Dictionary of Symbols* (New York: Philosophical Library, 1962), pp. 30, 431–42.

63. Cirlot, op. cit., pp. 74, 95, 324, 333; Ions, op. cit., pp. 44, 90, 97; Rawson, op. cit., pp. 153, 162, 164–66.

64. For continued references to Shiva's cult and Tantrism (or sexual union as a form of worship) see, e.g., *OC*, pp. 646, 821; *HP*, p. 667; also, "Etroits sont les vaisseaux" (the central sequence of *Amers*) for mythical concepts directly related to Shiva and the Tantric cult.

65. *OC*, pp. ix–x, xi.

66. *Pour fêter une enfance*, *OC*, p. 24; *Eloges*, *OC*, pp. 42, 43, 46.

67. *Eloges*, *OC*, p. 46.

68. "Notes," *OC*, p. 1194.

69. Chauleau, op. cit., pp. 14–16.

70. *OC*, p. xi; *Eloges*, *OC*, p. 44.

71. *OC*, p. xi; "Notes," *OC*, pp. 1087–88 (sale of island and renaming for Petreluzzi). *Note:* ten years later Alexis Leger still expressed regret over the sale of the island: see letter to G. Frizeau, 7 Feb. 1909, *OC*, p. 740.

Chapter 2: Crusoé in France

1. *OC*, p. xi.
2. Ibid.
3. Ibid.
4. Ibid.
5. Ibid.
6. *OC*, p. xii.
7. *OC*, p. 1215.
8. *OC*, p. xi.
9. Ibid. [His lifelong aversion of books manifested itself in a variety of ways. For examples see Guerre, *HP*, p. 172; Emmanuel Berl, "Alexis Leger et Briand," *HP*, 777; and Perse's poem *Vents*, esp. *OC*, pp. 186–87.]
10. Also a future collaborator of *La Nouvelle Revue Française*, *OC*, p. xii.
11. Ibid.
12. Ibid. See also Léon Moulin, "Introduction," *Francis Jammes: Choix de poèmes* (Paris: Mercure de France, 1917), p. 15; R[obert] D[enommé], "Francis Jammes," *CDMEL*, pp. 401–2.
13. *Six Sonnets* (1891): *Vers* (1892–94). See Denommé, op. cit., p. 401.
14. Saint-John Perse mentions a poem written at the age of ten (*OC*, p. 1194) and another, "Des villes sur trois modes," when he was a *lycéen* (*OC*, pp. 651–54).
15. Moulin, op. cit., pp. 15, 35.
16. Letter to F. Jammes, 13 Jan. 1910, *OC*, p. 759.
17. Letter to F. Jammes, Dec. 1910, *OC*, p. 759.
18. Letter to G.-A. Monod, 26 June 1909, *OC*, p. 656.
19. Dedication in the hand of Francis Jammes, *Rayons de miel: Eglogues* (Paris: Bibliothèque de l'Occident, 1908), *PLP*.
20. Composed in 1904 and published in *La Nouvelle Revue Française* in 1909.
21. E.g., statement in a letter to F. Jammes, June 1911, *OC*, pp. 762–63.
22. During Midnight Mass on Christmas Eve, at the moment of the Magnificat, in Notre Dame Cathedral.
23. Published in 1910. However, "Les Muses," the first of the *Cinq grandes odes*, was composed between 1900 and 1904. The poem is considered one of the finest examples of French lyricism.
24. Completed in 1905 (although subsequently revised numerous times), *Partage de midi* transposed Claudel's illicit love affair into what is frequently thought to be his most grandiose drama.
25. Both poets were born in the year 1868.
26. *OC*, p. xiii. [André Blanchet, in his introduction to *Paul Claudel—Francis Jammes—Gabriel Frizeau: Correspondence (1897–1938)* (Paris: Gallimard, 1952), p. 17, states: "L'ode aux Muses, ce premier cup de tonnerre du pur lyrisme Claudélien . . . révélait Alexis Leger à lui-même, lui révélait Saint-John Perse."]

27. "The Journal of André Gide" (December 1, 5, 1905), in *The Correspondence between Paul Claudel and André Gide* (New York: Pantheon, 1952), pp. 44, 46–47.

28. *Correspondence de Jacques Rivière et d'Alain Fournier* (Paris: Gallimard, 1928), rpt. *HP*, pp. 603–5.

29. For these and other comparisons between Paul Claudel and Saint-John Perse see Ruth M. Horry, *Paul Claudel and Saint-John Perse* (Chapel Hill: University of North Carolina Press, 1971), esp. pp. 8–9, 18, 25, 33, 34, 57, 68, 101, 103. For Claudel's laughter see Pierre Moreau, "Introduction," and Jacques Madaule, "Les Sources du comique dans le cosmique," *Cahiers Paul Claudel 2: Le Rire* (Paris: Gallimard, 1960), pp. 11–19 and 185–208, respectively.

30. For the passage in question see *Images à Crusoé, OC*, p. 20.

31. Excerpts from the diary of Paul Morand, quoted in *The Correspondence between Paul Claudel and André Gide*, p. 284.

32. As told to Claude Vigée (in 1959), *OC*, pp. 1302–3. [The same incident is told by Vigée in "La Quête de l'origine dans la poésie de Saint-John Perse," *HP*, pp. 345–46, but with a notable error in the date: Alexis Leger was eighteen, not thirteen, years old, as stated by Vigée.]

33. Jacques Rivière's account of the conversion attempt, in *The Correspondence between Paul Claudel and André Gide*, p. 7, differs considerably from Vigée's in that the former states: "L. L. came out in tears, and left the house at once."

34. Letter to P. Claudel, 1906, Nov. *OC*, p. 712.

35. Letter to G.-A. Monod, Mar. 1907, *OC*, p. 649.

36. Ibid.

37. Ibid.

38. Letter to Claudel, Nov. 1906; letter to G.-A. Monod, Jan. 1907, *OC*, p. 648.

39. (Descriptions of military life): *OC*, pp. 645–46, 648, 757, 1222.

40. Letter to G.-A. Monod, May 1906, *OC*, p. 646. [In speaking of "nihilisme oriental," Leger again refers to the servant-priestess of Shiva.]

41. Letter to G.-A. Monod, Jan. 1907, *OC*, p. 648.

42. *Tichodroma muraria*, or "Rose-des-Alpes," *OC*, p. xiii.

43. Lac d'Estaens, ibid.

44. Letter to G.-A. Monod, Mar. 1907 [shortly after the death of Leger's father], *OC*, p. 649.

45. Letter to P. Claudel, 31 Dec. 1907, *OC*, pp. 715–16.

46. Ibid., p. 716.

47. Letter to Monod, May 1906, *OC*, p. 644. [More than forty years later Saint-John Perse still saw religion in similar fashion, as "le besoin le plus élémentaire d'Absolu." Letter to Claudel, 7 Jan. 1950, *OC*, p. 1020.]

48. Letter to Monod, May 1908, *OC*, p. 650.

49. Letter to Claudel, 10 Dec. 1908, *OC*, p. 717.

50. Letter to Monod, May 1908, *OC*, p. 649.

51. Letter to Monod, July 1909, *OC*, p. 659. [Written during the period of

mourning for his maternal grandmother, whom he loved deeply; see *OC*, p. xiv.].

52. Letter to P. Claudel, 10 Dec. 1908, *OC*, p. 717.

53. E.g., "Mais si un homme tient pour agréable sa tristesse, qu'on le produise dans le jour;/Et mon avis est qu'on le tue!" *Anabase*, *OC*, p. 96. [Although this is the most famous—and fiercest—pronouncement, others can be found all throughout his work.]

54. Letter to Clauel, 10 Dec. 1908, *OC*, p. 717.

55. Letter to Claudel, June 1907, *OC*, p. 713.

56. *Pour fêter une enfance*, *OC*, p. 25.

57. Letter to Rivière, 13 Sept. 1909, *OC*, p. 665.

58. Mourning and "fêter" are associated in numerous instances, e.g., in a discussion of Beethoven's third symphony (originally entitled "Symphonie pour fêter le souvenir d'un grand homme"); see letter to Monod, May 1908, *OC*, p. 650; in a poem composed at this time (originally entitled "Pour fêter les oiseaux") see letter to Gide, *OC*, pp 682–89 (for text and discussion of this poem).

59. The poem shows a marked repetition of the word *alors*—or its variant, *jadis*. Its thematics emphasize an Edenlike atmosphere and celebrate the nobility, grandeur, and auroral freshness of childhood.

60. *OC*, p. 28.

61. Letter to Rivière, 13 Sept. 1909, *OC*, p. 665.

62. Letter to Gide, May 1911, *OC*, p. 769.

Chapter 3: Crossroads

1. E.g., letter to G. Frizeau, Mar. 1907, *OC*, p. 730.

2. Letter to J. Rivière, 21 Dec. 1910, *OC*, p. 680.

3. I.e., by the death of her husband and her mother-in-law, in 1907 and 1908, respectively, *OC*, pp. xiii–xiv.

4. Concerning his paternal grandmother Leger wrote: "J'ai un nouveau deuil très lourd: j'ai perdu la mère de mon père, mon vrai sang, dont j'avais encore besoin pour me comprendre." Letter to Frizeau, 22 Aug. 1908, *OC*, pp. 735–36.

5. Letter to Frizeau, 30 Apr. 1911, *OC*, pp. 753–54.

6. Letter to G.-A. Monod, July 1909, *OC*, p. 660; letter to J. Rivière, 21 Dec. 1910, *OC*, p. 680.

7. Letter to Monod, Jan. 1907, *OC*, p. 648.

8. The narrator who is a rancher or plantation owner in a country that resembles either South America or the poet's birthplace. See *OC*, pp. 7–8.

9. Letter to Frizeau, 7 Feb. 1909, *OC*, p. 740.

10. Letter to Rivière, 21 Dec. 1910, *OC*, p. 681.

11. Letter to Monod, July 1909, *OC*, p. 659.

12. Letter to Rivière, 13 Feb. 1916, *OC*, p. 705.

13. *OC*, p. xiv.

14. E.g., letter to Monod, Oct. 1906, *OC*, p. 647; letter to Claudel, Nov. 1906, *OC*, p. 712.

15. *OC*, p. xiv.

16. Letter to Frizeau, 27 Feb. 1909, *OC*, p. 743.

17. Ibid.

18. Ibid.

19. Ibid., pp. 743–44.

20. Ibid., p. 743.

21. *Amitié du prince*. [For interesting comparisons between Saint-John Perse and Nietzsche—and especially between Zarathustra and the "Prince" of the poem mentioned above see Byron Colt, "Saint-John Perse," *Modern Language Quarterly* 3, no. 3 (1960), pp. 9–16.]

22. *OC*, p. xvi.

23. Letter to Claudel, 10 June 1911, *OC*, p. 722.

24. Letter to Frizeau, 17 Jan. 1908, *OC*, p. 731. [The letter also contains excerpts of Leger's translation and his notes, see pp. 731–33.]

25. Letter to Frizeau, 23 Mar. 1908, *OC*, p. 734.

26. Ibid.

27. Letter to Frizeau, 10 Mar. 1911, *OC*, p. 753.

28. E.g., "Léon-Paul Fargue," *OC*, pp. 507–32.

29. Letter to Monod, Sept. 1908, *OC*, p. 650. [A variant of this exclamation can be found in a letter to Frizeau, 19 Sept. 1908, *OC*, p. 738.]

30. (In the poems *Saint Paul, Saint Pierre,* and *Saint Jacques,* respectively). Letter to Claudel, 15 Feb. 1910, *OC*, p. 718.

31. Letter from Gide to Claudel, 12 Mar. 1910, in *Paul Claudel et André Gide: Correspondence (1899–1926)* (Paris: Gallimard, 1949), p. 128.

32. *The Correspondence between Paul Claudel and André Gide* (New York: Pantheon, 1952), p. 172.

33. Ibid., p. 185.

34. Ibid., p. 165; see also *Cahiers Paul Claudel 1* (Paris: Gallimard, 1959), pp. 54, 101.

35. For an excellent discussion of this topic see Yves Bonnefoy, "Eloge et Illumination," in *Le Nuage rouge* (Paris: Mercure de France, 1977), pp. 221–33.

36. "Léon-Paul Fargue," *OC*, p. 519.

37. Letter to Rivière, 8 July 1910, *OC*, p. 675.

38. Ibid.

39. Letter to Rivière, 18 July 1913, *OC*, p. 707. [In the poem *Vents,* written over thirty years later, one finds numerous echoes of that "hâte" ("haste") admired in Rimbaud: e.g., *OC*, pp. 181, 193, 247; and Saint-John Perse excelled at the art of the ellipsis and the leap.]For an excellent discussion of this question see also Jean-Pierre Richard, "Figures avec paysages," In *Pages Paysages: Microlectures II* (Paris: Editions du Seuil, 1984), pp. 157–60.

40. Letter to Monod, 9 May 1909, *OC*, p. 655.

41. Letter from Alain Fournier to Jacques Rivière, 9 Sept. 1911, *HP*, p. 605.

42. The other poems are: "Chanson du présomptif" and "Berceuse," *OC*, pp. 73–84.

43. E.g., see letter to Frizeau, 30 Apr. 1911, *OC*, p. 755.

44. Letter to Frizeau, Mar. 1910, *OC*, p. 750.

45. *OC*, p. 58.

46. *OC*, p. 60.

47. See Chapter 1, notes 60–63.

48. See Chapter 2, note 41.

49. Letter to Claudel, Nov. 1906, *OC*, p. 712.

50. Letter to Frizeau, 19 Sept. 1908, *OC*, p. 738.

51. See note 38.

52. *OC*, pp. 65, 53, 69, respectively.

53. (Refrain), *OC*, pp. 66, 68, 70, 72. [Note the oxymoron in this typically paradoxical epithet.]

54. Op. cit., Epigraph, *OC*, p. 67.

55. *OC*, p. xiv.

56. Which Leger had named "L'Animale." Letter to Frizeau, 7 Feb. 1909, *OC*, p. 741. For the recently discovered text of the poem by the same name see Albert Henry, "*L'Animale*," *Cahiers Saint-John Perse 4* (Paris: Gallimard, 1981), pp. 10–26. For the identification of the Gauguin painting in question see Etienne Albert Hubert, "A Propos de *L'Animale:* Un tableau de Gauguin," *Cahiers Saint-John Perse 5* (Paris: Gallimard, 1982), pp. 129–34.

57. Letter to Frizeau, 9 Mar. 1909, *OC*, p. 744.

58. In *La Nouvelle Revue Française* (1 Aug. 1909); see *OC*, p. 1203.

59. Letter to Rivière, 13 Sept. 1909, *OC*, p. 665.

60. Letter to Frizeau, 19 Dec. 1909, *OC*, p. 668.

61. [Ubu, Alfred Jarry's famous character incarnating the sum of man's ignoble qualities.] Letter to Frizeau, 17 Feb. 1910, *OC*, pp. 670–71.

62. Letter to Frizeau, 10 Dec. 1909, *OC*, p. 668.

63. Ibid.

64. E.g., Rivière, Gide, Frizeau: see *OC*, pp. 665, 744, 1203.

65. See letter to Monod, 10 May 1911, *OC*, p. 663.

66. Evidently, Spinoza's *Tractus theologicus*, which Leger had asked Monod to lend him: see letter to Monod, 26 June 1909, *OC*, p. 655.

67. Letter to Monod, July 1909, *OC*, p. 657.

68. Ibid.

69. Letter to Monod, Sept. 1909, *OC*, p. 662.

70. Letter to Rivière. 8 July 1910, *OC*, p. 675.

71. *OC*, p. xv.

72. According to those who knew Leger well. [However, his friendships with musicians (Stravinsky, Honneger, Varèse, and others) were numerous.]

73. Letter to Rivière, 8 July 1910, *OC*, p. 675.

74. Ibid.

75. See note 37.

76. The deterioration of Leger's friendship with Jammes was due to differences in religious convictions as well as to a misunderstanding concerning the former's publications in *La Nouvelle Revue Française*. See letters from Leger to Jammes, *OC*, pp. 759–63.

77. At this initial meeting Rivière's impressions of Leger were not favorable. See *HP*, pp. 603–4.

78. H[elen] I. N[aughton], "Jacques Rivière," *CDMEL*, p. 670.

79. Saint-John Perse, "Sur Jacques Rivière," *OC*, pp. 467, 468–69, 470.

80. E.g., letters to Rivière, *OC*, pp. 669, 671, 675.

81. E.g., Leger's letter to Rivière, *OC*, p. 675.

82. Letter to Rivière, 21 Oct. 1910, *OC*, p. 677.

83. Published by Gallimard in 1924; translated by T. S. Eliot and Giuseppe Ungaretti initially, *Anabase* was eventually translated into German, Greek, Rumanian, Russian, Spanish, and other languages.

84. Naughton, op.cit., p. 670.

85. See letter to Gide, 9 Apr. 1911, *OC*, p. 766.

86. Ibid.

87. See letter to Rivière, 21 Dec. 1910, *OC*, p. 680, and "Notes," *OC*, p. 1223.

88. Letter to Gide, Apr. 1911, *OC*, p. 767.

89. "les pures cristallisations d'un Valéry," "Léon-Paul Fargue," *OC*, p. 509.

90. Letter to P. Valéry, 26 Nov. 1922, *OC*, p. 463.

91. "Hommage à la mémoire de Claudel," *OC*, p. 486. *Note:* For a particularly interesting exchange of imaginary gifts see also "Préface" by André Malraux, *Les Oiseaux et l'oeuvre de Saint-John Perse* (Aix-Paris: Fondation Saint-John Perse, 1976–77), p. 21.

92. "Notes," *OC*, p. 1223.

93. Letter to Gide, Apr. 1911,*OC*, p. 768.

94. *Cahiers de la Plëïade* (Summer–Fall 1950), rpt. *OC*, p. 1223.

95. Ibid., *OC*, p. 1204.

96. Ibid.

97. Letter to Rivière, 2 June 1911, *OC*, pp. 692–93.

98. "Notes," *OC*, p. 1205.

99. For the various stages of this process of reeducation see *OC*, pp. 1205–7.

100. "Notes," *OC*, p. 1224.

101. Letter to Rivière, 23 June 1911, *OC*, p. 696.

102. Letter to Rivière, 11 Nov. 1911, *OC*, pp. 699–700.

103. Letter to Gide, Aug. 1911, *OC*, p. 775.

104. Ibid.

105. Letter to V. Larbaud, 22 Sept. 1911, *OC*, p. 790; see also "Notes," *OC*, p. 1226.

106. Letter from V. Larbaud to L.-P. Fargue, "Notes," *OC*, pp. 1090–91.

107. "Notes," *OC*, p. 1213. [A variant of this date—20 Dec.—perhaps an error, appears in a letter to Rivière, 10 Jan. 1912, *OC*, p. 702.]

108. For the complete text of the article see *OC*, pp. 1227–31.

109. Letter to Rivière, 10 Jan. 1911, *OC*, p. 702. [In writing to Larbaud himself, Leger was more diplomatic; see letter to Larbaud, Dec. 1911, *OC*, pp. 793–94.]

110. Letter to Rivière, 10 Jan. 1911, *OC*, p. 702.

111. Letter to Claudel, 17 May 1911, *OC*, pp. 719–20.

112. "Notes," *OC*, p. 1215. See also letter from Claudel to Jammes, 10 May 1911, *HP*, p. 608.

113. Auguste Bréal, *Philippe Berthelot*, 2d ed. (Paris: Gallimard, 1937), pp.

10, 11, 15, 19, 25–26, 34–35, 41, 43, 52, 55–56, 57, 58–59, 84, 96, 101–2, 105, 114.

114. Opinion expressed by E. M. Cioran during an interview with the author (Paris, Nov. 1979).

115. See note 110.

116. *OC*, p. xvi.

117. Letter to G.-J. Aubry, 17 June 1949, *OC*, p. 1036; *OC*, p. xvi.

118. "A la mémoire de Valery Larbaud," *OC*, p. 493.

119. Letter to V. Larbaud, Aug. 1913, *OC*, p. 799; see also letter to Aubry, note 117, *OC*, p. 1035.

120. *OC*, p. 464 ("Jadis Londres"); *OC*, pp. 492–93, 1232–33.

121. Letter to Larbaud, Aug. 1913, *OC*, pp. 799, 800.

122. "Notes," *OC*, p. 1225; letter to Joseph Conrad, 26 Feb. 1921, *OC*, p. 866. [Leger had already spoken with enthusiasm of Lear in 1912 (see note 123); the latter would fascinate Saint-John Perse until the end of his life (see Chapter 7, note 62).]

123. Letter to Gide, 7 Dec. 1912, *OC*, p. 781.

124. Ibid.

125. Letter to Mme Kumar Nehru, Mar. 1961, *OC*, p. 1082.

126. "Hommage à la mémoire de Rabindranath Tagore," *OC*, p. 501.

127. Ibid.

128. Ibid., p. 502.

129. Letter from P. Claudel to A. Gide, 25 Nov. 1913, *The Correspondence between Paul Claudel and André Gide*, p. 199.

130. [For the text of the *Epitre dédicatoire* by Gide see *OC*, pp. 1225–26, or *HP*, pp. 611–12.]

131. Reino Virtanen, "Between St. John and Persius: Saint-John Perse and Valéry," *Symposium* (Summer 1978), pp. 156–71, esp. pp. 167–68.

132. *OC*, p. xvii.

133. Ibid. See also Paul Claudel, *Journal* (Paris: Gallimard, 1968), I, p. 263 (entry for Oct. 1913).

134. "Hommage à la mémoire de Paul Claudel," *OC*, p. 485.

135. See note 82.

136. Letter to Claudel, 10 June 1911, *OC*, p. 722. [It is interesting that "Anabase" is mentioned as a possible title over five years before the actual writing of the poem *Anabase* occurred.]

137. Story retold by Marcos Victoria (in 1960), in "La Musique dans la nuit," *HP*, pp. 283–84.

138. Letter to Larbaud, 29 May 1914, *OC*, p. 802.

139. Paul Allard, *Le Quai d'Orsay: Son personnel, ses rouages, ses dessous* (Paris: Editions de France, 1938), p. vi.

140. Ibid., p. 13.

141. Ibid., pp. 13–15.

142. *OC*, p. xvii.

143. Salvador de Madariaga, "Alexis Leger," *HP*, p. 675.

144. Jean-Baptiste Duroselle, *La Décadence: 1932–1939* (Paris: Imprimerie Nationale, 1979), p. 23.

145. Paul Morand, *Journal d'un Attaché d'Ambassade: 1916–1917* (Paris: La Table Ronde, 1948), p. 22.

146. Paul Morand, "Il n'a jamais failli sur l'essentiel et reste un être parfaitement accompli," *Arts*, 12 June 1957, p. 3.

147. *OC*, p. xvii.

148. Title of Barbara Tuchman's *Guns of August* (New York: Macmillan, 1962), which vividly describes the start of World War I.

149. *OC*, p. xvii.

150. Morand, op. cit., p. 12.

151. Morand, op. cit., p. 161.

152. Morand, op. cit., p. 167.

153. Morand, op. cit., p. 88.

154. Morand, op. cit., p. 123.

155. *OC*, p. xvii.

156. Quoted by Morand op. cit., p. 27.

157. Allard, op. cit., p. 42.

158. *OC*, p. xvii.

159. Morand, op. cit., p. 21.

Chapter 4: Thunder beneath the Snow

1. Letter to A. Gide, 10 May 1921, *OC*, p. 895.

2. "30° ou 31° au-dessous zéro chaque nuit." Letter to MSLL, 10 Jan. 1910, *OC*, p. 831.

3. Letter to Gide, 10 May 1921, *OC*, pp. 895–96.

4. The same striking phrase used to describe London (Chapter 3) will also be applied to Washington (see Chapter 6).

5. Fragment of a letter to Philippe Berthelot from Alexis Leger (part of the correspondence between the two men that has never been found), quoted by Paul Morand, *Journal d'un Attaché d'Ambassade: 1915–1917* (Paris: La Table Ronde, 1948), p. 126.

6. Letter to MSLL, 10 Jan. 1917, *OC*, pp. 829–30.

7. Letter to MSLL, 17 Feb. 1917, *OC*, pp. 836–37.

8. Letter to P. Berthelot, 3 Jan. 1917, *OC*, p. 807.

9. Ibid.

10. Letter to MSLL, 10 Jan. 1917, *OC*, p. 830.

11. At the divide of noon and midnight when the great *partage* occurred, between the profane and the sacred, life and death, temporal and eternal. [The work was certainly known to Leger.]

12. Letter to Jules Dumour (his great-uncle), 28 Nov. 1917, *OC*, pp. 827, 820, respectively.

13. Letter to MSLL, 27 Jan. 1917, *OC*, p. 833. [The book in question was never written or may have been lost or destroyed, for it has never come to light.]

14. Letter to MSLL, 2 Feb. 1917, *OC*, p. 852.

15. Letter to MSLL, 27 Jan. 1917, *OC*, p. 833.

16. Paul Claudel, "Choses de Chine," *Cahiers Paul Claudel 4* (Paris: Gallimard, 1962), p. 128.

17. Jean Cocteau, "Lettre ouverte à Madame Nantet," *Cahiers Paul Claudel 2*, p. 22.

18. Letter to MSLL, 27 Jan. 1917, *OC*, p. 833.

19. Ibid. [A variant of this pronouncement can be found in Leger's letter to Berthelot, *OC*, p. 811.]

20. Letter to P. Valéry, 2 Sept. 1917, *OC*, p. 824.

21. See Chapter 3, note 16.

22. Letter to Berthelot, *OC*, p. 812.

23. Ibid.

24. Letter to Berthelot, *OC*, pp. 809–10.

25. *OC*, pp. 831, 837.

26. Letter to MSLL, Feb. 1919, *OC*, p. 869.

27. Ibid.

28. Letter to MSLL, 2 Feb. 1918, *OC*, p. 853.

29. Ibid.

30. Letter to MSLL, 10 Jan. 1917, *OC*, p. 832.

31. Letter to MSLL, 4 Apr. 1917, *OC*, p. 841.

32. Letter to MSLL, Feb. 1919, *OC*, pp. 868–69.

33. Letter to MSLL, 4 Apr. 1917, *OC*, p. 841.

34. Letter to MSLL, 20 Apr. 1919, *OC*, p. 872.

35. Ibid.

36. Letter to MSLL, 2 Feb. 1918, *OC*, p. 854.

37. Ibid.

38. Letter to MSLL, 13 June, 1917, *OC*, pp. 844–45.

39. For other descriptions of the event; see *OC*, p. 848, and "La Chine," *Annuaire diplomatique*, rpt. *HP*, p. 684.

40. For details see *OC*, pp. 814, 1240; *HP*, pp. 178, 618.

41. "Relation respectueuse addressée par le Secrétaire Lei Hi-gnai à son Excellence le Ministre Kang Te au sujet de sa mission auprès de la famille du Président Li et les circonstances qui accompagnèrent l'exode de cette dernière vers un lieu de refuge," *OC*, pp. 814–19. [A toned-down and slightly altered version of the incident appears in a letter to MSLL, 2 Aug. 1917, *OC*, pp. 847–48.]

42. "La Chine," *HP*, p. 684.

43. "Temple Tao-Yu" appears as Leger's address in a number of letters dating from the summer of 1917: e.g., *OC*, pp. 813, 819, 821.

44. Letter to His Excellency Alexandre Conty, ["Temple Tao-Yu"], 27 Sept. 1917, *OC*, p. 820.

45. Letter to MSLL, Aug. 1917, *OC*, p. 846.

46. Letter to A. Conty, *OC*, p. 820.

47. Letter to Dr. Bussière, 22 Sept. 1917, *OC*, p. 821.

48. Ibid., p. 822.

49. Ibid.

50. Letter to MSLL, 2 Aug. 1917, *OC*, pp. 846–47.

51. Guerre, *HP*, p. 176. [There is also internal evidence in *Anabase* to indicate that its composition took place late in the summer of 1917, for the words "Car le soleil entre au lion"—found on the first page—certainly refer to the sign of Leo, which begins on August 21. This reference, coupled with the letter referred to in note 50—dated August 2—seems to confirm the time of creation.]

52. [Contained in the same letter as the reference to a work like an "Anabase"]. Letter to P. Claudel, 10 June 1911, *OC*, p. 722; see also Chapter 3, note 136.]

53. Paul Claudel, *Réflexions sur la poésie* (Paris: Gallimard, 1963), pp. 86–87.

54. Maurice-Jean Lefebve, "La Révanche de la poésie," *HP*, p. 101.

55. See note 51.

56. Paul Claudel, "Un Poème de Saint-John Perse: 'Vents,'" rpt. *HP*, p. 44.

57. See Chapter 3, note 82.

58. *Anabase*, *OC*, pp. 89, 108, 113, respectively.

59. Ibid., p. 114.

60. Ibid., pp. 95, 105, 99, 112, 106, respectively.

61. Ibid., p. 111.

62. *OC*, p. 850.

63. *OC*, pp. 851–52.

64. *OC*, p. 852.

65. *OC*, pp. 837, 842.

66. E.g. in *Pour fêter une enfance*, *OC*, pp. 23, 26; in *Eloges*, *OC*, pp, 36, 48; in *Récitation à la gloire d'une Reine*; see discussion in Chapter 3.

67. 23 Oct. 1912, *OC*, p. 797.

68. 17 May 1919, *OC*, p. 875.

69. See "Lettre à une dame d'Europe," 17 Mar. 1921, *OC*, pp. 890–92.

70. *OC*, p. 887.

71. Letter to P. Berthelot, *OC*, p. 807.

72. E.g., *OC*, pp. 95, 96, 99, 102.

73. E.g., *OC*, pp. 102–4.

74. E.g., *OC*, pp. 109-11.

75. Ibid.

76. Note: The number 9 with its symbolic meanings is used by the poet to suggest unity and consummation. For further examples see *Amers* ("Etroits sont les vaisseaux") and the date 9/IX, discussed in Chapter 7.

77. *OC*, p. xviii.

78. Letter to MSLL, 13 June 1917, *OC*, p. 845.

79. Letter to MSLL, 2 Feb. 1918, *OC*, p. 852.

80. Letter to MSLL, 25 Apr. 1917, *OC*, p. 843.

81. Ibid.

82. Letter to MSLL, 9 Apr. 1918, *OC*, pp. 856–57.

83. Ibid., p. 858.

84. Ibid., p. 859.

85. *OC*, p. 861.

86. Letter to J. Dumour, *OC*, p. 826.

87. *OC*, pp. 861–62.

88. *OC*, p. 856.

89. E.g., *OC*, pp. 838, 856.

90. *OC*, p. 856.

91. *OC*, pp. 822–23.

92. Letter to J. Conrad, *OC*, pp. 886-88.

93. Ibid., p. 889.

94. Composed between 1953 and 1956, *Amers* contains numerous repetitions of the phrase "la mer en nous," e.g., *OC*, p. 261.

95. *Siddharta*.

96. *René Leys*.

97. *Equipée: Voyage au pays du réel*.

98. A volume of poetry, originally published in Peking in 1912,

99. See Raymond Cogniat, "Préface," *Victor Segalen: Poète de l'Asie* (Paris: Galérie Jean Loize, 1944), pp. 9–18, for more details.

100. Such as Claudel and Berthelot: see Victor Segalen, *Lettres de Chine* (Paris: Plon, 1967), pp. 63–64, 93, 97, 261 (Claudel); pp. 116, 124, 129 (Berthelot).

101. "La Chine," *HP*, p. 684.

102. *OC*, p. 865.

103. *OC*, pp. 866–67.

104. *OC*, p. 876.

105. Ibid.

106. Letter to MSLL, 3 Jan. 1920, *OC*, p. 877.

107. Ibid., pp. 877–78.

108. Letter to MSLL, 21 Apr. 1920, *OC*, p. 879.

109. Ibid.

110. Letter to MSLL, 4 May 1920, *OC*, p. 880.

111. Ibid.

112. Ibid.

113. Ibid., pp. 880–81.

114. See notes 48 and 49.

115. *OC*, 4 pp. 869–70.

116. Letter to J. Conrad, *OC*, p. 888. Cf. note 33 (letter to MSLL, reporting the same experience).

117. Ibid.

118. See note 92.

119. Letter to Conrad, *OC*, p. 888.

120. Ibid.

121. Ibid., p. 889.

122. Ibid.

123. See note 111.

124. It can be established that the voyagers reached their goal close to 31 May 1920 (see *OC*, p. 880–81). Leger, born 31 May 1887, was thus thirty-three years old [an age usually associated with the major revelations of mythological heroes, and a number in itself sacred in many mythologies].

125. Letter to MSLL, 5 June 1920, *OC*, p. 881.

126. Letter to G.-C. Toussaint, 29 Mar. 1921, *OC*, p. 894.

127. Ibid.

128. See Prologue, notes 16 and 17.

129. Letter to Toussaint, *OC*, p. 894.

Chapter 5: Eminence Grise *and the Masked Poet*

1. Letter to MSLL, 17 May 1921, *OC*, p. 883.

2. Letter to MSLL, 20 Mar. 1921, *OC*, p. 882.

3. Letter to G.-C. Toussaint, 29 Mar. 1921, *OC*, pp. 894–95.

4. Ibid., p. 894.

5. Letter to MSLL, 17 May 1921, *OC*, p. 883.

6. *OC*, p. xviii.

7. Letter to MSLL, 17 May 1921.

8. Leger left China on 2 April 1921 and expected to arrive in Paris in mid-June (see *OC*, pp. 882, 896).

9. Letter to Toussaint, 29 Mar. 1921, *OC*, pp. 893–94.

10. Ibid., p. 893.

11. Ibid., p. 895.

12. Play on "Knight-errant," literally "Knight of Wandering," Michel de Ghelderode, *HP*, p. 154.

13. Letter to MSLL, 17 May 1921, *OC*, p. 883.

14. Giuseppe Ungaretti, "Histoire d'une traduction," *HP*, pp. 68–69.

15. See Chapter 3, note 56.

16. *OC*, p. 882.

17. *Neiges, OC*, p. 157.

18. Letter to A. Gide, 10 May 1921, *OC*, p. 896.

19. Letter to MSLL, 19 May 1921, *OC*, p. 884.

20. Letter to Toussaint, *OC*, p. 895.

21. Letter to MSLL, 199 May 1921, *OC*, p. 884.

22. Letter to Gide, *OC*, p. 896; Paul Claudel, *Journal* (entry of August 1921), p. 561.

23. *OC*, p. xix; "Notes," *OC*, pp. 1093, 1102 .

24. Letter to MSLL, 19 May 1921, *OC*, p. 884.

25. *OC*, p. 1104. [Most likely this was not mere chance and one can assume that the poet was quite aware that "Anabase" was his best, or most fully developed, work of that period.]

26. *OC*, pp. xviii, 1097; *HP*, p. 681.

27. Quoted by Mazars, *HP*, p. 620.

28. Jean-Baptiste Duroselle, *La Décadence: 1932–1939* (Paris: Imprimerie Nationale, 1979), p. 11.

29. André Maurois, *Histoire de la France, II*, (Paris: Albin Michel, 1947), p. 306.

30. Leger/Perse always emphasized his Breton ancestry; e.g., see *OC*, pp. 1059, 1342.

31. Aristide Briand (as told to Raymond Escholier), *Souvenirs parlés* (Paris: Hachette, 1932), p. 166.

32. Ibid., p. 169.

33. Saint-John Perse, "Briand" (Speech delivered on 28 Mar. 1942, to commemorate the eightieth anniversary of Briand's birth), *HP,* p. 716.

34. Quoted by Mazars, *HP,* p. 620.

35. Ibid., pp. 619–20.

36. Ibid., p. 619; also, L.-M. Raymond, *HP,* p. 112, and E. Berl, *HP,* p. 777.

37. "Briand," *HP,* pp. 716–17.

38. Mazars, *HP,* p. 620; also Berl [with a slight variation], *HP,* p. 777.

39. Kurt Wais, "Deux manières d'exister dans l'oeuvre de Saint-John Perse," *HP,* p. 270.

40. *OC,* p. xviii.

41. Auguste Bréal, *Philippe Berthelot,* 2d ed. (Paris: Gallimard, 1937), p. 200.

42. Ibid., p. 202.

43. Ibid.

44. "relieved of his duties." Ibid.

45. *OC,* pp. xviii–xix.

46. *OC,* p. xix.

47. "Alexis Leger," *Annuaire diplomatique,* rpt. *HP,* p. 681.

48. *OC,* p. xix.

49. Ibid.

50. André Breton, "Le Donateur," *HP,* p. 53.

51. Louis Aragon, "Car c'est de l'homme qu'il s'agit," *Les Lettres Françaises,* 3 Nov. 1960, rpt. *HP,* 576–77.

52. *OC,* p. xix; "Notes," *OC,* p. 1104.

53. Sylvia Beach, *Shakespeare and Company* (New York: Harcourt, Brace, 1956), p. 142.

54. *OC,* p. xix; "Notes," *OC,* p. 1245.

55. Quoted by Jacques Petit, "Autour de la publication de *Tête d'or,*" in *Cahiers Paul Claudel 1* (Paris: Gallimard, 1959), p. 26.

56. *The Correspondence between Paul Claudel and André Gide* (New York: Pantheon, 1952), p. 141.

57. Petit, op. cit., p. 26.

58. See "Notes," *OC,* pp. 1101–2.

59. See "Notes," *OC,* pp. 1093–94.

60. Richard Ellman, *James Joyce* (New York: Oxford University Press, 1959), pp. 514, 526, 536, 538, 573; Beach, op. cit., pp. 57, 94.

61. Ellman, op. cit., p. 539.

62. Ellman, op. cit., p. 565.

63. Edmond Jaloux quoted by Herbert Gorman, *James Joyce* (New York: Rhinehart, 1948), p. 303.

64. For these and other comparisons between Joyce and Perse see Octavio Paz, "Un Mythe moderne," *HP,* p. 256.

65. For a rare mention of this friendship see Denis Devlin, "Saint-John Perse à Washington," *HP*, p. 73.

66. See letter from L.-P. Fargue to A. Leger, 1 Nov. 1923, *HP*, p. 795.

67. Ellman, op. cit., p. 556.

68. *Finnegans Wake* (New York: Viking Press, 1947), p. 498. [Although Adaline Glasheen, in *A Second Census of Finnegans Wake: An Index of the Characters and Their Roles*, rev. and exp. ed. (Evanston, Ill.: Northwestern University Press, 1963), p. 227, identifies "Sant Legerleger" as "St. Leger, Sir Anthony—16th Century viceroy; also a horserace," one can hypothesize that this character—in one of Joyce's typically multiple constructions—is also based on Alexis Saint-Leger Leger or Saintleger Leger.]

69. In 1922 and 1923, respectively. See W[alter] L[ange], "Rainer-Maria Rilke," *CDMEL*, p. 667.

70. "Notes," *OC*, p. 939.

71. Cioran, *HP*, p. 221.

72. *OC*, p. xix; "Notes," *OC*, p. 1104.

73. Beach, op. cit., pp. 58, 63.

74. Letter from "A. M." to Saint-Leger Leger, 23 Oct. 1923, "Notes," *OC*, p. 1234. [For the eventual fate of this manuscript see *OC*, pp. 1104, 1235.]

75. Letter from V. Larbaud to Saint-Leger Leger, 23 Mar. 1922, "Notes," *OC*, p. 1233.

76. Ibid., p. 1235.

77. E.g., "Notes," *OC*, p. 1235.

78. For details see Beach, op. cit., p. 142.

79. Beach, op. cit., p. 143.

80. *OC*, p. 1103.

81. Ibid.

82. *OC*, p. 1235.

83. Promoted to "Secrétaire d'Ambassade 1ère classe" on 21 Nov. 1924 (*Annuaire diplomatique*, *HP*, p. 681), Leger was also favored by Berthelot's amnesty in 1924 (*OC*, p. xix) and his probable return to power.

84. *OC*, p. xix.

85. Letter to "une dame d'Europe" (unidentified), 17 Mar. 1921, *OC*, p. 981.

86. *OC*, p. xx; also "Le Quai d'Orsay," *HP*, pp. 693–95.

87. *OC*, p. xx.

88. Ibid.

89. *OC*, pp. 939–40.

90. Letter from R.-M Rilke to A. Saint-Leger Leger, Mar. 1925, "Notes," *OC*, p. 1103.

91. "Notes," *OC*, pp. 1102–3.

92. Ibid., p. 1104.

93. *OC*, p. xix. For the complete text of "Sur Jacques Rivière" see *OC*, pp. 466–72.

94. Ibid., p. 466.

95. Ibid., pp. 471–72.

96. For the complete text of this preface see *OC*, pp. 1236–38.

97. "Notes," *OC*, p. 1238. For the rest of the text see pp. 1237–38.

98. *HP*, p. 694.

99. Elizabeth R. Cameron, "Alexis Saint-Léger Léger" (sic), in *The Diplomats: 1919–1939*, eds. Gordon A. Craig and Felix Gilbert (Princeton, N.J.: Princeton University Press, 1953), pp. 380–81.

100. For the complete text see "Discours pour la signature du Pacte Briand-Kellogg" (Paris, 27 Apr. 1928), *HP*, pp. 695–97.

101. Ibid., p. 695.

102. Ibid., pp. 696–97.

103. For a list of these and the forty-six others who would adhere to, or declare their intention to adhere to, the pact by January 1929 see ibid., p. 697.

104. Such as Comtesse Marthe de Fels who was his companion during these years (according to several informants interviewed by the author).

105. "La Chine," *HP*, p. 684; Joseph Paul-Boncour, "Poète insoupçonné," *HP*, p. 789; Henri Hoppenot, "D'Alexis Leger à Saint-John Perse," *HP*, p. 804; S. de Madariaga, *HP*, p. 676.

106. Duroselle, op. cit., p. 24, states that Leger arrived at the Quai at 11:00 A.M., left again for lunch, and only returned at 4:00 P.M.

107. E.g., letters from Leger's friends (Valéry, Gide, Colette, Anna de Noailles, and others); see *HP*, pp. 793–99.

108. Beach, op. cit., pp. 149–50.

109. Beach, op. cit., p. 149.

110. Beach, op. cit., pp. 40, 121, 175, 206.

111. Beach, op. cit., p. 207.

112. In 1925. Beach, op. cit., pp. 127–28.

113. Beach, op. cit., pp. 26–27, 34–36.

114. For the history of this translation, as well as for the letters exchanged between the two poets, see "Notes," *OC*, pp. 1141–44. For Saint-John Perse's observations and corrections of the translation see ibid., pp. 1145–47; see also letter from T. S. Eliot to A. Leger, 15 Jan. 1927, *HP*, p. 419.

115. For the text of this translation by "St.-J. Perse," published in bilingual format in *Commerce*, Nov. 1924 (as a homage to T. S. Eliot), see *OC*, pp. 465–66, and "Notes," *OC*, p. 1141.

116. Letter from A. MacLeish to M. de Bassiano, Princess Caetani, *OC*, p. 1106.

117. Letter from R.-M. Rilke to Princess Caetani, *OC*, p. 1107. [Rilke, after considering a translation of *Anabase*, admitted that he was incapable of doing so. For more details see *OC*, pp. 1107–8. For the preface to the German translation of W. Benjamin and B. Groethuysen (by Hugo von Hoffmansthal) see *HP*, pp. 423–25.

118. Letter from G. Ungaretti to Princess Caetani, *OC*, p. 1105.

119. Letter from T. S. Eliot to A. Leger, see note 114. For more details concerning Eliot's concern regarding this translation, and the numerous revisions he undertook (considering his first translation "imperfect"), see "Notes,"

OC, p. 1144. For the influence of *Anabase* and its translation on the work of T. S. Eliot see the latter's statements, *HP*, p. 19.

120. T. S. Eliot, Preface to *Anabasis* (London: Faber & Faber, 1930).

121. *OC*, p. xxi.

122. Jean Lasserre, "Meneurs d'hommes: Alexis Leger," *Le Petit Parisien*, Jan. 1936, rpt. *HP*, p. 781.

123. Raymond, op. cit., *HP*, p. 113.

124. S. de Madariaga, *HP*, pp. 675–76.

125. Berthelot (born in 1866) was about sixty years old at this time, while Leger was thirty-nine.

126. Bréal, op. cit., p. 21.

127. *HP*, p. 698.

128. For the complete text of "Mémorandum sur l'organisation d'un régime d'Union fédérale européenne" see *HP*, pp. 699–708.

129. Ibid., p. 699.

130. Ibid., pp. 702–7.

131. Ibid., p. 708.

132. The English translation of *Anabase* appeared in 1930; the Italian one was about to come out in the magazine *Fronte*; the German one was ready for publication by the Insel Verlag.

133. "Briand," *HP*, p. 721.

134. Ibid. [The reference here is most likely to Briand's continued efforts, such as the meeting at The Hague (1930), the London Naval Conference (1930), and the voyage to Berlin (1931)—all of which Leger and Briand undertook together; see *oc*, p. xx.]

135. "Briand," *HP*, p. 721.

136. Cameron op. cit. (pp. 379–80) describes Leger's diplomatic career as comprising two distinct phases: (1) 1925–32, the period of design and realization; (2) 1933–40, the period of "décadence" and steadily narrowing diplomatic activity.

137. Berthelot was retired in November 1931; see Pertinax, *Les Fossoyeurs* (New York: La Maison Française Inc., 1943), I, p. 217.

138. *OC*, pp. xxi, 1097; *HP*, p. 681.

139. Paul Allard, *Le Quai d'Orsay: Son personnel, ses rouages, ses dessous* (Paris: Editions de France, 1938), p. 49.

140. Berl, *HP*, p. 777.

141. Duroselle, op. cit., p. 272.

142. Duroselle, loc. cit.

143. Duroselle, op. cit., p. 56.

144. Such as the examination of all telegrams. Allard, op. cit., p. 75.

145. Duroselle, op. cit., p. 24.

146. Lasserre, op. cit., *HP*, p. 781.

147. For details see *OC*, p. 1140 (Larbaud), p. 1139 (Valéry).

148. Cameron, op. cit., pp. 381–82.

149. Cameron, op. cit., p. 382.

150. Cameron, loc. cit.

151. Sumner Wells, quoted by Cameron, op. cit., p. 383.

152. Cameron, op cit., p. 384; Duroselle, op. cit., p. 73.

153. Duroselle, op. cit., p. 124.

154. Duroselle, op. cit., p. 136; *OC*, p. xxi.

155. Quoted by Pertinax, op. cit., p. 221.

156. Quoted by Cameron, op. cit., p. 384.

157. Cameron, loc. cit.

158. Duroselle, op. cit., p. 142.

159. Quoted by Cameron, op. cit., p. 386.

160. Quoted by Cameron, op. cit., p. 386.

161. Cameron, loc. cit.

162. Mazars, *HP*, p. 620.

163. Quoted by Denis de Rougemont, "Saint-John Perse en Amérique," *HP*, p. 614.

164. Louis Fisher, *Men and Politics*, excerpt rpt. in *HP*, p. 784.

165. *OC*, p. xxii. For the British point of view of Flandin's visit to London see Winston Churchill, *The Gathering Storm* (Boston: Houghton Mifflin, 1948), pp. 191–92.

166. "Briand," *HP*, p. 720.

167. "the warrior's haven" [phrase traditionally used to describe the role of woman].

168. Various informants (Mme Jenny Bradley, M. E. M. Cioran) interviewed by the author described these attributes of Comtesse de Fels. The fact that Claudel was a mutual friend is also substantiated by a letter from Leger to the former; see *OC*, p. 1015. Comtesse de Fels received the author in her home in Paris several times (autumn–winter, 1979) and consented to speak of her relationship with Alexis Leger/Saint-John Perse. Much of the information reported here was gathered during these interviews.

169. An object that Mme de Fels stated was carved in her home, still possesses, and showed the author.

170. A photograph of this dog still existed in the home of Mme de Fels in 1979. Immortalized in the following line of "Poème à l'Etrangère," *OC*, p. 173: "je flatte encore en songe, de la main . . . ma chienne d'Europe qui fut blanche . . ." [To the best of my knowledge, no link has so far been established between this particular animal and the reference in Saint-John Perse's poem.]

171. *OC*, p. xxii; see also letter to L. Blum, 10 Mar. 1946, *OC*, pp. 627–29. The rapport between the two men was further confirmed by Mme Leger during a conversation with the author (Washington, Spring 1980).

172. Duroselle, op. cit., p. 229.

173. Cameron, op. cit., 392.

174. Words of a Polish diplomat (unidentified), quoted by Duroselle, op. cit., p. 483.

175. Duroselle, op. cit., p. 393.

176. *OC*, p. xxii.

177. Quoted by Cameron, op. cit., pp. 394–95.

178. Cameron, op. cit., p. 395.

179. Cameron, loc. cit.

180. de Rougemont, op. cit. *HP*, p. 614.

181. Quoted by Mazars, *HP*, p. 620.

182. Cameron, op. cit., p. 396.

183. Leger (in 1936) quoted by Lasserre, op. cit.

184. Cameron, op. cit., p. 396.

185. Pertinax, op. cit., p. 295.

186. Quoted by Pertinax, op. cit., p. 297.

187. Cameron, op. cit., p. 401.

188. Cameron, loc. cit.

189. Cameron, loc. cit.

190. Cameron, op. cit., pp. 378–79.

191. Pertinax, op. cit., pp. 284–85, 287.

192. Cameron, op. cit., p. 401.

193. Elie Bois, "Comment le Secrétaire Général fut relevé des ses fonctions," in *Le Malheur de la France* (London, 1941), rpt. *HP*, pp. 765–66.

194. Cameron, op. cit., p. 402; also reported by Pertinax, op. cit., p. 298.

195. Bois, *HP*, p. 767.

196. For Leger's point-by-point refutation of Reynaud's plan see Pertinax, op. cit., pp. 300–301.

197. Cameron, op. cit., p. 403.

198. Bois, *HP*, p. 768.

199. For further details see *OC*, p. xxii, and Leger's letter to President Herriot from Arcachon, 28 May 1940, *HP*, pp. 713–14. [The letter is the only pronouncement concerning his unjust treatment made by Leger. Moreover, all references to the conspiracy of which he was a victim have been omitted in the articles on this subject reprinted in *HP*.]

200. Quoted by Cameron, op. cit., p. 403, and Bois, *HP*, p. 768.

201. *OC*, p. xxiii; "Notes," *OC*, p. 1095, for more details. [Various friends attempted to track down these manuscripts, or offered to do so. The reactions of Perse varied from discouragement of such attempts or even the mention of the pillaging (e.g., letter to Alain Bosquet, 30 Nov. 1951, *OC*, pp. 1067–68), to lack of response (e.g., letter to A. Gide re L. Blum's offer, 2 Jan. 1948, *OC*, p. 1000). Roger Garaudy had a search undertaken in Russia—without the poet's knowledge—which uncovered the track of the manuscripts, but according to a Russian statement (1963): "all the archives of Saint-John Perse dating from the period 1923–1940 were destroyed by the Germans" (*OC*, p. 1095).

202. Phrase used by Leger just before his departure from China; see note 11.

203. After spending a few weeks with his mother near Arcachon, Leger would first go to London and then to the United States via Canada. *OC*, pp. xxii–xxiii.

204. His mother was then seventy-seven years old. She would die in 1948, during her son's exile, but was already in ill health (see letter to President Herriot, *HP*, p. 713).

Chapter 6: Exile and Other Kingdoms

1. Leger arrived in New York on 14 July 1940: *OC*, p. xxiii; Raymond, *HP*, p. 113. Re insomnia caused by heat see letter to Mrs. Francis Biddle, 18 July 1942, *OC*, p. 902.

2. The Shelton Hotel (no longer in existence, according to the current New York telephone directory). See letter headings, *OC*, pp. 897–900, 935–36.

3. *OC*, p. xxiii.

4. See letter to Mrs. Biddle (the sister of Marguerite de Bassiano, Princess Caetani), 27 Aug. 1940, *OC*, p. 897.

5. Jean Rollin, "A New York, en 1940", *Démocratie 60* (6 Oct. 1960), rpt. *HP*, p. 786.

6. *OC*, p. xxiii; Hoppenot, *HP*, pp. 805–6.

7. Katherine Garrison Chapin (Mrs. F. Biddle) had published two plays, seven volumes of poetry, and numerous critical studies; she was also the director of the Poetry Society of America and poetry consultant at the Library of Congress: *OC*, pp. 1244–45.

8. *OC*, p. 1245.

9. Letter to Mrs. Biddle, 13 Sept. 1940, *OC*, p. 898. [For other details see *OC*, p. 1245.]

10. Letter to Mrs. Biddle, 6 Nov. 1940, *OC*, pp. 899–900.

11. Ibid., p. 900.

12. Letter to Mrs. Biddle, 10 Dec. 1940, *OC*, p. 901.

13. Letter to A. MacLeish, 4 Dec. 1940, *OC*, p. 936.

14. *OC*, p. 1255; Archibald MacLeish, "Le Temps de la louange," *HP*, pp. 104–5.

15. Tate became an employee of the Library of Congress upon the invitation of MacLeish; see *OC*, p. 1294, and Jacques Charpier, *Saint-John Perse* (Paris: Gallimard, 1962), pp. 17–18.

16. Letter to MacLeish, 18 Oct. 1940, *OC*, pp. 935–36; also, *OC*, p. xxiii.

17. *OC*, p. xxiii.

18. Letter to MacLeish, 4 Dec. 1940, *OC*, p. 937.

19. E.g., letter to MacLeish, 18 Oct. 1940, *OC*, p. 935.

20. de Rougemont, *HP*, p. 126.

21. Letter to Mrs. Biddle, 6 Nov. 1940, *OC*, p. 900.

22. Letter to Mrs. Biddle, 10 Dec. 1940, *OC*, p. 901.

23. See Chapter 2, note 45.

24. Raymond, *HP*, p. 624.

25. Ibid., p. 625. [The same phrase, "lieu géométrique," that Perse used in speaking to Raymond, had been used by Leger in describing both London and Peking, it will be remembered.]

26. Devlin, *HP*, p. 71. For the actual address see letter headings of this period, *OC*, pp. 944, 957–60, 972–73.

27. Hoppenot, *HP*, p. 805.

28. Raymond, *HP*, p. 625.

29. *OC*, p. xxiii. For the text of the official statement concerning Leger's collaboration in the work of the Library of Congress see *OC*, p. 1095.

30. Letter to ["Archie"] MacLeish, 24 Mar. 1946, *OC*, p. 945.

31. *Vents, OC*, p. 188.

32. Ibid., pp. 186–87.

33. Letter to MacLeish, 24 Mar. 1946, *OC*, p. 945. [For more details see "Notes," *OC*, p. 1257.]

34. *OC*, p. 945.

35. Ibid.

36. Devlin, *HP*, p. 71.

37. Hoppenot, *HP*, p. 806.

38. Raymond, *HP*, p. 626.

39. [For the entire text of the pronouncement made by the poet concerning *Anabase* see *OC*, p. 1108.]

40. Quoted by Charpier, op. cit., p. 15. For MacLeish's version see his "La Source vive," *HP*, p. 445.

41. For details concerning Long Beach Island see *OC*, pp. xxiii–xxiv, and "Notes," *OC*, p. 1109.

42. *Exil, OC*, p. 124.

43. Ibid., p. 130. [The lines that follow reinforce the notion of a new beginning from nothingness: "avec les choses les plus frêles, avec les choses les plus vaines, la simple chose, la simple chose que voilà, la simple chose d'être là, dans l'écoulement du jour."]

44. Ibid., p. 135.

45. Ibid., p. 124.

46. Ibid., p. 136. [The lines that precede this passage are also extremely revealing: "Lointaine est l'autre rive où le message s'illumine: Deux fronts de femmes sous la cendre . . . deux ailes de femmes aux persiennes . . ." Ibid.]

47. Ibid., p. 134.

48. Ibid., p. 136.

49. Ibid., p. 137.

50. In 1942, 1943, 1944, 1945, respectively.

51. See note 49.

52. *OC*, p. xxiii.

53. *OC*, pp. xxiii–xxiv, 1109.

54. *OC*, p. 1112. [Denis Devlin was also a diplomat. For details of these functions and his eventual fate see *OC*, p. 1294.]

55. For the complete text of Devlin's account of the translation of *Exil* see *HP*, pp. 71–73.

56. *OC*, p. 167. [The unusual nature of the adjective "green" can be explained by the particular importance and meaning attributed to this color by Perse. For the most interesting discussion of the emblematic character of the color green—purity, plenitude—see Yves-Alain Favre, *Saint-John Perse: Le langage et le sacré* (Paris: José Corti, 1977), p. 87.]

57. For the complete text of the poem see *OC*, pp. 166–73.

58. *OC*, p. 1120.

59. *OC*, p. 169.

60. Ibid., pp. 169–70.

61. Ibid., p. 171.

62. Ibid., p. 172.

63. Ibid.

64. Ibid., pp. 172–73. [For one of the most interesting discussions of this passage see Roger Caillois, *Poétique de Saint-John Perse* (Paris: Gallimard, 1954), pp. 97–98. One might, however, disagree with one detail in Caillois' interpretation: "sabliers" ("hourglass trees") is certainly not only an image of the flow of time (as he points out) but also a reference to one of the trees native to Guadeloupe (see Chapter 1) and thus an evocation of childhood memories.]

65. *OC*, pp. xxiii–xxiv. See also letters and telegram to Winston Churchill, *OC*, pp. 603–4, 617; letters to Charles de Gaulle, *OC*, pp. 614–15; article "An III de l'exil," *OC*, pp. 615–16; "Briand," *OC*, pp. 605–14.

66. "Briand," *OC*, p. 616.

67. In this speech the word "humain" is used with striking frequency, and it ends on the word "humanité." See *OC*, pp. 605–14.

68. Note that Perse always uses the plural form—*Pluies, Neiges, Vents, Amers*—which has the effect of universalizing the subjects of the poems.

69. *OC*, p. xxiv.

70. Charlton Ogburn (a member of the party), in "Comment fut écrit *Pluies*," *HP*, p. 274, relates an amusing incident that occurred in a cemetery; "[Perse] souriait devant la pompe d'un beau tombeau de femme portant cette inscription: 'A . . . Lady . . . , qui fut parfaite épouse, parfaite compagne et parfaite maîtresse.' Et comme je lui rappelais discrètement que le titre de 'maîtresse' n'évoquait ici que la Maîtresse de plantation . . . il changea de sourire pour nous dire simplement que l'art de vivre, grand merci, n'avait jamais relevé des mêmes conceptions dans la civilisation française et dans l'anglaise."

71. Ibid.

72. *Images à Crusoé*, *OC*, p. 15.

73. Ogburn, *HP*, pp. 275–76.

74. Ogburn, *HP*, p. 278. [Ogburn also states that an incident which had taken place at the hotel before their arrival fascinated Perse and may have had some effect on his poem: a beautiful young woman had dived, at night, into the empty outdoor swimming pool (thinking it was filled with clear, transparent water), fractured her skull, and died. Actually, Ogburn's observation is not correct. Nothing appears in *Pluies* relating to this incident. However, it quite clearly makes its appearance in *Vents*, in the following passage: "Et la Mort . . . avivera ce soir d'un singulier éclat l'étoile au front de l'Etrangère, qui descend seule, après minuit, la nuit royale des sous-sols vers la piscine de turquoise illuminé d'azur."(*OC*, p. 211.) This provides us with one of the most interesting examples of poetic transformation that an actual incident undergoes in the hands of Saint-John Perse, and the delayed use to which it is put.]

75. *OC*, p. 154 (place and date), p. 139 (dedication).

76. Ibid., pp. 141 and 152. [The banyan tree is an East Indian tree (*Ficus bengalensis*), the branches of which send out numerous trunks that grow down to the soil and form props so that a single tree covers a very large area, and is thus a particularly fortuitous image of rain.]

77. Ibid., p. 143.

78. E.g., ibid., pp. 145, 148, 152.

79. E.g., ibid., pp. 141, 145, 154.

80. Ibid., pp. 150–51.

81. Ibid., p. 151.

82. Ibid., p. 153.

83. Conrad Aiken even offered Saint-John Perse the use of his country house, The Forty-one Doors, in Cape Cod. The latter considered the former among the foremost American poets; Aiken, on the other hand, expressed the opinion (after the publication of *Amers*) that Saint-John Perse was the greatest poet in the modern world. [For these and other details concerning Aiken and Perse see *OC*, pp. 921, 929, 1235.]

84. As soon as the poem appeared in America, Aiken wrote an article on *Pluies* in the *New Republic* (16 Apr. 1945). Its conclusion is reprinted in *OC*, pp. 1119–20.

85. *OC*, p. 1294 (opinion of Saint-John Perse re Tate).

86. Allen Tate, "Mystérieux Perse," *HP*, p. 136.

87. Ibid., p. 139.

88. Letter to A. Tate, 5 Apr. 1944, *OC*, p. 972.

89. *OC*, p. 1294. For Perse's reaction to Tate's caring treatment of his work see letter to Tate, 26 Nov. 1944–6 Feb. 1945, *OC*, pp. 973–76.

90. *Neiges* bears the dedication: "A Françoise-Renée Saint-Leger Leger," *OC*, p. 155. [The poem was written in New York in 1944. She was able to receive it before her death in Paris in 1948, far from her son. See "Notes," *OC*, p. 1120.]

91. See letter to MacLeish, 2 Aug. 1944, *OC*, p. 943. The same letter also describes the fate of his sisters, one of whose husbands had died, and two nephews who were interned.

92. Ibid.

93. His mother was then eighty-one years old.

94. *Neiges*, *OC*, pp. 160, 161, respectively.

95. Ibid., p. 160.

96. Ibid., p. 163.

97. In Argentina, together with the other poems of exile. *OC*, p. xxiv.

98. Ibid.

99. *OC*, p. xxv.

100. Letter to Mrs. Biddle, 20 Sept. 1942, *OC*, p. 904.

101. Ibid., p. 903.

102. Mrs. William Astor Chanler, described as a lover of drama and poetry and a woman of great erudition in a little-known field of North African civilization, had lived for a long time in Paris, welcomed Leger in Washington during the International Conference (1921–22); when he was exiled, the two met again in New York, and she did her utmost to lighten the burdens of his solitude; she also provided him with a place to stay each summer on her private island. For more details and the complete text describing Mrs. Chanler see "Notes," *OC*, p. 1246.

103. Letter to Mrs. Biddle, 20 Sept. 1942, *OC*, pp. 904–5.

104. Ibid., p. 904.

105. *OC*, p. 1120; also, letter to MacLeish, 24 Mar. 1946, *OC*, p. 945, and "Notes," p. 1258.

106. Prologue. [For the complete passage in *Vents*, containing this phrase, see note 123.]

107. Letter to Mrs. Biddle [sent from Seven Hundred Acre Island], 13 Sept. 1945, *OC*, pp. 906–7.

108. *Vents*, *OC*, p. 179. [It seems likely that this is an echo of T. S. Eliot's "The Hollow Men," for in his translation of the former's poem, St.-J. Perse had used the phrase "nous sommes les hommes faits de paille." See *OC*, p. 465.]

109. *Vents*, *OC*, p. 180.

110. Ibid., p. 181.

111. Ibid., p. 185. [This follows the sequence devoted to the Storm god, ibid., pp. 183–85.]

112. Ibid., p. 186.

113. [Very likely, a reference to the Library of Congress, but also all institutions of its kind, as proven by the passages that follow]. Ibid.

114. Ibid., pp. 186–87.

115. Ibid., p. 190 [The sacrificial rite, involving a beautiful woman, culminating in a sacred union, symbolizing the renewal of life and celebrating the creative energy of the universe, occurs in numerous mythologies and in a number of Perse's poems. It was already present in *Récitation à l'éloge d'une Reine* and will reach its culmination in "Etroits sont les vaisseaux" of *Amers*.]

116. Ibid. [Lightning, and its accompanying phenomenon, thunder, is associated in nearly all the mythologies of the world with the revelation of the Godhead. In the life and work of Leger/Perse, it is of particular importance—as has already been shown—and even manifests itself in biographical details given by him, such as that four of his ancestors were killed by lightning (*OC*, p. 1089), but is most consistently associated with the god Shiva, as numerous examples show.]

117. Ibid., p. 193.

118. Ibid., p. 195.

119. Ibid., p. 196.

120. Paul Claudel, "Un Poème de Saint-John Perse: 'Vents,'" rpt. *OC*, p. 1123.

121. *Vents*, *OC*, pp. 211–12. [The figure of the shaman who—it will be remembered—preoccupied the poet since his Chinese experience had also appeared earlier in this poem: *OC*, p. 181.]

122. Ibid., p. 213.

123. Ibid.

124. Earlier in the poem (*OC*, p. 205), one finds the phrase: "On ne fréquente pas sans s'infecter la couche du divin."

125. Ibid., p. 223. [This is the culminating point of the voyage. It is followed by a sharp turn—and a return.]

126. Ibid., p. 224.

127. Ibid., pp. 224–26.

128. Ibid., p. 228.

129. Ibid., p. 229.

130. Ibid., p. 251. [The tree of the Indies may be an echo of the phrase used to describe the work of Tagore (see Chapter 3, note 127), but more than that, the universal symbol of the tree that unifies life and death, destruction and creation, the nether regions and the sky, and signifies the ever renascent forces of the cosmos—also symbolized by the "banyan de la pluie" of *Pluies*—fittingly ends the poem.]

131. The letter to Mrs. Biddle of 13 Sept. 1945, cited above, indicated that the struggle was between the life of a poet and the necessity, now that the war was over and a return to France was possible, to resume a political career that had certain practical advantages and would aid his family. See *OC*, p. 907.

132. In the collection *Métamorphoses*, with the title *Exil suivi de Poème à l'Etrangère, Pluies, Neiges* and the signature Saint-John Perse (a faulty edition, withdrawn at the request of the author); see *OC*, p. 1357.

133. Letter from Paul Claudel to Saint-John Perse, 12 Apr. 1945, *HP*, p. 439.

134. See note 84.

135. In his *Anthologie de la poésie française* (Paris: Gallimard, 1949), Gide found a way of paying homage to Saint-John Perse, in his preface, by citing a quote from *Vents*, and stating tht it was a bridge reaching out toward the future. [For more details see *OC*, p. 1130.]

136. *HP*, p. 631.

137. *OC*, p. xxv.

138. Letter to Mrs. Biddle, 20 Aug. 1946, *OC*, p. 908. [In this letter he states that this "grant-in-aid" would not be sufficient to allow him to live from literature and he might again have to consider offers to return to diplomatic functions in France.]

139. Only two days later, in a letter to A. Tate, 22 Aug. 1946, he wrote that he was still deciding between the two paths and asked Tate about a possible annual allocation from the Bollingen Foundation. For more details see *OC*, p. 976.]

140. Letter to L. Blum, 28 Sept. 1945, *HP*, p. 731.

141. Letter to Leger, 15 Oct. 1947, *HP*, p. 733.

142. For further details see: Message from Claudel, 19 Jan. 1948, *HP*, pp. 733–34.

143. *OC*, p. xxv.

144. Letter to Mrs. Biddle, 21 June 49, *OC*, p. 909.

145. Chapin, *HP*, pp. 289–90.

146. Ibid., pp. 286, 288–89.

147. Ibid., p. 290.

148. The exact date of her death can be established by a letter to Mrs. R. W. Bliss, written the day after that death (25 Oct. 48), *OC*, p. 933.

149. Letter to Claudel, 3 Jan. 48, *OC*, pp. 1013–14. Note: The unmarried sister in question is Mlle Eliane Saint-Leger Leger, living at the same address as her sister, Mme Abel Dormoy (the poet's third sister, Mme Ubaldo Sommaruga, was living in Milan, Italy). For more information see the letter to Alain Bosquet, 9 Mar. 53, *OC*, p. 1070.

150. Letter to MacLeish, 12 Nov. 48, *OC*, p. 948.

151. Letter to Claudel, 3 Jan. 48, *OC*, p. 1013. (Claudel did not die until 1955, at the age of eighty-seven. See Perse's homage, *OC*, pp. 483–85.)

152. Valéry had died in 1945, Fargue in 1947. For Perse's grief at both their deaths see *OC*, pp. 1011 and 1013.

153. Letter to Paulhan, 29 Sept. 1949, *OC*, p. 1025, and "Notes," p. 1304.

154. Letter to G.-J. Aubry, 17 June 1949, *OC*, p. 1035.

155. Letter to Claudel, 3 Jan. 1948, *OC*, p. 1014.

156. For change of address see letter to M.-P. Fouchet, 12 Dec. 1947, *OC*, p. 986.

157. *OC*, p. xxv.

158. For more details see *OC*, p. 1096.

159. Letter to Claudel, 1 Aug. 1949, *OC*, p. 1017.

160. Max-Pol Fouchet, "Rencontre de l'exact," *HP*, pp. 131–32. [Further details of this encounter were kindly furnished by the late M. Fouchet during an interview in Paris (Fall 1979) and in ensuing correspondence with the author.]

161. Letters to Fouchet, 27 Mar. 1948, 2 May 1948, *OC*, pp. 989, 991.

162. *OC*, p. xxv; plants collected, *OC*, p. 1096.

163. Letter to MacLeish, 18 June 1949, *OC*, p. 949. [The reference is, obviously, to "Amers," thus allowing one to date the beginnings of the poem earlier than is generally done, i.e., 1953–56, the dates of composition the poet gives at the end of this work.]

164. Letter to Claudel, 1 Aug. 1949, *OC*, p. 1017. [This attitude is combined with a refusal of the past—in the form of pillaged poems—and a drive toward "l'oeuvre vive à sa naissance." For details see letter to Gide, 28 May 1949, *OC*, p. 1006.]

165. *OC*, p. xxv.

166. Letter to Gide, 29 Aug. 1949, *OC*, p. 1011.

167. For the complete list of contributors and their texts, rpt., see *HP*, pp. 11–136.

168. Chapin, *HP*, pp. 288–89.

169. Letter to Mrs. Biddle, 13 Sept. 1950, *OC*, p. 912.

170. "Notes," *OC*, p. 1098.

171. For an interesting discussion of the images of two types of women that appear in the work of Saint-John Perse (one characterized by fecundity and obesity, the other by dynamism, slimness, action, linked to the figure of Diana the Huntress) see Mireille Sacotte, "Sur deux chants d''Anabase,'" *Lectures de Saint-John Perse* (Paris: Klincksieck, 1976), pp. 72–73. [Obviously, Dorothy Diana Russell corresponds to the second type, and the poet, as we shall see, will play on her middle name.)

172. E.g., see letter to Mrs. Biddle, 26 June 1952, *OC*, pp. 914–15.

173. *OC*, p. xxvi; for details re Avery Island see *OC*, p. 1098.

174. *HP*, pp. 632, 636–37, respectively.

175. For MacLeish's presentation address and Saint-John Perse's acceptance speech see *HP*, pp. 633–35.

176. *OC*, p. xxvi.

177. See note 163.

178. *Amers, OC*, p. 263.

179. Ibid., p. 259.

180. Ibid., p. 268.

181. *OC*, p. xxvi.

182. E.g., Mount Washington. Ibid.

183. *OC*, pp. xxvi–xxvii (during the years 1953–56).

184 . Letter to Mrs. Biddle, 31 July 1953, *OC*, p. 915.

185. Letter to Mrs. Biddle, 11 Aug. 1953, *OC*, p. 916.

186. Ibid. p. 917.

187. Letter to Mrs. Biddle, 12 Dec. 1955, *OC*, p. 921.

188. "Etroits sont les vaisseaux," *Amers, OC*, pp. 327, 328, respectively.

189. See discussion in Chapter 1. For evidence that Shiva was particularly in the mind of Saint-John Perse at this time see his letter to a Swedish writer, "La Thématique d'*Amers*," *HP*, p. 667, where he explicitely alludes to that particular divinity.

190. "Etroits sont les vaisseaux," *Amers, OC*, pp. 336–37.

191. Concrete and unabashed detailing of sexual images can be found all throughout the poem, especially in ibid., pp. 328, 330–31, 332–33, 334-37.

192. Among the mythological figures one finds: female Hindu divinities and Apsaras (pp. 333–34), Ishtar (p. 340), Aphrodite (p. 349), as well as ibid., various minor divinities and female hierophants who celebrate their union with a male divinity appearing in a variety of incarnations (stallion, watersnake or "Congre royal"—both an explicit sexual symbol and a sacred manifestation).

193. Ibid., p.. 380.

194. Ibid., p. 385.

195. *OC*, p. xxviii.

196. *OC*, pp. xxvii–xxviii.

Chapter 7: A Road of Glowing Embers

1. Phrase frequently used in *Chronique*, the poem Perse would shortly write, whose double meaning is old age and age of greatness.

2. He went straight to the south of France, without stopping in Paris (which, undoubtely, would have aroused painful memories); *OC*, p. xxvi.

3. Letter to Francis Biddle, Sept. 1957, *OC*, p. 927.

4. *Guerre, HP*, P. 169.

5. Inlets cut in the cliffs of this region of France.

6. Letter to T. S. Eliot, 21 May 1959, *OC*, p. 1040. [The mistral is the famous wind of this part of Europe.]

7. Letter to Mrs. H. T. (Mina) Curtiss, 27 July 1957, *OC*, p. 1057.

8. Letter to Mrs. Biddle, 30 Sept. 1957, *OC*, p. 924.

9. Letter to Mrs. Curtiss, 9 Sept. 1958, *OC*, p. 1059. [This phrase is preceded by a mention of his Celtic ancestry, also cited by Guerre, *HP*, p. 179, which, as we have already seen, is on occasion evoked by Leger/Perse.]

10. Ibid.

11. Letter to Mrs. Biddle, 30 Sept. 1957, *OC*, p. 924.

12. Letter to Mrs. Curtiss, 9 Sept. 1958, *OC*, p. 1059. [Perse's dislike for flowers was well known; see Chapin, *OC*, p. 1249.]

13. Letter to Mrs. Curtiss, 27 July 1957, *OC*, p. 1057.

14. Ibid.

15. Ibid.

16. Letter to Mrs. Biddle, 30 Sept. 1957, *OC*, p. 924.

17. Ibid.

18. Ibid.

19. For a description of Perse's activities in this realm see letter to Mrs. Biddle, *OC*, p. 925.

20. "peninsula," but also a play on the word "île" (island): "almost an island" (all-but island).

21. "the alizé for the mistral," [i.e., the wind of the tropical Antilles for that of the Mediterranean region]. Letter to Mrs. Biddle, *OC*, p. 924.

22. [The phrase has a double meaning and could read as: "But at least it's wind" or "But it's always wind."] Ibid.

23. Letter to Mrs. Curtiss, 27 July 1957, *OC*, p. 1057. [For details about this object, found by Mrs. Curtiss in 1951, see letter to the same, 10 Jan. 1957, *OC*, pp. 1044–45, and "Notes," *OC*, p. 1330.]

24. American writer, professor of English at Smith College, translator of French authors, owner of an estate (Chapelbrook) in Massachussets, where Saint-John Perse spent some time each summer. For further details concerning Mrs. Curtiss see "Notes," *OC*, pp. 1329–30.

25. Name of the site on which the property Perse now owned was located (meaning The Vineyards). His villa was named La Polynésie—perhaps in remembrance of his visit on the way back from China—as indicated in a letter to A. Tate, 12 Oct. 1959, *OC*, p. 984.

26. Letter to Mrs. Biddle, 30 Sept. 1957, *OC*, p. 924.

27. Ibid., p. 925.

28. Letter to Mrs. Curtiss, 9 Sept. 1958, *OC*, p. 1059.

29. *OC*, p. xxviii; also evident from letters of the period.

30. Published 16 May 1957. For the complete list of contributors as well as the texts in this homage see *HP*, pp. 143–64.

31. *New York Times Book Review*, 62, no. 30 (27 July 1958).

32. For Perse's reaction to this article see letter to W. H. Auden (n.d.), 1958, *OC*, p. 1043. For Perse's opinion of Auden as a writer see "Notes," *OC*, p. 1329. [Auden had already written a study devoted to Perse, intended for publication in the *Cahiers de la Pléiade* (1950), which was finally not included due to lack of space. For more details see *OC*, p. 1329.]

33. See letter to Tate, 12 Oct. 1959, *OC*, p. 984.

34. For the rapport between Saint-John Perse and E. E. Cummings see Erika Ostrovsky, "Saint-John Perse et E. E. Cummings: Points de rencontre," *Espaces de Saint-John Perse 3* (Aix: Université de Provence, 1981), pp. 99–112; also letter to Cummings, Dec. 1949, *OC*, p. 1041, and "Notes," *OC*, pp. 1328–29.

35. E.g., letter to Mrs. Curtiss, 9 Sept. 1959, *OC*, p. 1065.

36. E.g., letter to MacLeish, 25 Apr. 1958, *OC*, p. 953.

37. See, e.g., letter to Mrs. Curtiss, 9 Sept. 1959, *OC*, pp. 1063, 1065.

38. Letter to MacLeish, 25 Apr. 1958, *OC*, p. 953.

39. Ibid.

40. He had already expressed such feelings two years earlier in a letter to Mrs. Biddle, 30 Aug. 1956, *OC*, p. 923.

41. *OC*, p. xxviii (year); for exact date see letter to MacLeish (note 38).

42. "A high of about 80°; thunder showers expected in the evening." Weather Report, *The Evening Star* (Washington), Friday 26 Apr. 1958, p. A-3. [The wedding was not publicized, for no mention of it appears, either on that or succeeding days.]

43. Letter to Mrs. Curtiss, 9 Sept. 1958, *OC*, p. 1061.

44. Letter to T. S. Eliot, 21 May 1959, *OC*, p. 1040. [She is also referred to as "celle qui unit son sort au mien" in the letter to MacLeish of 25 Apr. 1958, and as "Celle avec qui j'ai choisi de vivre" in a letter to Tate, 15 May 1958, *OC*, p. 984.]

45. Letter to Mrs. Curtiss, 9 Sept. 1958, *OC*, p. 1058.

46. Ibid.

47. Diana the Huntress (whom Perse had also evoked in reference to a hurricane in a letter to Mrs. Biddle, Sept 5, 1955, *OC*, p. 920.)

48. Letter to Mrs. Curtis 9 Sept. 1958, *OC*, p. 1058.

49. A charming small house in Georgetown, at 1621 Thirty-fourth Street, to which he had moved: see letter to Tate, 15 May 1958, *OC*, p. 984. [The poet's widow still lived there. The author spent a weekend on the premises, at the invitation of Mme Leger, in the spring of 1981.]

50. Letter to Mrs. Curtiss, 9 Sept. 1958, *OC*, p. 1058. [Many interesting parallels can be drawn between Saint-John Perse and Audubon, but they go beyond the scope of this study.]

51. Ibid., p. 1059.

52. Ibid.

53. Ibid., p. 1060.

54. Ibid.

55. Ibid.

56. Ibid., p. 1061.

57. Ibid.

58. Ibid.

59. Ibid. [One notes that "Mistral" is now capitalized—as if to emphasize its importance and value—while this was not the case a year earlier: see note 21.]

60. Ibid., p. 1062.

61. Ibid.

62. Ibid. [Other references to Valéry also occur at this period and in this region: e.g., see the letter to T. S. Eliot, 21 May 1959, *OC*, p. 1040.]

63. Letter to MacLeish, 8 Feb. 1960, *OC*, p. 954.

64. Letter to Mrs. Curtiss, 9 Sept. 1958, *OC*, p. 1062.

65. Ibid. [Note that the letter is dated 9/IX.]

66. *HP*, p. 638.

67. For text of the official citation see *HP*, pp. 63–69.

68. Chapin, *HP*, p. 286.

69. *OC*, p. xxviii.

70. Letter to Mrs. Curtiss, 9 Sept. 1959, *OC*, p. 1063. [The same letter also indicates the belief that this property had been found by Mrs. Curtiss through magical means like those of a water witch or diviner.]

71. Letter to A. Tate, 13 Feb. 1960, *OC*, p. 985.

72. Epigraph.

73. Letter to Mrs. Curtiss, 9 Sept. 1959. [In this letter the phrase "Diane et moi" recurs twice, as well as "Diane auprès de moi"—underscoring the feeling of closeness and happiness. *OC*, pp. 1064, 1065.]

74. *Chronique*, *OC*, p. 391.

75. Ibid., p. 391.

76. Ibid., p. 391.

77. Ibid., p. 397.

78. Ibid., p. 399.

79. Ibid., p. 402.

80. Ibid., p. 401.

81. Ibid., p. 404.

82. *Amers*, *OC*, p. 264.

83. *OC*, p. xxviii.

84. Letter to Maria Martins (Brazilian sculptress and friend of Saint-John Perse in Washington, see "Notes," *OC*, pp. 1342–43), Apr. 1960, *OC*, p. 1079.

85. Ibid., pp. 1079–80.

86. *OC*, p. xxviii. [See also "Pour Victoria Ocampo," *OC*, pp. 503–6.]

87. *OC*, p. xxviii.

88. Letter to J. Paulhan, 19 July 1960, *OC*, pp. 1026–27.

89. Ibid., p. 1027.

90. *OC*, p. xxviii.

91. "Poésie" (Discours de Stockholm), *OC*, p. 443.

92. Ibid., pp. 444–45.

93. Ibid., p. 446.

94. Ibid., p. 447.

95. Guerre, *HP*, pp. 173–75.

96. Ibid., p. 178.

97. Ibid., p. 177.

98. Ibid. p. 177; (map) Mazars, *HP*, p. 621.

99. Mazars, *HP*, p. 621.

100. Mlle Eliane Saint-Leger Leger; Mme Abel Dormoy (Marguerite); Mme Ubaldo Sommaruga (Paule). Letter to A. Bosquet, 9 Mar. 1953, *OC*, p. 1070.

101. As well as the first director of the Fondation Saint-John Perse in Aix-en-Provence (where the archives on the poet would be housed) inaugurated 19 June 1976.

102. For a complete list of the visitors who came to Les Vigneaux during these years see *OC*, pp. xxx–xliii.

103. See note 49.

104. Told to the author by Mme Dorothy Leger.

105. See *OC*, pp. xxix–xliii.

106. *OC*, p. xxxvi.

107. *OC*, p. xxiv.

108. *OC*, p. xxxviii.

109. For a complete list of places visited during the travels of this decade see *OC*, pp. xxix–xliii.

110. For a complete list of publications and translations during this period see *OC*, pp. xxviii–xlii.

111. *Amers*, *OC*, p. 385.

112. Letter to MacLeish, 8 Feb. 1960, *OC*, p. 954. [This proposal was made by Camus shortly before his untimely death.]

113. In Paris, together with Paulhan. See *OC*, p. xxx.

114. Société des Editions d'Art, "Aux Vent d'Arles" (Paris, 1962), published the original edition of large format with the original etchings by Braque. For more details see *OC*, p. xxx.

115. See my discussion in Prologue.

116. "more than is covered by the flight of the kite [ornith.]." *Oiseaux*, *OC*, p. 407.

117. Ibid., p. 409.

118. Ibid., p. 410.

119. Ibid., p. 413.

120. Ibid., p. 414.

121. Ibid., p. 416.

122. Ibid., pp. 417–18.

123. Ibid., p. 419. [It will be remembered that exactly the same phrase ("Passer outre") had been used by the poet, over forty years earlier: see Chapter 5, note 9.)

124. Ibid., p. 422. [An almost identical phrase as the one cited in note 119 had already been used by Leger in 1920, at the time of his extremely important journey to Outer Mongolia ("Unité retrouvée, malaise dissipé"); see Chapter 4, note 121; and again in *Amers* ("Unité retrouvée, présence recouvrée,") *OC*, p. 368].

125. Ibid., p. 426.

126. The last words of *Oiseaux* are: "Et de cette aube de fraîcheur . . . ils gardent parmi nous quelque chose du songe de la création." Ibid., p. 427.

127. *OC*, p. xxxi.

128. The figure of the widow seems to have been especially moving to Saint-John Perse (probably because of his mother's state and, subsequently, that of two of his sisters). The widow appears in his writings in *Poème à l'Etrangère* and, of course, in *Neiges*, as well as in a homage to Jacqueline Kennedy when she was widowed: "Sacre d'un deuil," *OC*, p. 535. In *Chanté par Celle Qui Fut Là*, the figure of the bereaved woman is universalized and projected into the future (she who will be widowed).

129. "Sung by One Who Was There": translation of the title by Richard Howard.

130. [Note the double meaning of "fins," i.e., ending and purpose.] *OC*, p. 431.

131. Ibid. pp. 431–32.

132. Ibid., p. 432.

133. "La Mort au masque de céruse" appears twice: Ibid., pp. 432, 433.

134. Ibid., p. 432. [The "Grandes Indes de l'Ouest" combines the two major domains of the poet's predilection—India and the West—into an imaginary kingdom (geographically incompatible but imaginatively extremely meaningful.]

135. [Note that both verbs are in the passé simple, a tense used to denote action completed in the past, also used on funerary inscriptions] Ibid., p. 433.

136. (*Chronique*), note 81.

137. *OC*, p. 433. *Note:* In his interesting article, "Saint-John Perse et l'Asie," *Espaces Saint-John Perse* (Aix: Université de Provence, 1979). Nos. 1–2, p. 165, Régis Antoine calls attention to this "primordiale scène de tendresse." One might add that, characteristically of Saint-John Perse, the primordial or universal rejoins the personal, for the imagery is also based on memories of his own life experiences.

138. "Chant pour un équinoxe" (1971), *OC*, pp. 437–38.

139. Mme Leger stated (in a conversation with the author) that she kept the nature of her husband's illness—cancer—from him, by arriving at an understanding with his doctor in France and that this was also the principal reason why the couple did not return to the United States during the last period of the poet's life. For corroboration of the different attitudes of French and American oncologists regarding informing patients of their malady see Susan Sontag, *Illness as Metaphor* (New York: Vintage, 1979), p. 7.

140. Note 106.

141. *OC*, p. xliii.

142. Explicit mention of this is found in a letter to G. Nadal, 22 May 1958, *OC*, p. 569. *Note:* This decision would also preclude the possibility of posthumous publication of any of the manuscripts pillaged by the Germans, even if these did come to light one day.

143. See Prologue.

144. The initial poem of *Eloges* (*OC*, pp. 7–8), also one and a half pages long.

145. T. S. Eliot, *Burnt Norton* (Part II).

146. *OC*, p. 437.

147. Ibid., pp. 437–38.

148. Ibid., p. 438.

149. Ibid.

150. Originally published in *La Nouvelle Revue Française*, no. 241 (1 Jan. 1973), p. 1.

151. Chapter 6, note 194.

152. *La Nouvelle Revue Française* (1 Jan. 1973), p. 1.

153. Ibid.

154. Ibid.

155. Ibid.

156. Ibid.

157. For a brilliant treatment of the "régime nocturne de l'image," the inversion of symbols, and the imagery of mystical experience, see Gilbert Durand, *Les Structures anthropologiques de l'imaginaire*, 6th ed. (Paris: Bordas, 1979).

158. Originally published in *La Nouvelle Revue Française*, no. 258 (1 June, 1974), pp. 1–9.

159. Ibid., p. 1 (stanza 1).

160. For a fine treatment of this and other aspects of this poem see Serge Canadas, "Passage de l'équinoxe: Introduction à la notion et à l'expérience de *Sécheresse*," *Cahiers Saint-John Perse 2* (Paris: Gallimard, 1979), pp. 19–33.

161. *La Nouvelle Revue Française* (1 June 1974), p. 1.

162. Ibid.

163. "L'Appelé" (or "L'élu") appears twice in the poem in *La Nouvelle Revue Française* (1 June 1974) (pp. 2, 7) and finally becomes "l'homme en Dieu" (p. 9), i.e., the agent and accomplice of the divine.

164. For the most erudite discussion of the attributes and ritual initiation of the shaman see Mircea Eliade's *Initiation, rites, sociétés secrètes* (Paris: Gallimard, 1959), pp. 199–224, and *Mythes, rêves et mystères* (Paris: Gallimard, 1957), pp. 95–125.

165. Erich Neumann, *The Great Mother*. Trans. Ralph Manheim (Princeton, N.J.: Princeton University Press, 1972), pp. 175, 233, 333–34. The role of "Queen Maya" as "the mother of the Buddha" is also mentioned by Campbell, *The Masks of God*, p. 254. *Note:* Perse's interpretation of "Maïa" (alternate form of "Maya") seems closest to the Hindu concept discussed by Neumann and once again affirms Perse's lifelong preoccupation with the cult of Shiva and Hinduism in general. At the same time, the variant "Maia" (which, in classical mythology, is the name of a nymph identified with Diana) links her to Diane/Dorothy.

166. *La Nouvelle Revue Française* (1 June 1974), p. 3.

167. Ibid.

168. Ibid., p. 4.

169. Ibid., p. 5.

170. Ibid. *Note:* "Etre is now capitalized (in contrast to "Nocturne") which seems to indicate a reaffirmation.

171. Ibid.

172. Ibid. p. 6.

173. A phrase that appears three times in the poem (Ibid., pp. 6, 8). For an excellent discussion of sacred Time, the Great Round, eternal return, etc., see: Mircea Eliade, *Aspects du mythe* (Paris: Gallimard, 1963), esp. pp. 96–111; *Le Mythe de l'éternel retour* (Paris: Gallimard, 1969), pp. 41–43, 49–50, 65–111, 135–53; *Le Sacré et le profane* (Paris: Gallimard, 1965), esp. pp. 60–98. *Note:* Although in "temps de Dieu" God is capitalized, there is no reason to conclude that the reference is to a particular (especially, a Judeo-Christian) divinity, but is a general reference to the divine as it has appeared in all Perse's work.

174. I.e., "Brève la vie, brève la course, et la mort nous rançonne: . . . O temps de Dieu, sois nous comptable." *La Nouvelle Revue Française* (1 June 1974), p. 6.

175. "nos actes sont partiels, nos oeuvres parcellaires! O temps de Dieu, nous seras-tu enfin complice?" Ibid.

176. "De l'aigre et de l'acerbe nous connaissons les lois . . . nos mets abondent en acides, et nos sources sont furtives. O temps de Dieu, sois-nous propice." Ibid. p. 8.

177. Ibid., p. 7.

178. Ibid., p. 9.

179. Canadas, op. cit., p. 29, furnishes an interesting discussion of this enigmatic line in which he emphasizes Perse's denunciation of the tendency to destroy the mythic by reason.

180. *La Nouvelle Revue Française* (1 June 1974), p. 9.

181. "Sur un Adagio de Beethoven," published in facsimile, *Cahiers Saint-John Perse 1* (Paris: Gallimard, 1978), first page.

182. *Cahiers Saint-John Perse 1*, p. 1.

183. *Chant pour un équinoxe* (Paris: Gallimard, 1975). *Note:* The volume, printed by Darantière of Dijon (the same printer who had done the first edition of Joyce's *Ulysses* and Perse's *Anabase* in 1924–see Chapter 5, notes 72 and 73) appeared on 20 Oct. 1975, exactly one month after the death of the poet.

184. The sequence of the poems is as follows: "Sécheresse" (1974), "Chant pour un équinoxe" (1971), "Nocturne" (1973), "Chanté par Celle Qui Fut Là" (1968).

185. *OC*, p. xliv.

186. The burial took place on Monday, 22 September 1975. The poet's death (according to his wish) was not revealed to the press until after the funeral. For further details see the obituary of Saint-John Perse in the *New York Times*, 23 Sept. 1975, p. 40; *Le Monde*, 24 Sept. 1975, p. 19; series of articles grouped under the general title "Saint-John Perse est mort," in the same issue of *Le Monde*.

187. The small seaside cemetery of Giens evokes the famous poem of Paul Valéry: "Le Cimetière marin."

LIST OF SHORT
TITLES

CDMEL   *Columbia Dictionary of Modern European Literature.*
Eds. Jean-Albert Bédé and William B. Edgerton. Second Edition, fully revised and enlarged. New York: Columbia University Press, 1980.

CSJP   *Cahiers Saint-John Perse.* Paris: Gallimard, 1978–82 (1: 1978; 2: 1979; 3: 1980; 4: 1981; 5: 1982).

ESJP   *Espaces de Saint-John Perse.* Aix-en-Provence: Publications de l'Université de Provence, 1980–83 (1–2: 1980; 3: 1981; 4: 1983).

HP   *Honneur à Saint-John Perse.* Paris: Gallimard, 1965.

LSJP   *Lectures de Saint-John Perse.* Paris: Klincksieck, 1976.

OC   Saint-John Perse, *Oeuvres complètes.* Bibliothèque de la Pléiade. Paris: Gallimard, 1972.

BIBLIOGRAPHY

I. Works of Saint-John Perse

POETRY

"Amers," *OC*, pp. 257–385.

"Anabase," *OC*, pp. 89–116.

"Chanté par Celle qui fut là," *OC*, pp. 431–33.

Chant pour un équinoxe ("Sécheresse," "Chant pour un équinoxe," Nocturne," "Chanté par Celle qui fut là"). Paris: Gallimard, 1975.

"Chant pour un équinoxe," *OC*, pp. 437–38.

"Chronique," *OC*, pp. 398–404.

Eloges ("Ecrit sur la porte," "Images à Crusoé," "Pour fêter une enfance," "Eloges"), *OC*, pp. 7–52.

Exil ("Exil," "Pluies," Poème à l'Etrangère"), *OC*, pp. 123–73.

La Gloire des Rois ("Récitation à la gloire d'une Reine," "Amitié du Prince," "Histoire du Régent," "Chanson du Présomptif," "Berceuse"), *OC*, pp. 58–84.

"Nocturne," *La Nouvelle Revue Française* (1 Jan. 73), p. 1.

"Oiseaux," *OC*, pp. 409–27.

"Sécheresse," *La Nouvelle Revue Française* (1 June 74), pp. 1–9.

"Vents," *OC*, pp. 179–251.

LITERARY SPEECHES; HOMAGES; STATEMENTS

SPEECHES

"Poésie" (Speech delivered at Nobel Prize Award Banquet, 10 Dec. 1960). *OC*, pp. 443–48.

"Pour Dante" (Address delivered in Florence for the 700th Anniversary of Dante, 20 Apr. 1965). *OC*, pp. 449–59.

HOMAGES

"Adrienne Monnier" *OC*, pp. 486–87.

"A la Mémoire de Valery Larbaud" ("Larbaud ou l'honneur littéraire"). *OC*, pp. 487–88.

"A la Mémoire de Georges Braque" ("Pierre levée"). *OC*, pp. 536–37.
"A René Char." *OC*, p. 542.
"A Igor Stravinsky." *OC*, p. 499.
"André Gide." *OC*, pp. 472–82.
"Cioran." *OC*, p. 541.
"En Hommage à T. S. Eliot ("Traduction d'un poème"). *OC*, pp. 465–66.
"Hommage à la Mémoire de Paul Claudel" ("Silence pour Claudel"). *OC*, pp. 483–86.
"Hommage à la Mémoire de Rabindranath Tagore." *OC*, pp. 500–503.
"Honneur à Jorge Luis Borges." *OC*, pp. 506–7.
"Léon-Paul Fargue" (Preface). *OC*, pp. 507–32.
"Lettre à Paul Valéry" ("Don d'un crâne de cristal"). *OC*, pp. 463–64.
"Message pour Ungaretti" ("A celui qui de sa main nue . . ."). *OC*, pp. 499–500.
"Poème pour Valery Larbaud" ("Jadis Londres"). *OC*, pp. 464–65; already in *HP*, pp. 651–53.
"Pour Nadia Boulanger." *OC*, pp. 540–41.
"Pour Georges Schehadé" ("Poète Schehadé"). *OC*, pp. 482–83.
"Pour Victoria Ocampo" ("Dame de San Isidro et du Rio de la Plata"). *OC*, pp. 503–6.
"Sur un Adagio de Beethoven." (published in facsimile). *CSJP 1*, p. 1.
"Sur Jacques Rivière." *OC*, pp. 466–72.

STATEMENTS (RELATING TO POETRY)

"Lettre à Roger Caillois." *HP*, p. 654.
"Lettres à Roger Caillois." *OC*, pp. 561–63.
"Lettre à Max-Pol Fouchet." (Extract). *HP*, p. 654.
"Lettre à Gaston Gallimard." *OC*, pp. 547–48.
"Lettre à Dag Hammarskjöld." *HP*, p. 667.
"Lettre à Albert Henry." *OC*, pp. 578–79.
"Lettre à Georges Huppert." *HP*, p. 655.
"Lettre à Archibald MacLeish." *OC*, p. 548.
"Lettre à Luc-André Marcel." *OC*, pp. 568–69.
"Lettre à Adrienne Monnier." *OC*, pp. 552–54.
"Lettre à Octave Nadal." *OC*, pp. 568–69.
"Message pour Valery Larbaud." *OC*, pp. 558–61.
"Note pour un écrivain suédois sur la thématique d'*Amers*." *OC*, pp. 569–72; *HP*, pp. 665–67.
"Réponse de Saint-John Perse à l'allocution du Grand Prix National des Lettres." *HP*, p. 639.

CORRESPONDENCE

"Lettres de Jeunesse" (to Gustave-Adolphe Monod, Jacques Rivière, Alain Fournier, Paul Claudel, Gabriel Frizeau, Francis Jammes, André Gide, Valery Larbaud). *OC*, pp. 643–806.

"Lettres d'Asie" (to Philippe Berthelot, Alexandre Conty, Dr. Bussière, Paul Valéry, Jules Dumour, Mme Amédée Saint-Leger Leger, Joseph Conrad, "une dame d'Europe," Gustave-Adolphe Monod, Jacques Rivière, Gustave-Charles Toussaint, André Gide). *OC*, pp. 807–96.

"Lettres d'Exil" (to Mrs. Francis Biddle, Mr. Francis Biddle, Mrs. Robert Woods Bliss, Archibald MacLeish, Roger Caillois, Allen Tate, Max-Pol Fouchet, Louis-Marcel Raymond, Adrienne Monnier, André Gide, Paul Claudel, Jules Supervielle, Jean Paulhan, G.-Jean Aubry, T. S. Eliot, E. E. Cummings, W. H. Auden, Mrs. H. T. Curtiss, Alain Bosquet, Pierre Guerre, Henry Peyre, Hugue Le Gallais, Mark van Doren, André Rousseaux, Maria Martin Juan José Castro, Mme Kumar Nehru, Igor Stravinsky). *OC*, pp. 897–1083.

"Huit lettres inédites: Saint-John Perse à Yvan Goll." Pres. by Roger Little. *CSJP 2*, pp. 105–26.

ANNOTATIONS BY SAINT-JOHN PERSE IN THE WORK OF OTHER WRITERS (IN HIS PERSONAL LIBRARY: ARCHIVES OF THE FONDATION SAINT-JOHN PERSE, AIX-EN-PROVENCE)

Aragon, Louis. *Le Libertinage*. Paris: La Nouvelle Revue Française, 1924.

Bonnefoy, Yves. *Pierre écrite*. Paris: Mercure de France, 1965.

Breton, André. *Fata Morgana*. Buenos Aires: Les Lettres Françaises, 1942.

Camus, Albert. *L'Homme révolté*. Paris: Gallimard, 1945.

Carrouges, M. *André Breton et les données fondamentales du Surréalisme*. Paris: Gallimard, 1950.

Char, René. *Le Poème pulverisé*. Paris: Fontaine, 1947.

Charpier, Jacques, and Seghers, Pierre. *Art Poétique*. Paris: Seghers, 1956.

Claudel, Paul. *Cinq grandes odes*. Paris: N.R.F., 1913.

_____. *Oeuvres complètes*. Paris: Gallimard, 1950.

Dante. *La Divine Comédie*. Paris: Garnier, 1962.

de Mandiargues, André Pieyre. *L'Age de craie, Hedera*. Paris: Gallimard, 1961.

du Bouchet, André. *Dans la chaleur vacante*. Paris: Mercure de France, 1961.

Dupin, Jacques. *L'Embrasure, Gravir*. Paris: Gallimard, 1971.

_____. *L'Epervier*. Paris: G.L.M., 1960.

Eluard, Paul. *Chanson complète*. Paris: Gallimard, 1939.

Emmanuel, Pierre. *Poètes d'aujourd'hui*. Introd. Alain Bosquet. Paris: Seghers, 1959.

Fargue, Léon-Paul. *Déjeuners de soleil*. Paris: Gallimard, 1942.

_____. *Pour la musique, Tancrède, Ludions*. Paris: Gallimard, 1943.

Fitzgerald, Robert. *In the Rose of Time: Poems 1931–1956*. New York: New Directions, 1956.

Glissant, Edouard. *Malemort*. Paris: Seuil, 1975.

Grosjean, Jean. *Terre du temps*. Paris: Gallimard, 1946.

Jouve, Pierre Jean. *Diadème, Mélodrame*. Paris: Gallimard, 1970.

_____. *Poésie: Les Noces, Sueur de sang, Matière céleste, Kyrie*. Paris: Mercure de France, 1964.

——. *Sueur de sang*, nouvelle ed. Paris: Mercure de France, 1955.

——. *Ténèbres*. Paris: Mercure de France, 1965.

Larbaud, Valery. *Caderno*. Paris: Editions Au Sans Pareil, 1933.

——. *Journal inédit*. Paris: Gallimard, 1954.

Lautréamont. *Les Chants de Maldoror.* Buenos Aires: Vian, 1944.

Malraux, André. *Antimémoires*. Paris: Gallimard, 1967.

——. *Les Chênes qu'on abat*. Paris: Gallimard, 1971.

——. *La Tête d'Obsidienne*. Paris: Gallimard, 1974.

Michaux Henri. *Un Barbare en Asie*, nouvelle ed. Paris: Gallimard, 1967.

——. *Face aux verrous*. Paris: Gallimard, 1954.

——. *Moments*. Paris: Gallimard, 1973.

Pauwels, Louis, and Berger, Jacques. *Le Matin des magiciens*. Paris: Gallimard, 1960.

Raine, Kathleen. *The Hollow Hill*. London: Hamish Hamilton, 1965.

Rimbaud, Arthur. *Oeuvres*. Introd. by René Char. Paris: Le Club Français du Livre, 1957.

Roy, Claude. *Un seul poème*. Paris: Gallimard, 1954.

Seferis, George. *Poems*. London: The Bodley Head, 1960.

Shakespeare. *Les Sonnets de Shakespeare* (French version by Pierre Jean Jouve). Paris: Le Sagittaire, 1955.

Spencer, Theodore. *Poems: 1940–1947*. Cambridge: Harvard University Press, 1948.

Supervielle, Jules. *L'Escalier.* Paris: Gallimard, 1956.

Tate, Allen. *Les Ancêtres*. Paris: Gallimard, 1948.

——. *Mediterranean and Other Poems*. Privately printed. The Benfolly Edition (limited to 12 copies). No. 2. 1936.

Ungaretti, Giuseppe. *A partir du désert*. Trans. by Philippe Jacottet. Paris: Seuil, 1965.

INTERVIEWS OR CONVERSATIONS WITH SAINT-JOHN PERSE PUBLISHED IN TRANSCRIBED FORM

Chapin, Katherine Garrison. "Saint-John Perse chez ses amis d'Amérique." *HP,* pp. 286–91.

Devlin, Denis. "Saint-John Perse à Washington" *HP,* pp. 71–73.

Guerre, Pierre. "Rencontres avec Saint-John Perse." *HP,* pp. 168–80.

Mazars, Pierre. "Une Journée à la villa 'Les Vigneaux.'" *HP,* pp. 618–23.

Ogburn, Charlton. "Comment fut écrit 'Pluies.'" *HP,* pp. 273–79.

Raymond, Louis-Marcel. "Rencontres de Saint-John Perse." *HP,* pp. 624–29.

Victoria, Marcos. "La Musique dans la nuit." *HP,* pp. 280–85.

II. *Works of Alexis Leger*

SPEECHES, MEMORANDA, HOMAGES, MESSAGES, STATEMENTS

"'An III de l'exil!' 14 juillet 1942" (Message to the French in America). Originally published in *France Amérique*. Rpt. *OC*, pp. 615–16.

"Briand" (Speech delivered at New York University in commemoration of Aristide Briand, 1942). *OC*, pp. 605–13; *HP*, pp. 716–22.

"Discours pour la signature du Pacte Briand-Kellogg" (1928). *HP*, pp. 695–98.

"Grandeur de Kennedy" (1963). Originally published in *Le Monde*, at the time of Kennedy's death. Rpt. *OC*, p. 639.

"Mémorandum sur l'organisation d'un régime d'union fédérale européenne" (1930). *OC*, pp. 583–96; *HP*, pp. 699–710.

"Réponse à une enquête de presse sur 'Les Meneurs d'hommes'." *OC*, pp. 598–600.

"Réponse à un historien allemand" (on the attitude of Alexis Leger toward the French refugees in London, 1940). *OC*, pp. 632–34 (also, *HP*, 725–26).

"Sur l'optimisme en politique." *OC*, pp. 597–98.

"Une Enquête sur l'optimisme" (réponse de Leger). *HP*, p. 783.

POLITICAL CORRESPONDENCE

Letters (to President Edouard Herriot. Winston Churchill, General de Gaulle, Franklin Delano Roosevelt, Léon Blum, Dag Hammarskjöld, the King of Sweden, John F. Kennedy, a Belgian historian). *OC*, pp. 598–614, 615–30, 634–39, 640.

Letters (to President Herriot, General de Gaulle, Winston Churchill, President Roosevelt, Léon Blum). *HP*, pp. 713–15, 727–31.

INTERVIEWS WITH ALEXIS LEGER
PUBLISHED IN TRANSCRIBED FORM

"Une Audience d'Alexis Leger." In Louis Fisher, *Men and Politics* (New York, 1941). Rpt. *HP*, p. 784.

"Meneurs d'hommes: Alexis Leger" (Interview with Jean Lasserre). *Le Petit Parisien* (9 Jan. 1936). Rpt. *HP*, pp. 779–82.

"A New York en 1940" (Interview with Jean Rollin). *Démocratie 60* (6 Oct. 1960). Rpt. *HP*, pp. 786–87.

INTERVIEWS OR DISCUSSIONS WITH PERSONS RELATED TO THE
LIFE AND WORK OF SAINT-JOHN PERSE/ALEXIS LEGER

Adonis (pseud.). Foremost modern poet in the Arabic language. Aix-en-Provence, March 1981.

Barrault, Jean-Louis. Actor, director, critic. Paris, December 1979.

Bonnefoy, Yves. Poet critic. December 1979 (by correspondence).

Bradley, Mme Jenny. Literary agent, important figure in the world of writers since the start of the century. Paris, November 1979.

Cioran, E. M. Writer. Paris, October, November 1979, July 1981.

Fels, Countess Marthe de. Companion of Saint-John Perse/Alexis Leger before World War II, friend of Claudel, Briand, author. Paris, November, December, 1979.

Fitzgerald, Robert. Poet, translator of Saint-John Perse. New York, February 1982.

Fouchet, Max-Pol. Writer, publisher, director of *Fontaine*. Paris, December 1979, June 1980, and correspondence.

Freund, Gisèle. Photographer. New York, October 1983.

Glissant, Edouard. Poet, novelist. Aix-en Provence, March 1981.

Guerre, Pierre. Writer, original director of the Fondation Saint-John Perse. March 1978.

Kemp, Friedhelm. Critic, translator of Saint-John Perse. Aix-en Provence, March 1981.

Leger, Mrs. Dorothy Diana. Widow of Saint-John Perse/Alexis Leger. Paris, November 1979; Les Vigneaux (home of the poet in France), July 1980; Washington, D.C. (the poet's home in America), April 1981.

Little, Roger. Critic, poet. Aix-en Provence, July 1980, 1981.

Norman, Mrs. Dorothy. Author, photographer, friend of Saint-John Perse. New York, March 1981; October, May 1982; April 1983.

Stetié, Salah. Lebanese poet, critic. Aix-en-Provence, March 1981.

Tabouis, Geneviève. Journalist, author, co-exile of Alexis Leger. Paris, December 1979.

Temple, F. J. Publisher, translator. Aix-en-Provence, March 1981 (followed by correspondence).

Vigée, Claude. Poet, critic. Aix-en Provence, March 1981.

Transcribed copies of all interviews and discussions in the collection of Erika Ostrovsky. The author hereby expresses her gratitude for the time and insights given by all the persons involved. Appreciation is also due to the Fondation Saint-John Perse, its directors and staff, for their invaluable help during the period of research necessary for the preparation of this book.

BIOGRAPHICAL, CRITICAL, AND HISTORICAL SOURCES RELATING TO THE LIFE AND WORK OF SAINT-JOHN PERSE/ALEXIS LEGER (MAJOR STUDIES OR THOSE OF UNUSUAL INTEREST ARE INDICATED BY AN ASTERISK)

Aiken, Conrad. "Hommage," *Combat* (16 May 1957), p. 7. Rpt. *HP*, p. 1456.

———. "Whole Meaning or Doodle: *Rains* by Saint-John Perse." *New Republic* 112 (16 Apr. 1945), pp. 512–14. French trans. in *HP*, pp. 441–42.

Allard, Paul. *Le Quai d'Orsay: Son personnel, ses rouages, ses dessous*. Paris: Editions de France, 1938.

Anex, Georges. "Poète du Seuil et du Songe," *HP*, pp. 241–45.

Antoine, Régis. "Saint-John Perse et l'"Asie," *ESJP 1–2*, pp. 151–66.

Apollinaire, Guillaume. *L'Esprit nouveau et les poètes*. Paris: Jacques Haumont, 1946.

Aragon, Louis. "Apologie de Saint-John Perse." *L'Humanité* (2 Sept. 1975), pp. 1, 8.

———"Car c'est de l'homme qu'il s'agit." *Les Lettres Françaises* (3 Nov. 1960). Rpt. *HP*, pp. 576–77.

Arrouye, Jean-Louis. "Amers d'Amérique." *ESJP 3*, pp. 127–51.

Ashton, Dore. "Saint-John Perse's Guadeloupe." *Kenyon Review* 23, no. 3 (Summer 1961), pp. 520–26.

Asturias, Miguel Angel. "Homage," *HP*, p. 148.

Auden, W. H. "A Song of Life's Power to Renew." *New York Times Book Review* 62, no. 30 (27 July 1958), pp. 1, 12. Also in French trans. in *HP*, pp. 502–3.

Autrand, Michel. "Saint-John Perse et Claudel." *Revue d'Histoire Littéraire de la France* 78, no. 3 (May–June 1978), pp. 355–78.

Bachelard, Gaston. *L'Eau et les rêves.* 9th ed. Paris: José Corti, 1942.

Barry, André. "Saint-John Perse, diplomate poète et poète diplomate." *Combat* (24 Sept. 1959), p. 8.

Bateman, Jacqueline. "Questions de métrique persienne." *LSJP*, pp. 27–56.

Beach, Sylvia. *Shakespeare and Company.* New York: Harcourt, Brace, 1956.

Benamou, Michel. "Le Chant de la terre dans 'Chronique'." *French Review* 34, no. 5 (April 1961), pp. 480–82. Rpt. *HP*, pp. 522–25.

Beucler, A. "Première Rencontre avec Saint-John Perse." *Littérature Générale/ Idées/Arts* 2, no. 2 (1964), 1–8.

Bidault, Georges. "Lettre à Alexis Leger" (16 Apr. 1946). *HP*, p. 732.

Blanchet, André. Introduction to *Paul Claudel—Francis Jammes—Gabriel Frizeau: Correspondence (1897–1938).* Paris: Gallimard, 1952. Pp. 7–28.

Bois, Elie. "Comment le Secrétaire Général fut relevé de ses fonctions." Extract from *Le Malheur de la France.* Rpt. *HP*, pp. 764–68.

Boisdeffre. Pierre de. "Le Destin de Saint-John Perse." *Journal de Genève* (24 Oct. 1959). Rpt. *HP*, pp. 573–75.

———. "Saint-John Perse." In *Histoire vivante de la littérature d'aujord'hui.* Paris: Perrin, 1958. Pp. 509–18.

———. "Saint-John Perse, Prix Nobel." *Revue des Deux Mondes* 23 (Nov.–Dec. 1960), pp. 455–61.

Bollack, Jean. "Ailleurs." *HP*, pp. 338–44.

———. "En l'an de paille." *HP*, pp. 473–79.

Bonnefoy, Yves. "Illumination et Eloge." In *Le Nuage rouge.* Paris: Mercure de France, 1977. Pp. 221–33.

Bosquet, Alain. "Les Noces de l'objet et du verbe." *HP*, pp. 161–64.

———. "1911, Eloges et le siècle nouveau." *CSJP 1*, pp. 91–100.

*———. *Saint-John Perse.* 11th ed. Paris: Seghers, Coll. Les Poètes d'aujourd'hui, 1977.

———. "Saint-John Perse ou la rhétorique rédemptrice." *HP*, pp. 363–77.

Bounoure, Gabriel. "Saint-John Perse et l'ambiguité poétique." *HP*, pp. 91–97.

Bourguès, Lucien. "Alexis Leger, Secrétaire Général." *HP*, pp. 775–76.

Bréal, Auguste. *Philippe Berthelot.* 2d ed. Paris: Gallimard, 1937.

Brée, Germaine. "*Exile* and Other Poems." *French Review* 27, no. 6 (May 1954), pp. 477–78.

———. "Winds." *French Review* 28, no. 6 (May 1955), pp. 552–53.

Breton, André. "Le Donateur." *HP*, pp. 52–55.

———. "Surréaliste à distance." Rpt. *HP*, p. 384.

Briand, Aristide. *Souvenirs parlés* (as told to Raymond Escholier). Paris: Hachette, 1932.

Brombert, Victor. "Perse's Avian Order." *Hudson Review* 19, no. 3 (Autumn 1966), pp. 494–97.

Byron, Thomas. *Nonsense and Wonder: The Poems and Cartoons of Edward Lear.* New York: Dutton, 1977.

*Caduc, Eveline. *Saint-John Perse: Connaissance et Création.* Paris: José Corti, 1977.

Cahiers Paul Claudel, 1, 2. Paris: Gallimard, 1959, 1960.

**Cahiers de la Pléïade,* 10 (Summer–Autumn 1950).

**Cahiers du Sud* 352 (Oct.–Nov. 1959).

**Cahiers Saint-John Perse, 1–7.* Paris: Gallimard, 1978–84.

Caillois, Roger. "The Art of Saint-John Perse." *Sewanee Review* 53 (Spring 1945), pp. 198–206.

———. "Eléments pour un panégyrique de Saint-John Perse." *Le Figaro Littéraire* 1534 (11 Oct. 1975), pp. 1, 13.

———. "Une Poésie encyclopédique." *HP*, pp. 80–90.

*———. *Poétique de Saint-John Perse.* Paris: Gallimard, 1954.

———. "Violence, néant et louange chez Saint-John Perse." *Cahiers du Nord* 23, nos. 98–99 (1953–54), pp. 284–92.

Cameron, Elizabeth R. "Alexis Saint-Léger-Léger." In *The Diplomats: 1919–1939.* Eds. Gordon A. Craig and Felix Gilbert. Princeton, N.J.: Princeton University Press, 1953. Pp. 374–406.

Campbell, Joseph. *The Flight of the Wild Gander: Explorations in the Mythological Dimension.* South Bend, Indiana: Regnery/Gateway, 1979.

———. *The Masks of God: Oriental Mythology.* London: Penguin, 1979.

Canadas, Serge. "Passage de l'équinoxe: Introduction à la notion et à l'expérience de *Sécheresse*." *CSJP* 2, pp. 19–33.

Cassou, Jean. "Hommage." *HP*, p. 147.

Césaire Aimé. *Discours sur le colonialisme.* 5th ed. Paris: Présence Africaine, 1970.

———. *A Season in the Congo.* Trans. Ralph Manheim. New York: Grove Press, 1969.

Chapin, Katherine Garrison. "Perse on the Sea within Us." *New Republic* 139, no. 17 (27 Oct. 1958), pp. 19–20.

———. "Saint-John Perse chez ses amis d'Amérique." *HP*, pp. 286–91.

———. "Time Confronted: Saint-John Perse." *New Republic* 145, no. 24 (11 Dec. 1961), pp. 21–22.

Char, René. "A Saint-John Perse." *HP*, p. 23.

*Charpier, Jacques. *Saint-John Perse.* Paris: Gallimard, Bibliothèque Idéale, 1962.

Chauleau, Liliane. *La Vie quotidienne aux Antilles françaises au temps de Schoelcher au XIXe siècle.* Paris: Hachette, 1979.

Churchill Winston. *The Gathering Storm.* Boston: Houghton Mifflin, 1948.

———. "Télégramme de M. Winston Churchill à M. Alexis Leger (30 mai 1940)." *HP*, p. 715.

*Cioran, E. M. "Saint-John Perse ou le Vertige de la Plénitude." *HP*, pp. 220–25.

Cirlot, O. E. *A Dictionary of Symbols.* New York: Philosophical Library, 1967.

Claudel, Paul. "Choses de Chine." In *Cahiers Paul Claudel 4* Paris: Gallimard, 1962. Pp. 122–31.

———. *Journal, I, II.* Paris: Gallimard, Bibliothèque de la Pléiade, 1968, 1969.

———. "Lettre à Alexis Leger (1934)." *HP,* p. 799.

———. "Lettre à Saint-John Perse (1945)." *HP,* p. 439.

———. "Lettre à Saint-John Perse (1947)." *HP,* pp. 463–64.

———. "Message (19 Jan. 1948)." *HP,* p. 711.

———. "Un Poème de Saint-John Perse: 'Vents.'" *La Revue de Paris* (1 Nov. 1949), p. 4.

———. *Réflexions sur la poésie.* Paris: Gallimard, 1963.

Claverie, André. "Une Poésie de la célébration." *CSJP 4,* pp. 85–114.

Cocteau, Jean. "Lettre ouverte à Madame Nantet." *Cahiers Paul Claudel 2,* pp. 18–24.

Cogniat, Raymond. Preface to *Victor Segalen: Poète de l'Asie.* Paris: Galérie Jean Loize, 1944.

Colette. "Lettre (3 Mar. 36)." *HP,* p. 798.

Colt, Byron. "*Amers:* Afterthoughts." *Prairie Schooner* 34 (Summer 1960), pp. 168–69.

———. "Saint-John Perse." *Modern Language Quarterly* 21, no. 3 (1960), pp. 235–38.

The Correspondence between Paul Claudel and André Gide. New York: Pantheon, 1952.

Correspondence de Jacques Rivière et d'Alain Fournier. Paris: Gallimard, 1928.

Crouy-Chanel, Etienne. "Alexis Leger, l'homme et son action: Un passé pas si simple: L'avant-guerre." *Le Monde* (9 Sept. 1980), p. 2.

Cummings, E. E. "Poème" ("En hommage à Saint-John Perse"). *OC,* pp. 1328–29.

———. *Selected Letters of E. E. Cummings.* London: André Deutsch, 1922.

Deguy, Michel. "Le Chant de Saint-John Perse." *Critique* 20, no. 205 (June 1964), pp. 507–15.

———. "La Critique de Saint-John Perse." *Cahiers du Sud* 58 (1964), pp. 304–6.

Denommé, Robert. "Francis Jammes." *CDMEL,* pp. 401–2.

Devlin, Denis. "Saint-John Perse à Washington." *HP,* pp. 71–73.

Diéguez, Manuel de. "Une Critique créatrice." *Combat* (19 Jan. 1961). Rpt. *HP,* pp. 529–32.

"Le Diplomate" (*Annuaire diplomatique,* Rpt. *HP,* pp. 681–82; "Décrets pris à Vichy contre Alexis Leger," *HP,* p. 724; "L'Absence en Chine," *HP,* p. 691; "La Chine," *HP,* pp. 683–84; "Le Quai d'Orsay," *HP,* pp. 693–94.)

Dolamore, Charles. "A Propos de 'Sécheresse.'" *LSJP,* pp. 115–28.

Dorst, Jean. "'Oiseaux' vus par un ornithologue."*ESJP 1–2,* pp. 327–34.

Doumet, Christian. "La Production du texte: Une lecture de 'Midi, ses fauves, ses famines . . .'" *ESJP 1–2,* pp. 27–38.

Dumour, Guy. "La Mort de Saint-John Perse: L'eclipse du soleil." *Le Nouvel Observateur* (29 Sept. 1975), pp. 76–77.

Dupland, Edmond. "'Notre' Saint-John Perse: En marge d'une lettre d'Alexis

Leger." *Guadeloupe* 2000 (Apr. 1976), pp. 19–21.

Durand, Gilbert. *Les Structures anthropologiques de l'imaginaire.* 6th ed. Paris: Bordas, 1979.

Duroselle, Jean-Baptiste. *La Décadence: 1932–1939.* Paris: Imprimerie Nationale, 1979.

Dutourd, Jean. "Saint-John Perse le poète aux deux visages." *Paris-Match* 1375 (4 Oct. 1975), p. 58.

*Elbaz, Shlomo. *Lectures d'"Anabase" de Saint-John Perse: Le désert, le désir.* Lausanne: L'Age d'homme, 1977.

———. "T. S. Eliot vu et 'corrigé' par Saint-John Perse." *ESJP 1–2*, pp. 129–50.

Eliade, Mircea. *Aspects du mythe.* Paris: Gallimard, 1963.

———. *Initiation, rites, sociétés secrètes.* Paris: Gallimard, 1959.

———. *Le Mythe de l'éternel retour.* Paris: Gallimard, 1969.

———. *Mythes, rêves et mystères.* Paris: Gallimard, 1957.

———. *Le Sacré et le profane.* Paris: Gallimard, 1965.

Eliot, T. S. "Un Feuillet unique" (Homage). *HP*, pp. 18–19.

———. "Lettre à S.-L. L. (1927)." *HP*, p. 419.

———. Preface to *Anabasis.* London: Faber & Faber, 1930.

Ellman, Richard. *James Joyce.* New York: Oxford University Press, 1959.

Emmanuel, Pierre. (Homage to Saint-John Perse). *HP*, pp. 149–50.

*———. *Saint-John Perse: Praise and Presence.* Washington, D.C.: Library of Congress, 1971.

Espaces de Saint-John Perse 1-2, 3, Aix-en-Provence: Université de Provence, 1980–1983.

Estang, Luc. "Saint-John Perse le civilisé." *Pensée Française* (Nov. 1957). Rpt. *HP*, pp. 569–72.

Etienne, Bruno. "Saint-John Perse et le politique." *ESJP 3*, pp. 157–88.

Fargue, Léon-Paul. "Lettres (1923–24)," *HP*, pp. 795–96; "Lettre à S.-L. L. (1924)," *HP*, p. 404; "Lettre à Saint-John Perse," *HP*, p. 20.

Fauchereau, Serge. *Lecture de la poésie américaine.* Paris: Minuit, 1968.

*Favre, Yves-Alain. *Saint-John Perse: le language et le sacré.* Paris: José Corti, 1977.

Ferran, Pierre. "La Mort au masque de céruse." *L'Education* (9 Oct. 1975), pp. 28–29.

Fisher, Louis. Excerpt from *Men and Politics* (New York, 1941). Rpt. *HP*, pp. 784–85.

Foucart, Claude. "Le Poète et le diable: Saint-John Perse et Herbert Steiner." *CSJP 4*, pp. 43–64.

Fouchet, Max-Pol. "Rencontre de l'exact." *HP*, pp. 131–35.

Fowlie, Wallace. "*Chronique* by Saint-John Perse." *Poetry* 99, no. 3 (Dec. 1961), pp. 194–96.

———. "L'Oeuvre pure de Saint-John Perse." *HP*, pp. 262–65.

———. "Poems That Sing of Man." *Saturday Review* 63, no. 47 (19 Nov. 1960), pp. 22–23.

Frédéric, Madeleine. "La Répétition dans *Amers.*" *CSJP 1*, pp. 123–36.

———. *La répétition et ses structures poétiques dans l'oeuvre de Saint-John Perse.* Paris: Gallimard, 1984.

*Galand, René. *Saint-John Perse*. New York: Twayne, 1972.

Galey, Mathieu, "Saint-John Perse: La voix d'exil." *L'Express* 1264 (29 Sept. 1975), p. 59.

Gali, Christian. "Saint-John Perse et Braque en désordre." *Silex* no. 2 (1977), pp. 67–70.

Garaudy, Roger. "Saint-John Perse." Lecture given at the Sorbonne, 16 Mar. 1962. (Text in the archives of the Fondation Saint-John Perse.)

Gaspar, Lorand. "De la plénitude." *CSJP 4*, pp. 29–41.

Gateau, Jean Charles. "Alexandre à Patmos." *Silex* no. 2 (1977), pp. 71–81.

Ghelderode, Michel de. "Hommage." *HP*, pp. 154–55.

Gibert, Pierre. "La Bible et les mythes assyro-babyloniens dans l'oeuvre poétique de Saint-John Perse." *ESJP 1–2*, pp. 201–12.

Gide, André. "Don d'un arbre." *HP*, pp. 14–17.

_____. *The Journals of André Gide*. Trans. Justin O Brien. Vol. II (1914–27). New York: Knopf, 1951.

_____. "Lettres à Saint-John Perse (1948–1949)." *HP*, pp. 465–67.

_____. Preface to *Anthologie de la poésie française*. Paris: Gallimard, 1949.

_____. Preface to *L'Offrande lyrique de Rabindranath Tagore*. Trans. André Gide. Paris: Gallimard, 1947.

Girard, René. "L'Histoire dans l'oeuvre de Saint-John Perse." *Romanic Review* 44, no. 1 (Feb. 1953). Rpt. *HP*, pp. 548–57.

Giraudoux, Jean. "Lettre de Jean Giraudoux (Singapore, 22 Jan. 35)." *HP*, pp. 797–98.

Glasheen, Adaline. *A Second Census of Finnegans Wake: An Index of the Characters and Their Roles*. Revised and expanded ed. Evanston, Ill.: Northwestern University Press, 1963.

Gorman, Herbert. *James Joyce*. New York: Rhinehart, 1948.

Gros, Léon-Gabriel. "Royaumes d'avant-soir." *Cahiers du Sud* 4, no. 358 (Dec. 1960). Rpt. *HP*, pp. 520–21.

Guerre, Pierre. "Dans la Haute Maison de Mer: Rencontres avec Saint-John Perse." *HP*, pp. 168–80.

_____. *Saint-John Perse et l'homme*. Paris: Gallimard, 1955.

Guillén, Jorge. "Je vivrai dans mon nom." *HP*, pp. 25–27.

Guillot, Gérard. "Diplomate et écrivain." *Le Figaro* (23 Sept. 1975), p. 26.

Haak, Hans-Erich. "Saint-John Perse et Alexis Leger." Lecture at the Goethe Institute in Paris, 8 Nov. 1967. (Text in the archives of the Fondation Saint-John Perse, Aix.)

Hearn, Lafcadio. *Two Years in the French West Indies*. New York and London: Harper & Brothers, 1890. Republished, Upper Saddle River, N.J.: Literature House/Gregg Press, 1970.

Henry, Albert. "L'Animale." (Presentation including the text of the supposedly jettisoned work by young Saintleger Leger, dated Bordeaux 1907, discovered in the possession of a Belgian collector.) *CSJP 4*, pp. 10–26.

_____. "Une Lecture d'*Amitié du Prince*." *CSJP 1*, pp. 65–90.

_____. "Une Lecture d'Anabase." *CSJP 2*, pp. 37–60.

Henry, Françoise. "Saint-Leger Leger, traducteur de Pindare." *CSJP 5*, pp. 31–77.

Herriot, Edouard. "Lettre à Alexis Leger" (19 Apr. 1946). *HP*, p. 732.

Hoppenot, Henri. "Une Accusation portée contre Alexis Leger: L'ordre de destruction des archives diplomatiques." *Le Monde* (15–16 Aug. 1947). Rpt. *HP*, pp. 769–71.

——. "D'Alexis Leger à Saint-John Perse." *Le Figaro littéraire* (5 Nov. 1960). Rpt. *HP*, pp. 803–7.

*Horry, Ruth. *Paul Claudel and Saint-John Perse.* Chapel Hill: University of North Carolina Press, 1971; London: Oxford University Press, 1971.

*Hubert, Etienne-Alain. "A Propos de 'l'Animale': Un tableau de Gauguin." (Identification of the Gauguin painting—*Femme Tahitienne*—which inspired "L'Animale" of Saintleger Leger.) *CSJP 5*, pp. 129–34.

Hurstfield, Julian. "Alexis Leger, les émigrés français et la politique américaine envers la France, 1940–1944." *ESJP 3*, pp. 189–203.

Ions, Veronica. *Indian Mythology.* London: Paul Hamlyn, 1967.

Jammes, Francis. "Lettre à Saint-Leger Leger (1924)." *HP*, p. 405.

——. *Rayons de miel: Eglogues.* Paris: Bibliothèque de l'Occident, 1908.

Jouve, Pierre-Jean. "Exil." *HP*, pp. 39–42.

——. "Hommage." *HP*, p. 145.

Joyce, James. *Finnegans Wake.* New York: Viking Press, 1947.

Kemp, Friedhelm. "Renaissance du poème." *HP*, pp. 122–25.

——. "Le 'Souffle du monde' dans l'oeuvre de Saint-John Perse." *CSJP 1*, pp. 17–34.

Knodel, Arthur. "Archibald MacLeish: Ami du prince taciturne." *ESJP 3*, pp. 3–16.

*——. "V Street: Une première version de *Poème à l'Etrangère*." *CSJP 3*, pp. 47–70.

——. "Les Images dans 'Neiges.'" *HP*, pp. 447–56.

——. "Prolific the Image, and the Metre, Prodigal." *Hudson Review* 11, no. 3 (1958), pp. 437–42.

——. "Saint-John Perse." *CDMEL*, p. 707.

*——. *Saint-John Perse: A Study of His Poetry.* Edinburgh: Edinburgh University Press, 1966.

——. "The Unheard Melody of Saint-John Perse." *Romanic Review* 50, no. 3 (Oct. 1959), pp. 195–201.

Koch, Kenneth. "St.-John Perse's New Poem (*Amers*)." *Evergreen Review* 2, no. 7 (1959), pp. 217–19.

Laden, Richard A. "La Matrice d'un lot d'images persiennes." *CSJP 3*, pp. 101–28.

Lane, Gary. *I Am. A Study of E. E. Cummings' Poems.* Kansas: University of Kansas Press, 1943.

Lange, Walter. "Rainer-Marie Rilke." *CDMEL*, pp. 666–67.

Larbaud, Valery. "Eloges." *HP*, pp. 32–38.

——. "Lettres à Saint-Leger Leger (1922–1933)." *HP*, pp. 399–403.

——. "Préface pour une édition russe d'Anabase.'" *La Nouvelle Revue Française* 148 (Jan. 1926). Rpt. *HP*, pp. 426–28.

Lear, Edward. *The Complete Nonsense of Edward Lear.* New York: Dover, 1951.

Le Boucher, Léon. *La Guadeloupe pittoresque.* Paris: Société d'Editions Géographiques, Maritimes et Coloniales, 1931.

Lefebve, Maurice-Jean. "La Révanche de la poésie." *HP,* pp. 98–103.

Léoni, Anne, and Raybaud, Antoine. "La Référence absente: Une lecture de 'Récitation à l'éloge d'une Reine.'" *ESJP 1–2,* pp. 61–72.

Lerch, Emil. "Saint-John Perse über seine Dichtungen." *Schweizer Monatshefte* 60 (1980), pp. 499–506.

Levillain, Henriette. "L'Image du sacrifice dans la poétique de Saint-John Perse." *ESJP 1–2,* pp. 189–200.

_____. "Le Rêve et le songe chez Saint-John Perse." *LSJP,* pp. 129–44.

*_____. *Le Rituel poétique de Saint-John Perse.* Paris: Gallimard, 1977.

Little, Roger. "Le Monde et le verbe dans l'oeuvre de Saint-John Perse." *CSJP 1,* pp. 101–22.

_____. "Le Pseudonyme de Saint-John Perse." *La Nouvelle Revue Française* no. 304 (May 1978), pp. 126–27.

_____. "Pour une lecture de Saint-John Perse." *LSJP,* pp. 9–26.

*_____. *Saint-John Perse.* London: Athlone Press of the University of London, 1973.

_____. "Saint-John Perse et Denis Devlin: Un compagnonnage." *ESJP 1–2,* pp. 119–28.

_____. "Saint-John Perse and Eliot." *Arlington Quarterly* 2, no. 2 (Autumn 1969), pp. 5–17.

*Loranquin, Albert. *Saint-John Perse.* Paris: Gallimard, 1963.

Loreau, Marc. "Habiter la gorge d'un dieu." *CSJP 5,* pp. 11–27.

Loriot, Patrick. "La Vie d'un poète." *Le Nouvel Observateur* (4 Dec. 1972), p. 74.

Lucchese, Romeo. "Eloge de Saint-John Perse." *HP,* pp. 259–61.

Lundkvist, Arthur. "Vision du monde et chant suprême." *HP,* pp. 562–64.

MacLeish, Archibald. "The Living Spring." *Saturday Review* 32, no. 24 (16 July 1949), pp. 8–9.

_____. Preface to the first American edition of *Eloges.* New York: Norton, 1944.

_____. "Le Temps de la louange." *HP,* pp. 104–6.

Madariaga, Salvador de. "Alexis Leger." *HP,* pp. 675–77.

Madaule, Jacques. "Les Sources du comique dans le cosmique." *Cahiers Paul Claudel 2.* Paris: Gallimard, 1960. Pp. 185–208.

Malraux, André. Preface to *Les Oiseaux et l'oeuvre de Saint-John Perse.* Aix-Paris: La Fondation Saint-John Perse, 1976–77.

Mandiarges, André Pieyre de. "A l'honneur de la Chair." *HP,* pp. 216–19.

Marcel, Luc-André. "Quelques raisons de louer." *HP,* pp. 193–206.

Marks, Barry. *E. E. Cummings.* New York: Twayne, 1964.

Martin, Jay. *Conrad Aiken: A Life of His Art.* Princeton, N.J.: Princeton University Press, 1962.

Mauriac, François. "A Paris en 1960." *HP,* p. 788.

Maurois, André. *Histoire de la France,* II. Paris: Albin Michel, 1947.

Mazars, Pierre. "Une journée à la villa 'Les Vigneaux,'" *HP,* pp. 618–23.

Miller, Henry. "Hommage." *HP,* p. 151.

Moeller, Charles. "Renouement (1960)." *La Revue Nouvelle* (Bruxelles) 32, no. 2 (1960), pp. 19–22.

Molino, Jean. "La Houle et l'éclair à propos de *Vents* de Saint-John Perse." *ESJP 3*, pp. 247–66.

Monnier, Adrienne. "Poème pour Saint-Leger Leger et Saint-John Perse (Octobre 1923)." *HP*, p. 613.

Morand, Paul. "Il n'a jamais failli sur l'essentiel et reste un être parfaitement accompli." *Arts* (12 June 1957). Rpt. *HP*, pp. 616–17.

――. *Journal d'un Attaché d'ambassade: 1916–1917*. Paris: La Table Ronde, 1948.

Moreau, Pierre. "Introduction." *Cahiers Paul Claudel 2*. Paris: Gallimard, 1960. Pp. 11–19.

Moulin, Léon. "Introduction." *Francis Jammes: Choix de poèmes*. Paris: Mercure de France, 1917.

*Murciaux, Christian. *Saint-John Perse*. Paris: Editions Universitaires, Classiques du XXe siècle, 1960.

*Nasta, Dan-Ion. *Saint-John Perse et la découverte de l'être*. Paris: Presses Universitaires de France, 1980.

――. "Territoire d'*Oiseaux*." *CSJP 3*, pp. 23–44.

Naughton, Helen T. "Jacques Rivière." *CDMEL*, p. 670.

Neumann, Erich. *The Great Mother*. Trans. Ralph Manheim. Princeton, N.J.: Princeton University Press, Bollingen Series, 1972.

Neumeister, Sebastian. "Saint-John Perse et le mythe de Robinson." *CSJP 2*, pp. 61–76.

Nimier, Roger. "Le Poème du rendez-vous avec l'âge et les siècles." *Arts* 787 (14 Sept. 1960), pp. 15–16.

Noailles, Anna de. "Lettre" (1931). *HP*, p. 798.

Norman, Charles. *E. E. Cummings: A Biography*. New York: Dutton, 1967.

La Nouvelle Revue Française. Issue in homage to Saint-John Perse, 278 (Feb. 1976), 170.

Ode, Catherine. "L'Eclair à travers la poésie de Saint-John Perse." Doctoral dissertation, Sorbonne (Paris IV), 1977.

Ogburn, Charlton. "Comment fut écrit *Pluies*." *HP*, pp. 273–79.

Onimus, Jean. "Une Poésie de la transcendance." In *Expérience de la poésie*. Paris: Desclée de Brouwer, 1973. Pp. 23–42.

Ostrovsky, Erika. "Saint-John Perse et E. E. Cummings: Points de rencontre." *ESJP 3*, pp. 99–112.

Papatzonis, T. C. "Saint-John Perse vu par un Hellène." *HP*, pp. 292–96.

*Parent, Monique. *Saint-John Perse et quelques devanciers*. Paris: Klincksieck, 1960.

Paul-Boncour, Joseph. "Lettre" (15 Oct. 1947). *HP*, p. 733.

――. "Poète insoupçonné." *HP*, p. 789.

Paul Claudel et André Gide: Correspondence (1899–1926). Paris: Gallimard, 1949.

Paul Claudel—Francis Jammes—Gabriel Frizeau: Correspondence (1897–1938). Paris: Gallimard, 1952.

Paz, Octavio. "Un Hymne moderne." *HP*, pp. 253–58.

———. "Saint-John Perse: Poet as Historian." *Nation* 192, no. 24 (17 June 1961), pp. 522–24.

Pertinax. *Les Fossoyeurs*. New York: La Maison Française, 1943.

Petit, Jacques. "Autour de la publication de *Tête d'or*." *Cahiers Paul Claudel 1*. Paris: Gallimard, 1959.

Peyre, Henri. "*Exile* by Saint-John Perse." *Shenandoah* (Winter 1953), pp. 75–79.

———. "Saint-John Perse." In *Contemporary French Poetry*. New York: Harper, 1964. Pp. 415–25.

Poulet, Georges. "De la constriction à la dissémination." *L'Arc*, IVe anné, 22 (Summer 1963), pp. 33–45.

———. "Saint-John Perse, ou la Poésie de l'effacement des choses." *HP*, pp. 298–315.

Proust, Marcel. "Sodome et Gomorrhe." In *A la Recherche du temps perdu*. Paris: Gallimard, Bibliothèque de la Pléïade, 1354. Vol. II, p. 849.

*Pruner, Francis. *L'Esotérisme de Saint-John Perse*. Paris: Klincksieck, 1977.

Py, Liliane. "Dionysos dans l'espace théâtral d'*Amers*." *LSJP*, pp. 94–99.

*Racine, Daniel. "La Fortune de Saint-John Perse en Amérique jusqu'en 1970." Doctoral dissertation, Sorbonne (Paris IV), June 1972.

———. "Saint-John Perse devant la critique américaine." *ESJP 3*, pp. 205–30.

Raine, Kathleen. "L'Admirable météorologie de Saint-John Perse." *HP*, pp. 468–70.

———. "Saint-John Perse, poète de la merveille." *CSJP 1*, pp. 45–64.

Rawson, Philip. *Erotic Art of the East*. New York: Putnam's Sons, 1969.

Raybaud, Antoine. "Exil palimpseste." *CSJP 5*, pp. 79–107.

Raymond, Louis-Marcel. "Humanité de Saint-John Perse." *HP*, pp. 110–21.

*———. *Lecture de Saint-John Perse*. Montréal: L'Action Universitaire, 1948.

Revue d'Histoire Littéraire de la France. Special issue: "Saint-John Perse" (May–June 1978).

Rhodes, S. A. "The Poetry of Saint-John Perse." *Sewanee Review* 44, no. 1 (1936) pp. 43–47.

*Richard, Jean-Pierre. "Petite remontée dans un nom-titre." In *Microlectures*. Paris: Seuil, 1979. Pp. 195–203.

———. "Saint-John Perse." In *Onze Etudes sur la poésie moderne*. Paris: Seuil, 1964. Pp. 31–66.

———. "Figures avec paysages." In *Pages Paysages: Microlectures II*. Paris: Seuil, 1984, pp. 157–67.

Rieber, B. "Saint-John Perse en Allemagne: Une lettre inédite du jeune Alexis St. Leger Leger." *Eléments pour la vie spirituelle* (n.d., n.p.).

Rieuneau, Maurice. "Sur Saint-John Perse et les oiseaux d'Audubon." *ESJP 1–2*, pp. 335–45.

Rigolot, Carol. "L'Amérique de Saint-John Perse: Réferentielle ou intertextuelle?" *ESJP 3*, pp. 87–98.

———. "The Paul Claudel–Saint-John Perse Correspondence." *Claudel Studies* I, 5 (1974), pp. 51–59.

Rilke, Rainer-Maria. "Lettre à Alexis Leger (29 Apr. 25)." *HP*, p. 793.

Roditi, Edouard. "Commerce with Saint-John Perse." *Adam* 300 (London 1963), pp. 186–91.

Rougemont, Denis de. "Saint-John Perse et l'Amérique." *HP*, pp. 126–30.

*Ryan, Marie-Laure. *Rituel et poésie: Une lecture de Saint-John Perse*. Berne: Peter Lang, 1977.

Sacotte, Mireille. "A Propos d'un paysage chinois." *ESJP 1–2*, pp. 281–92.

———. "Sur deux chants d' 'Anabase.'" *LSJP*, pp. 70–74.

*Saillet, Maurice. *Saint-John Perse, poète de gloire*. Paris: Mercure de France, 1952.

Schehadé, Georges. "Voici l'Ile." *HP*, p. 28.

Schuman, Robert. "Lettre à Alexis Leger (21 Jan. 50)." *HP*, p. 734.

Schwarz-Bart, Simone. *Pluie et vent sur Télumée Miracle*. Paris: Seuil, 1972.

Seferis, George. "Rencontre avec Saint-John Perse." *Alif* 7 (Tunis, 1976), pp. 78–88.

Segalen, Victor. *Equipée: Voyage au pays du réel*. Paris: Plon, 1929.

———. *Lettres de Chine*. Paris: Plon, 1967.

Senghor, Léopold Sédan. "Saint-John Perse ou poésie du royaume d'enfance." *La Table Ronde* 172 (May 1962), pp. 16–36.

Signac, Marcel. "Saint-John Perse et de Gaulle." *Rivarol* (2 Oct. 1975).

Sontag, Susan. *Illness as Metaphor*. New York: Vintage, 1979.

Spender, Stephen. "Un Bas-Relief." *HP*, p. 107.

Suda, Mitsuru. "Séjour londonien de Saint-John Perse. Au sujet de son commerce amical avec Valery Larbaud." *Japanese Comparative Literature Association Bulletin* 93 (1 May 1979), p. 2.

Supervielle, Jules. "Hommage (poème)." *HP*, p. 24.

———. "Lettre à Saint-John Perse (1942)." *HP*, p. 437.

Szembek, Jean. *Journal: 1933–1939*. Paris: Plon, 1952.

Tabouis, Geneviève. *Ils l'ont appelée Cassandre*. New York: Editions de la Maison Française, 1942.

Targe, André. "Alexis le faux saulnier." *Silex* 2 (1977), pp. 89–98.

Tate, Allen. "Mystérieux Perse." *HP*, pp. 136–40.

Thibaudet, Albert. "L' 'Anabase' de Saint-John Perse." *L'Europe Nouvelle* (9 Aug. 1924), pp. 19–26.

Thomas, Henri. "Pour l'amour de Fargue." *Cahiers du Colloque de Pataphysique*. Dossiers 22–24 (1963), pp. 55–56.

Ungaretti, Giuseppe. "Histoire d'une traduction." *HP*, pp. 68–70.

———. "Préface pour sa traduction italienne d''Anabase'" (1931). Rpt. *HP*, p. 429.

Valéry, Paul. "Lettres" (1924, 1937). *HP*, pp. 793–95.

*Van Rutten, Pierre. *"Eloges" de Saint-John Perse*. Paris: Hachette, 1977.

*———. *Le Langage poétique de Saint-John Perse*. The Hague: Mouton, 1975.

———. "*Vents* et le destin américain." *ESJP 3*, pp. 233–46.

Vernier, Richard. "Poeta ludens: Le rire de Saint-John Perse." *Pacific Coast Philology* 11 (Oct. 1976), pp. 76–84.

Victoria, Marcos. "La Musique dans la nuit." *HP*, pp. 280–85.

*Vigee, Claude. "La Quête de l'origine dans la poésie de Saint-John Perse." In *Révolte et louanges*. Paris: Corti, 1962. Pp. 199–218.

———. "Saint-John Perse 'Route de braise . . . .'" *Europe* 56, no. 587 (Mar. 1978), pp. 159–70.

Virtanen, Reino. "Between St. John and Persius: Saint-John Perse and Valéry." *Symposium* (Summer 1978), pp. 156–71.

Vitrac, Roger. "Publication of 'Anabase.'" *Le Journal Littéraire* (Sept. 1924). Rpt. *HP*, p. 414.

Von Hofmannsthal, Hugo. "Préface pour une édition allemande d'Anabase' (1924)." *HP*, pp. 423–27.

Wais, Kurt. "Alexis Leger (Saint-John Perse): Leben und Werk." In *Deutschland/Frankreich*, II. Stuttgart, 1957. Pp. 227–56.

———. "Deux manières d'exister dans l'oeuvre de Saint-John Perse." *HP*, pp. 266–72.

White, Jean. "Ex-Diplomat Here Nobel Prize Winner." *Washington Post* (27 Oct. 1960).

Winspur, Steven. "Le Signe pur." *CSJP 4*, pp. 45–63.

*Yoyo, E. *Saint-John Perse et le conteur.* Paris: Bordas, 1971.

OTHER PERSIANA

Dramatic presentation of "Amers: Poème de Saint-John Perse." Directed by Bernard Roukhomovsky. Paris. Palais des Congrès. 12–13 Dec. 1980.

Exhibits at the Fondation Saint-John Perse, Aix-en-Provence:

"Les Oiseaux et l'oeuvre de Saint-John Perse" (inaugural exhibit at the opening of the Fondation, 19 June 1976).

"Images à Crusoé" (marking the 70th anniversary of its publication by the N.R.F.). 1979.

"Saint-John Perse et les Etats-Unis." 1980.

"Lucien Clergue (photos); Robert Petit-Lorrain (dessins)." 1981.

"L'Univers minéral de Saint-John Perse." 1982.

"Les années de formation: 1887–1925." 1984.

Film (animation) by Laure Garcin based on *Amers* (1960). Scenario in the archives of the Foundation Saint-John Perse.

International Colloquia at the Fondation Saint-John Perse. Proceedings and published texts in *Espaces Saint-John Perse* (except No. 3, due to technical difficulties in recording):

[1]"Mots et savoirs dans l'oeuvre de Saint-John Perse." 1979.

[2]"Saint-John Perse et les Etats-Unis." 1980.

[3]"Saint-John Perse devant les créateurs contemporains." 1981.

[4]"Travail du rythme, travail du sens." 1984.

Official Honors (presentations; acceptances or refusals by Perse). Texts: *HP*, pp. 632–46.

Round Table at the Fondation Saint-John Perse:
    "Questions de poétique: Le travail du texte." 1978.
    Published texts in *Espaces Saint-John Perse* (1–2).

Spectacle "Galaxie Saint-John Perse." Conceived and directed by Pierre Seghers. Paris, Théâtre de la Ville, 18 April 1983.

Television program (the first) devoted to Saint-John Perse. Directed by Daniel Gelin and Jacques Tréffouel. Fr. 3 (Bordeaux), 23 April 1983. Culmination of the day honoring French poetry organized by the French Ministry of Culture.

INDEX